THE PRIVATE
WORLD OF
CONGRESS

THE PRIVATE WORLD OF CONGRESS

Rochelle Jones
Peter Woll

THE FREE PRESS

A Division of Macmillan Publishing Co., Inc.

NEW YORK

Collier Macmillan Publishers

LONDON

For
Chris and Maria Calomiris and family
and
Howard Schweizer
who continue to bring sustenance
and vitality to Capitol Hill

The Free Press
A Division of Macmillan Publishing Co., Inc.
866 Third Avenue, New York, N. Y. 10022

Collier Macmillan Canada, Ltd.

Library of Congress Catalog Card Number: 79-7371

Printed in the United States of America

printing number
1 2 3 4 5 6 7 8 9 10

Library of Congress Cataloging in Publication Data

Jones, Rochelle.
  The private world of Congress.

  Includes bibliographical references and index.
  1. United States. Congress. 2. United States.
Congress--Officials and employees. 3. Legislators--
United States. 4. Power (Social sciences) I. Woll,
Peter   joint author. II. Title.
JK1061.J65   328.73   79-7371
ISBN 0-02-916680-2

Contents

Preface

THIS BOOK TAKES the reader behind the scenes on Capitol Hill. It goes where the public does not — to staff conferences, the inner offices of Senators and Congressmen, the private meetings where legislative strategy is mapped and public policy is actually made.

Politics is a game with winners and losers. In Congress the ultimate prize is power and status on Capitol Hill. Members of Congress scramble for the symbols of power — committee chairmanships, assignments to prestigious committees, large and expert staffs, legislative victories, and special perks. Meanwhile, congressional aides play their own power game, using their positions, their bosses, and their expertise to advance their own reputations for power.

The fact that politics is about power should not be surprising. That politicians seek to build reputations for power in Congress is not a cynical perspective. The framers of the Constitution recognized that the incentive for power, properly harnessed and directed, can produce good government. The entrepreneurial nature of political activity in Congress has added an important new dimension, which this book seeks to clarify and evaluate against our constitutional system.

The Private World of Congress explores the neglected but fascinating power incentive of members and staff. Political scientists are, of course, aware that the internal power incentive exists but they continue to picture Congress as an institution shaped primarily by the members' drive for reelection. Obviously members want to be reelected. However, it is not the striving for reelection that explains the behavior on Capitol Hill, but the quest for personal power within Congress itself.

1

The Lure of Power

CONGRESS IS A world apart, an isolated place, despite the constant intrusion of tourists and buffeting by lobbyists of all political persuasions, that exists largely for itself.

The setting of the Capitol itself emphasizes its isolation. Major Pierre L'Enfant, who was commissioned to draw up the original plan for the new city of Washington, chose the top of Jenkins Hill at the highest elevation of the capital city for the future home of Congress. The Capitol was built there in the middle of a forest separated from the surrounding city by Goose Creek, which meandered through what was to become the center of official Washington. In the grand design of the city Jenkins Hill was renamed Capitoline Hill and Goose Creek became the Tiber. Congress, the representative branch of the government, was to be cloaked in the democratic traditions and ideals of ancient Rome. The boxlike structure which housed both the House of Representatives and the Senate when they arrived in the 1800s has since sprouted wings and a dome. New office buildings, three on the House side and two on the Senate side, have been constructed to provide office space for members and their staffs. But the preeminence of the Capitol itself has been maintained. Congress passed a law in 1901 forbidding structures which would overshadow the Capitol dome. The forest has given way to broad expanses of lawn and terraces. On those rare Washington days when the horizon is not shrouded by winter fog or obscured by waves of shimmering heat, the view from the Hill is magnificent. White marble buildings march down Pennsylvania Avenue to the White House, and further on, Arlington National Cemetery rises from the banks of the Potomac River.

Upon arrival in Washington the first members of Congress found a wilderness where the new seat of government was to be located. Cow paths served for roads. Street lights and signposts

1

were nonexistent. Carriages bogged down in the mud, and guests returning home from parties often got lost and wandered until daybreak in the marshes surrounding the Capitol. When Anthony Trollope ridiculed the pretensions of the new capital in 1862, he wrote that "the country is wild, trackless, unbridged, uninhabited and desolate." The mile between the Capitol and the White House was a hazardous winding path which led through mosquito-infested bogs and which was traversed at great peril. Not surprisingly, the Congressmen preferred to stay in the vicinity of the Capitol rather than venture into the unsurveyed terrain outside the narrow circumference of their small community. Isolated from the rest of government and from their families and friends back home for months at a time, the Congressmen clustered on Capitol Hill in a self-contained society. The separation of powers became, to use James Sterling Young's phrase, a separation of persons. Young brilliantly describes the inner workings of that encapsulated early Congressional community in *The Washington Community, 1800–1828:*

> The knolltop settlement of legislators was a complete and selfcontained village community. . . . Neither work nor diversion, nor consumer needs, nor religious needs required them to set foot outside it. Eight boardinghouses, a tailor, a shoemaker, a washerwoman, a grocery store, and an oyster house served the congressional settlement in 1801. Within three years a notary, an ironmonger, a saddle maker, several more tailors and bootmakers, a liquor store, bookstores, stables, bakery, and taverns had been added. . . . An itinerant barber served the community, shuttling between the scattered villages of the capital on horseback, and a nearby bathhouse catered to congressional clientele. Legislators with families could send their children to school on the Hill. The members had their own congressional library and their own post office, dispatching and receiving mail—which was distributed on the floor of the Senate and House daily—without leaving the Hill. . . . Village religious services were provided each Sunday, with the Hall of Representatives serving as the church and visiting ministers as preachers. . . . For diversion, members had only to walk down to the Tiber for good fishing and duck-shooting or step into the woods immediately east of the Capitol for a morning's hunt before Congress convened at eleven or twelve o'clock. There was in addition the Congressional Dancing Assembly, meeting regularly in one of the taverns on the Hill. . . . So thoroughly was the community life of the congressional contingent centered upon itself that

their work activities, the daily debates, became one of the principal diversions for legislative society. Senate and House chambers
were the settlement's theaters. . . . Here, the women with their
needlepoint, wives and guests of the members were wont to spend
the better part of weekday afternoons chatting with friends and
taking measure of the actors on the stage below. Major debates
and contests for oratorial preeminence were played to a packed
house in a carnival atmosphere, supplies of popcorn and candy being dispatched from the floor to the galleries in slings affixed to
fishing poles.[1]

Congress remains a largely self-sufficient community today.
Many of the same amenities which were described by Young are
now available to Congressmen and their staffs within the Capitol
complex. Barber shops, beauty shops, post offices, shoe-shine
stands, newsstands, cafeterias, dining rooms, and fast-food take-
out stands are scattered throughout the various office buildings.
Three doctors serve in the infirmary in the Capitol. Nurses dis-
pense aspirin, cough syrup, and flu shots at first-aid stations.
Branch offices of the Internal Revenue Service open during income tax season. A swimming pool in the Rayburn Office Building and exercise rooms on both sides of the Hill help to keep
members of Congress in shape. House and Senate chaplains ca-
ter to their spiritual needs. The Capitol Hill police force, larger
than the police forces of many metropolitan communities, is on
duty twenty-four hours a day, seven days a week.

Some people who work for Congress pack their briefcases at
night and brave the rush-hour traffic to the outlying suburbs,
but many others live in the same neighborhoods around the Capitol as their predecessors once did. The Capitol Hill community
continues to be a place where legislators and Congressional staff
live, eat, and rub shoulders after hours. In place of the boarding
houses of the early days, there are elegantly restored Victorian
and early twentieth century townhouses. The saloons and tav-
erns have turned into modern cocktail lounges and cozy pubs,
but they are still places for the exchange of political rumors and
gossip. (A pub frequented by single staff members bears the
name Jenkins Hill, providing a link between the old and new
communities.) The Eastern Market, which served the community in 1850, remains open seven blocks from the Capitol.

The wilderness has been tamed over the last century, but the
landscape is not all that has altered. Mental and emotional isola-

tion from constituents has been added to the physical isolation of Congressmen. Early lawmakers journeyed to Washington for sessions that lasted only a few winter months and spent the rest of the year at home. Congressmen today settle in Washington and go home on weekends and during Congressional recesses. Such trips are normally whirlwind tours, jammed morning to late at night with speaking engagements, ribbon-cutting ceremonies, and a steady stream of meetings with local officeholders, party leaders, and interest groups that tax the stamina of the hardiest. The pace that Congressman Paul Findley maintained during a day "back to the District" in 1977 is all too typical. The day before, he met late into the night with constituents; the day after, he had an appointment at 10 a.m. with a mayor who was having a problem with the Department of Housing and Urban Development. His schedule that day looked like this:

MONDAY, FEBRUARY 14

10:00 a.m. Sepha Jones. Received a book of poetry that she had written.

10:15 a.m. John Kirby. Discussed a highway problem.

10:30 a.m. Father Mascari. Discussed plans for a golden age retirement center for rural Americans.

10:45 a.m. Dale Rowand and Ken Redfern, Department of Agriculture. Discussed plans for an International Visitors Day at the State Fair.

11:30 a.m. Stopped for a hamburger.

11:45 a.m. Drove to Jacksonville.

12:15 p.m. Made visits around Jacksonville Square.

 1:30 p.m. Attended ribbon-cutting ceremony at District Service Office of Honorable Jim Reilly, 224 West State, Jacksonville.

 2:00 p.m. Jacksonville Town Meeting. Was made an honorary fireman and an honorary policeman by the City of Jacksonville and received commendation from the City Council and Mayor Hocking for assistance on solving community problems.

 3:30 p.m. Met with Dr. Fuhrig in mayor's office, regarding Conference of Churches, Great Decisions Series, China slides.

 4:30 p.m. Stopped at McDonald's for a cheeseburger.

 4:45 p.m. Drove to Alton.

7:00 p.m.   Alton Town Meeting, Metropolitan National Bank on Beltline, Community Room, Alton.

8:00 p.m.   Met with various constituents on individual problems.

9:00 p.m.   Interview with Southern Illinois University radio on foreign policy.

Such trips are helpful in acquainting members with the needs and concerns of their constituents and in bringing local problems to their attention, but they cannot be a substitute for living day in and day out during most of the year in the community.

Congressmen are more isolated these days because they spend a longer period of time in Congress. The first Congresses were marked by a rapid turnover of members. During the first forty years of the Republic between one-third and two-thirds of the Congressional community left after every Congress, not to return. Neither Congressmen nor Senators displayed any particular affection for Washington, nor was there any reason for them to. Perquisites were few, and the salary was minimal. Starting in 1818 members were paid $8 a day while Congress was in session plus traveling expenses between home and the Capitol. The Senate experienced special difficulty in holding on to its members. Five of the twenty-six original Senators resigned before serving out their terms of office. An early Senate appointee set a record by resigning from the same seat twice (he was reappointed after his replacement subsequently resigned). Another early Senate appointee succeeded in resigning from each of his state's two Senate seats. These Congressmen were citizen legislators in the truest sense. And they were apt to view service in Congress as a duty and burden if not an aggravation, distracting them from their businesses and family life. The Congressional career, as we now think of it, was virtually unknown.

Today, being a member of Congress is a full-time career in itself. Turnover is low; members rarely leave unless they are defeated at the polls or forced to retire by old age. The typical Congressman is completely wrapped up in the job of being a Congressman. The Congressional career is so time-consuming and so mentally and physically absorbing that Congressmen rarely have energy left over to give to anyone or anything else. Their needs tend to find fulfillment within the institution of Congress. The legions of political marriages that survive in Washington in name only offer bleak testimony to the lure of Congress. Congressmen now associate mainly with Congressmen. The constituents and lobbyists who come into their offices are seen by their staffs and not by Congressmen themselves. The letters that arrive are answered for the most part by legislative correspondents and signed by automatic signature machines. The House Commission on Administrative Review found in 1977 that a Congressman typically spends four hours and twenty-five minutes a day on the House floor or in committee meetings, almost an hour with his staff and three minutes with the House leadership. By contrast he spends less than half an hour with constituents. The Commission on the Operation of the Senate found that a Senator spent approximately four hours on the floor or in committees and two and a half hours on staff matters. Other meetings outside the office and speeches consumed two more hours. He spent only an hour and forty minutes with either constituent or interest groups.

The gyroscope for Congressmen is not their constituents, but each other. And in fact some members of Congress have begun complaining that they spend most of their time with their own staffs and are increasingly isolated even from each other. Senator Peter Domenici underscored this isolation and the impact this has on the role of Congressional staff when he said, "I think the exclusive club that we thought we were part of implied that we related to one another; mostly club members are supposed to be friends. They are supposed to see each other. I think one of the major frustrations in this institution is that there isn't any time for that. The thrust of this institution is against rather than in favor of that kind of relationship. That is yielding some very strange things, like relationships with staff almost exclusively, instead of with fellow Senators."[2] Isolated on the Hill and immersed in their jobs, Congressmen have acquired their own way of viewing the world. This Congressional mind set enabled Congress, for example, to claim Gerald Ford as one of their own long after he had acceded to the presidency. The increasing preoccupation of Congressmen with Congress has important implications for Congressional behavior. They have more or less donned blinders which exclude from view all but the internal world of Capitol Hill.

The men who came to Washington in the 1800's shared the values of their constituents, and their behavior reflected those values. They were suspicious, as their constituents were, of power, and they believed, as their constituents did, that power tended to corrupt. Their letters are riddled with expressions of abhorrence of Congressional society. A Congressman wrote that his service in the House "has produced in me nothing but absolute loathing and disgust." They described Washington as "this sink of . . . corruption" and as a place of "inequity and defilement." They longed to go home. A House member wrote, "So disgusted [am I] . . . with political men and political life—nay with mankind itself, that I wish I could shut myself up from life and have nothing more to do with any one but my wife and children. I look around—and exclaim where is there one man I can trust! and I feel there is not one!" They formed a Congress in which it was every man for himself, where institutional restraints on behavior were nonexistent and factions were the order of the day. It was, wrote James Sterling Young, "a Congress united in little else but its hostile attitudes toward leadership and power-seeking."

Over the last century and a half Congress has changed dramatically. The men and women who come to Congress today are not suspicious of power for its own sake, and they harbor no suspicions of strong leaders. They are more likely to complain about the absence of leadership. Democrats in both the House and Senate criticized former Speaker Carl Albert and former Majority Leader Mike Mansfield for their all too gentle conduct of Congressional business. Congressmen now have a different sort of relationship with their constituents. David Mayhew argues in *Congress: The Electoral Connection* that a Congressman's principal motivation is to get reelected and his behavior in Congress is therefore directed toward his constituents.[3] He postulates that Congressmen engage in what he terms "advertising," "credit claiming," and "position taking" in order to further their chances at the polls. He implies that Congressmen, seeking to stay in Congress, find that it is helpful to *appear* to represent the interests, opinions, and beliefs of their constituents. Congressmen who represent the voters in this fashion are not the same as Congressmen who embody the values and standards of their constituents and who behave as their constituents would as a result.

Congress is no longer a free-for-all. There are things that are done and things that aren't done. A member who chooses to march to the beat of a different drum is likely to find himself

leading a parade of one. Former Congressman Clem Miller, in a
series of celebrated letters to his Northern California constituents, wrote that "conformity is a most powerful force in Congress" and described "the silent reproof" that descends on a
member who strays. "[C]onstituting a force of one or two or
three, standing against your friends, that sticks in the memory of
others," he said. "It lingers in the back of the mind for a long
time. It adds a factor to the continuing catalogue one makes of
all his fellow members."[4]

Congress has become institutionalized, and in the process it
has evolved unwritten standards of behavior and unspoken rules
of conduct which make life easier for all. Donald S. Matthews
once categorized these as apprenticeship, specialization and
hard work, courtesy to other members, reciprocity, and institutional patriotism. For the most part they are as true today as
when Matthews wrote in the 1950s and apply equally well to
members of both the Senate and House. Although junior Congressmen are no longer expected to be, like children, seen and
not heard, senior Congressmen still expect a certain measure of
deference. The burden of presiding for long hours over the Senate continues to fall on the freshmen Senators, who are supposed
to assume the duty cheerfully. Members are expected to keep up
with their committee work, and the majority develop recognized
expertise in carefully chosen areas. They are expected to accom-
modate their colleagues, especially those of their own party,
when they can and to go their own way quietly when they can't.
They are supposed to confine disagreements to the issues and
keep personal clashes to a minimum. Above all they are expected
to be loyal to their respective bodies. Members try to adhere to
these rules and standards and shun those who don't, but the system doesn't always work smoothly. The rule of accommodation
and the rule of courtesy collided head on in 1977 during Senate
debate on natural gas pricing. Senators Howard Metzenbaum of
Ohio and James Abourezk of South Dakota tied up the chamber
as they tried to head off a vote on deregulation. Members who
wanted to pass the bill and adjourn were simmering by the time
Majority Leader Robert Byrd of West Virginia broke the filibuster through a series of prearranged procedural rulings from Vice
President Walter Mondale, who was presiding. Senators who
only the day before had been furious at the delaying tactics of
Metzenbaum and Abourezk then erupted at Byrd and Mondale.

An unprecedented shouting match took place on the floor as Senators accused the Majority Leader of dictatorial tactics that violated the rights of members. Senator Abourezk, who had a distinctly personal style, became so frustrated in Congress that in 1977 he announced his resignation after one term.

In addition, Congress has acquired an internal incentive system. There is a reason that Congressmen want to be Congressmen that is not adequately explained by the electoral connection. That Congressmen want to be reelected is self-evident. Almost all run again. The question is why. The excitement of winning public office and the ego gratification that accompany winning are insufficient reasons for seeking reelection. They may be enough the first or second time, but the law of diminishing returns argues that such incentives will pall before long. Congressmen seek reelection because they are hooked on Congress itself. They are motivated by a desire for personal power, and their goal is power and status on the Hill. Like all careerists whether a middle-management executive at a large corporation or an attorney at a high-powered law firm, they seek to advance through the ranks of the organization to ever higher positions of authority. Like all organizations Congress distributes rewards and perquisites to its members, and those who succeed get more of both. There are many kinds of rewards and perquisites, and members seek out different ones depending on their personalities, interests, and goals. They include such tangible things as offices overlooking the Capitol and all-expenses-paid trips around the world and such intangible things as deference from colleagues and flattery from four-star generals. They range from retinues of staff to invitations to appear on "Meet the Press" and photographs on the front page of the *New York Times* to phone calls from the President. The rewards of achieving power and status in Congress are such that few Congressmen can easily relinquish them. These internal incentives are what keep members in office, and the drive to achieve and maintain power and status is what fuels reelection campaigns.

The goal of power and status is not the sole goal of members. Human beings are obviously more complex than that. Members *do* want to be reelected. Members *do* want to help their constituents. Members *do* want to pass good laws. Members *do* want to improve their districts and states. The immediate goals of members will vary with time and over the course of a Congressional career. A freshman member of the House from a marginal district, facing an uncertain future at the polls, will put more emphasis on helping his constituents and getting reelected. A third-term Senator who is the ranking member or chairman of a key committee will give a higher priority to passing legislation and formulating public policy. Congressmen will be motivated by different complexes of goals and drives depending on their re-election possibilities, their seniority, and their committee assignments. What they want to do in public life and what they believe themselves capable of doing will play a part in determining their behavior at any given time. But overall the goal of achieving power and status in Congress offers the single best explanation for the individual behavior of members of Congress and the collective behavior of Congress itself.

Political scientists, attempting to analyze and explain Congress, have advanced different explanations for Congressional behavior. Most frequently, they have focused on the drive to be reelected and the desire to make good public policy. But these theories, while true from time to time, simply cannot explain the behavior of most Congressmen most of the day when they are examined objectively.

First, consider the goal of reelection. David Mayhew claims this is the chief determinant of Congressional behavior and Richard Fenno suggests this is the primary goal of some members of Congress, notably members of the House Interior Committee and the Post Office and Civil Service Committee and their Senate counterparts. (The Senate Post Office and Civil Service Committee was combined with the Governmental Affairs Committee in 1977 as a result of reorganization of the Senate committee system.) Fenno, in *Congressmen in Committees*, cited reelection and the making of good public policy as two of the three goals of Congressmen. The third was power, which he acknowledged was the goal of members of the House Appropriations and Ways and Means Committees and the Senate Appropriations Committee. He added, though, that members of the Senate Appropriations Committee sought power in order to benefit their home states.[5]

Congressional behavior has relatively little to do with how a member fares at the polls. Except in the rarest of instances a member will not be reelected or defeated on the basis of his votes or the positions that he has taken. It is a simple fact of political life that once a member has been elected, he has little cause to worry about reelection. This holds equally true for Congressmen and Senators. Political scientists usually assume falsely that Congressmen, who are elected every two years, will be more sensitive to the voters than Senators, who are elected every six years. In fact, although neither has much cause for concern after his second term, a Congressman generally has more reason to believe that he will hold onto his seat than a Senator does. Over the last two decades the number of marginal, up-for-grabs seats in the House has declined strikingly. (Marginals are seats which are won with less than 55 to 60 percent of the vote and which the opposition has a reasonable chance of capturing in the next election.) Before 1966 about 60 percent of House seats were safe. Since then about 75 percent have been. The overwhelming majority of members who face reelection can confidently assume that they will be back in Washington the following January. Some 95 percent of members who seek reelection normally win. Even at the height of the Vietnam war protests in 1968 some 98 percent of House members were reelected and in the midst of widespread disillusionment with politics as a result of Watergate in 1974 some 88 percent of House members won.

Members of Congress are reelected simply because they have been elected once before. Voters are largely ignorant of their Congressman's or Senators' positions on the issues and key votes. Survey after survey reveals that most constituents do not even know the names of their Congressmen. The Survey Research Center at the University of Michigan found only 18.7 percent of voters could recall the name of the incumbent and 65.4 percent could remember the name of neither candidate after the 1974 Congressional election. More constituents are able to name at least one of their United States Senators, but only a very small group know the names of both of their two Senators and their Congressman. This ignorance further disputes the notion that Congressional behavior can be explained in terms of reelection goals. If a member is a reasonably skilled politician, he need not worry under normal circumstances about his reelection possibilities.

Congressmen are not necessarily oblivious to the views of their constituents. Most Congressmen want to represent their constituents, but they may act in accordance with their own beliefs about what is right and wrong for the people they represent. Most Congressmen believe they are trustees of the people rather than delegates of the people. Congressman William Steiger of Wisconsin said, "I'm not here just to blindly follow the public opinion polls. I'm here to do what I think is right." The Congressman who sees himself as a trustee will act differently from a Congressman who sees himself as a delegate.

Congressman are more likely to be concerned about pleasing well-organized interest groups than the rank-and-file voter. Politically powerful pressure groups do follow the votes and positions of Congressmen. They know who their friends are and are not, and they are in a position to reward those who help them and punish those who don't. Congressmen may be friendly to such groups as the AFL-CIO, the Americans for Democratic Action, the Americans for Constitutional Action, the United Auto Workers, and the National Association of Manufacturers in hopes of receiving political endorsements, campaign contributions, and volunteer help in elections in return. These are broad-based national groups whose interests may overlap and even coincide with the interests of constituents, but then again they may not. And even if there is harmony of interests, such groups are concerned with only a small percentage of the bills which come before Congress. Members of the House Post Office and Civil Service Committee who were interviewed by Fenno, for example, wanted to help their constituents and thereby win reelection. They believed their committee work could be used to win the support of organized groups back in their districts and thus turn into an electoral advantage. The Congressmen were chiefly concerned with the postal unions which were interested in only one issue: pay increases for postal workers. Members easily satisfied the unions by working and voting for the pay raises. Their other activities were of little or no interest to the unions. A Congressman may be acutely sensitive to the views and opinions of the interest groups whose support he courts. He may vote his district on those few issues a year which are especially important to the folks back home. But even those Congressmen whose gyroscopes are most closely calibrated to reflect their constituents are free most of the time to pursue other goals. Except for the most junior members and those from the most marginal districts, reelection activities demand little attention. In short, the goal of reelection does not conflict with the goals of power and status on the Hill; they can exist side by side. And by itself the reelection motive does not satisfactorily explain Congressional behavior.

Second, take the goal of shaping public policy. Fenno argues that the members of the House Education and Labor Committee and Foreign Affairs Committee and their counterparts on the Senate Labor and Public Works Committee and Foreign Relations Committee put this goal first. (The Senate Labor and Public Works Committee was renamed the Committee on Human Resources during the committee system reorganization in 1977.) These members allegedly seek out their committee assignments, have a strong personal interest in their jurisdictions, and pursue policy goals through the committees. The facts, however, belie the theory. The committees which deal with education and labor policy are not sought after by Congressmen and Senators. They have little panache. The great issues of the day rarely fall within their jurisdictions, and their members do not help to chart the course of the country's future. Unsurprisingly, members were drawn mainly from the ranks of freshmen at the time of Fenno's study. Freshmen constituted 60 percent of the appointees in both the House and the Senate. They were members who had little seniority and almost no choice in committee assignments. The more prestigious and powerful committees were foreclosed to them. These committees were the most desirable of the committees to which they could aspire, and by concentrating on the legislation which fell within the committees' jurisdiction, they were making the best of their relatively bad lot. If, as they claimed, their goal was to shape public policy in these areas, it was fleeting. Once they accumulated some seniority, they did not choose to stay on the committees and move up through the ranks so they could have more impact on public policy. Instead, they used their seniority and the choices in committee assignments which it brought to transfer to other committees of greater prestige.

The foreign affairs committees have more stature within the House and Senate. The Foreign Relations Committee in the Senate, in fact, is one of the most prestigious of all committees because of the Senate's constitutional role in foreign policy. It has responsibility for approving treaties with foreign countries and ambassadorial appointments. Members of this committee rarely leave since status and power automatically accrue to the Senators who serve there. They are free to concentrate on foreign policy because they have already acquired status and power. The Foreign Affairs Committee in the House is somewhat different. It has a certain amount of prestige but little power. Unexpectedly, more members are freshman and more members leave to seek committee assignments elsewhere. Fenno found that a high proportion of the Congressmen on this committee also left to seek election to the Senate. Since a freshman Senator at the time of the study had virtually no chance of appointment to the Foreign Relations Committee, they obviously were not leaving to pursue their policy-making goals there. Instead, they had other reasons for seeking election to the more exclusive and prestigious Senate. Having tasted power and status, they sought more.

In short, the goal of shaping public policy, like the goal of reelection, does not preclude the pursuit of other goals. And in fact policy expertise, which is a form of intelligent specialization that is expected of members of Congress, is used to achieve power and status on the Hill.

The drive for power and status within Congress is not new. The history of Congress could be written in terms of struggles to acquire and consolidate power. Two periods deserve special attention, the first decade of this century, when the seniority system began to emerge, and the last ten years, when young Congressmen and Senators launched a concentrated attack on the prerogatives of that system. Both periods corresponded to changes in the composition of Congress. Changing political conditions were reflected in the membership of Congress and altered the relationship between the ins who benefited from the existing system and the outs who didn't. Members who were amassing influence found that they were cut off from the rewards of power, while those who held the formal reins of power were not necessarily those who possessed influence and were not representative of them. The perquisites and prerogatives that go along with power were no longer distributed evenly. Something had to give and it did.

The rapid turnover in the House which marked most of the 1800s declined toward the end of the century as a career in Congress suddenly became attractive to members who a few years earlier had spurned such a life. Congressman no doubt began to seek reelection for a number of reasons, but the shifting values of their constituents was particularly important. The suspicion of power for its own sake which had limited terms of office waned as community leaders started to recognize that Congressmen who were wise in the ways of Washington could be more helpful than those who were not. The South first realized that political experience could bring political rewards. A Congressman who knew the shape of the barrel was likely to pull out the most pork. The South was practicing Sunbelt politics long before political scientists and journalists discovered the phenomenon in the 1970s. The disparity in federal expenditures between the South and the rest of the country which has been documented in a number of recent books stretches back to antebellum times. Before the Civil War the federal government was spending about twice as much per capita in the South as in the New England and Middle Atlantic states. Even after the Civil War was lost, the South managed to capture a considerably larger share of federal expenditures than the Middle Atlantic states and a slightly larger share than the New England states. At the same time the South was paying proportionately less into the federal treasury. The South thus stood to gain considerably from the federal government, and this was not lost on Southern leaders. The best guarantee that the federal largess would continue was the reelection of Congressmen who could thread their way through the bureaucratic labyrinth. The South had another reason to be acutely interested in the decisions of the federal government in the early 1800s. The great debate over slavery loomed ahead, and the outcome meant life or death to the Southern way of life. Just as Southern leaders found that it was expedient to keep their Congressmen in office to insure the continued flow of federal dollars, so they found that it was advantageous to have experienced men in Congress for the debate on slavery. Men who had the most power could best protect their constituents. Power in Congress was no longer something to be scorned but something to be sought after. The value of incumbency was obvious early on in the South, and the statistics on Congressional turnover reflect this. From the early days of the Republic the South has held the edge on the rest of the country. Since 1789 the difference between Northern and Southern turnover has never been less than 6.6 percent.

As Southern constituents were finding that their interest lay in reelecting their Congressmen, members from the North and East were finding that their interest lay in seeking reelection. The election of 1896 polarized the country, and real competition between the two parties vanished for all practical political purposes in many areas. The Republican Party declined in the

South after the Civil War, and the solid South became solidly
Democratic. The Republicans, however, came to dominate Congress. Control of the House, which had fluctuated earlier in the
century, was firmly in the grip of the Republican Party from
1895 to 1911. The beneficiaries of this were the members from
Republican strongholds outside the South. Republicans who
sought reelection and were successful could hope in time to rise
to positions of leadership. Thus members on both sides of the
aisle were accumulating seniority by the time Joseph Cannon of
Illinois captured the Speakership in 1903.

The Speaker was an all-powerful figure in the nineteenth
century. He recognized members in debate, ruled on points of
order, and generally interpreted the rules of the House. As chairman of the Rules Committee, he determined when and how legislation reached the floor. His real power, however, rested in his
authority to name committee chairmen and to appoint both the
majority and minority members of committees. (Starting in 1902
the minority leader named minority committee members.) Committees were named anew at the beginning of each Congress,
since the House, required by the Constitution to stand for reelection every two years, was a continuing body neither in law nor in
custom. Committee assignments and the chairmanships were important pawns in the battle for the Speakership as rival candidates bartered commitee posts for votes. The negotiations over
who would serve where often lasted for months, since a member's
career rose or fell on the basis of his commitee assignments. The
wife of Speaker James G. Blaine wrote home in 1871, "Your father sits here at the table toiling away over his committees. . . .
As fast as he gets them arranged, just so fast some after-consider-
ation comes up which disarranges not one, but many, and over
topples the whole row of bricks. It is a matter in which no one
can help him. . . . [He] had wool and cotton manufacturers to
meet in Boston, dinners, breakfasts and lunches . . . to give and
take in New York, and, over and above all, pressures, to permit
or resist, of Congressional committees." The Speaker, while powerful, was not supposed to be dictatorial. There were informal
limits on his authority under Rule X to appoint committees. As
members built up seniority, they acquired a vested interest in
their committee assignments and a personal stake in who would
be chairman of their committees. The Speaker could still reorganize the committee system at the start of each Congress, but he

risked alienating friends and potential allies if he did so capriciously.

Joe Cannon, the invincible "Iron Duke of Danville" who had been nominated to Congress twenty-five consecutive times, was not the sort to tread lightly. A rough-and-tumble politician, described by a historian as "an assiduous cultivator of the arts of potation, profanity and poker,"[6] Cannon played hard and to win. He did not have an easy time of it. The Republican Party was split into factions, and the country was bitterly divided over the tariff and conservation legislation. These sectional disputes intensified the feuds within the Republican Party. Presiding over the House with an unlit cigar clenched between his teeth, Cannon ruthlessly rewarded his friends and punished his enemies. In 1907 he replaced four committee chairmen and transferred the ranking member of the Agriculture Committee, who was in line to become chairman, to a low-ranking position on the Merchant Marine and Fisheries Committee. Two years later he refused to make most committee assignments until the House had acted on the Payne-Aldrich tariff bill. When committee assignments were finally announced some five months into the session, numerous high-ranking committee members were stripped of their posts. Henry Cooper of Wisconsin, chairman of the Insular Affairs Committee for ten years, was summarily removed. Victor Murdock of Kansas, ninth on Post Office and Post Roads, was demoted to the twelfth-ranking spot. A ranking member of the Appropriations Committee found himself serving on the Committee on Ventilation and Acoustics, and a New Jersey Congressman who had been chairman of the Banking and Currency Committee for eight years was replaced by a member who had not previously served on the committee.

The renegade Republicans had had enough. A Wisconsin Congressman appealed to his colleagues, "Have we not been punished by every means at the disposal of the powerful House organization? Members long chairmen of important committees, others holding high rank — all with faithful and efficient party service to their credit — have been ruthlessly removed, deposed and humiliated. . . ." Members had come to expect that seniority would bring power, and they were not prepared to relinquish the privileges of rank. If they wanted to retain those prerogatives, they had few choices. The insurgents could knuckle under to Cannon after all, or they could toss in their lot with the increasingly restless Democrats and hope for the best. Cannon had drawn the line on the red-plush carpet. It was capitulation or revolt. Most chose revolt. They forged an alliance of convenience with the Democrats based on the most pragmatic of political calculations. Years later James Watson, a trusted crony of Cannon, wrote in his memoirs, "Should anyone ask [George] Norris, whether, had Speaker Cannon satisfied his ambition, he would have gone along and supported him, just as the rest of us did, I imagine he would be candid enough to say that in all probability he would have done so. I say 'anyone', because I think he would make that statement to any inquirer. He said it to me on three separate occasions, and said it emphatically."[7] Cannon, however, did not choose to satisfy Norris, and the Congressman from Nebraska, along with the other insurgents, crossed over.

Waiting on the other side of the aisle to receive them was Congressman Champ Clark of Missouri, the House Minority Leader. Clark was a formidable figure in his own right. A tall, barrel-chested farmer, Clark was a populist who carefully cultivated his reputation as the champion of the many against the few. In his Western slouch hat, frock coat, and standing collar, he was a romantic figure in Washington and on the stump, where he delivered ringing speeches liberally sprinkled with literary and classical allusions. Clark was ambitious as well as formidable. He wanted to be Speaker of the House. With the Republicans in disarray, he had a chance. If he could break Cannon's iron-clad control of the House and lead the Democrats to victory in the next election, he could exploit his prestige to capture the Speakership. He welcomed the insurgent Republicans with open arms. For Clark and the other Democrats it was an alliance of convenience also.

The coalition of insurgent Republicans and Democrats succeeded on March 19, 1910. The revolution seems inconsequential in retrospect. Cannon fell when the coalition succeeded in mustering enough votes to overrule him on a point of order. The defeat was symbolic, but it was a signal to Cannon, the members of the House, and the country at large that the Speaker was no longer in control of a majority of members.

Clark capitalized on his newfound stature and accepted speaking engagements around the country. At Tammany Hall that Fourth of July, he said in a typically bombastic style, "I bring to you glad tidings of great joy that the Democrats in the

House of Representatives have laid aside the weight which for years did so easily beset us, that of fighting each other and recently have presented a solid front to the common enemy. We are no longer a feeble, querulous, dispirited body but a courageous, vigilant, hopeful and militant band, not only ready but eager for the fray."[8] He had become the titular head of the Democratic Party. With his help the Democrats seized control of the House in 1912, and Clark was rewarded for his efforts by being elected Speaker.

The Democrats, however, had learned the lessons of the preceding years. As soon as Congress met, the Democratic caucus moved to take the power to name committees away from the Speaker. They gave it instead to the Majority Leader, who also chaired the Ways and Means Committee and presided over the caucus. The Democratic members of the Ways and Means Committee in turn became the Democratic Party's Committee on Committees and for the next 62 years had the authority to make committee assignments.

When the Republicans regained control of the House in 1918, they too had absorbed the lessons of their years under Joe Cannon and were not about to repeat the experience. They voted in their caucus to take the authority over committee assignments away from the Speaker and to vest it in a Committee on Committees composed of members from states which elected Republicans to the House. A *New York Times* reporter, analyzing the significance of this move, wrote that it "was probably adopted because the members who are holdovers and who have worked their way toward the top of the Republican side of the various committees want to retain the benefit of the rule of seniority. . . . [This] was interpreted as meaning that the House committees would be organized and their Chairmen picked in virtually the same old way, after the manner that put Southern men at the top of most of the important committees in both House and Senate in the [outgoing] Congress."

The seniority system was conceived in the 1910 revolt against Cannon, fathered by the Speaker's flagrant disregard of the emerging custom of seniority, and was born in the Democratic caucus of 1912. It continued to grow in fits and starts until it reached maturity in the 1920s. By then the rule of seniority was automatically observed in making committee assignments and selecting committee chairmen. Lapses simply were unheard of.

By the turn of the century members of the House expected to be rewarded for their previous service. When Cannon chose not to, members were forced to remove that authority from the Speaker in order to safeguard their prerogatives. Members who had acquired seniority had too much to lose if the Speaker could shuffle committee assignments and chairmanships at will. Their power and status in the House were at stake. By decentralizing the power of appointment, members hoped to reduce the chances that the authority would be abused, and by instituting the rule of seniority they sought to maintain their power. They succeeded beyond their wildest dreams. Power and status accrued to those who survived. The seniority system which started out protecting the rewards of service ended up rewarding service. Those who benefited the most from the seniority system were those who were regularly returned to Congress. A member from a safe seat had only to bide his time, secure in the knowledge that the workings of the seniority system would ultimately bring rewards his way. The seniority system may not have produced the brightest or wisest committee chairmen. It may not have led to the best legislation or public policy. It may not have served the country. It did, however, function extremely well for the purposes for which it was designed. It protected the power and status of members. It eliminated conflict by distributing rewards impartially. And as long as those who were rewarded were representative of the House as a whole, it served the interests of all members.

By the 1970s this was no longer the case. Southerners controlled the committees as they had whenever the Democrats were in power. By and large they were a conservative lot. The House, however, had grown steadily more liberal over the years, and due to population and political shifts the proportion of Southerners in the House had dropped. Southern Democrats comprised 55 percent of the membership in 1947, but in 1970 they made up only 18.2 percent. Yet they clung tenaciously to 44.4 percent of the chairmanships of all standing committees. Liberals and Congressmen from the rest of the country were being shut out of their fair share of the rewards. Chafing under the seniority system which frustrated their drive for power, they launched an attack against it. They had little to gain by announcing their true intentions, so they cloaked their drive for power in reform rhetoric. They argued that the rigid seniority system was undemocratic and that conservative chairmen were strangling legislation which was in the public interest and supported by a majority of members. Despite this rhetoric, the so-called reform movement was in fact a power grab by members who were losing out under the seniority system. A number of well-respected liberals such as Congressman John Moss of California and Congressman John Dingell of Michigan, who had managed to work their way into the power structure and who would be hurt by the proposed reforms, vehemently opposed any changes. As political scientist Norman Ornstein wrote, "The reason major reforms efforts of the 1960's and 1970's have emanated from the liberal Democrats is simply that they were most in need of payoffs."[9]

The liberals needed a beachhead from which they could launch their attack on the seniority system. Since they had none inside the existing power structure, they struck out on their own. Led by Congressmen Lee Metcalf, Frank Thompson, John Blatnik, and James O'Hara, they organized the Democratic Study Group in 1959. The DSG with its own staff and resources became a base of operations. Its first success came in 1970 when they were able to steer a resolution calling for a study of the seniority system through the Democratic caucus.

The Committee on Organization, Study, and Review, better known as the Hansen Committee after its chairman, Congresswoman Julia Hansen of Washington, met that spring. Its recommendations became the Legislative Reorganization Act of 1970. The committee spent considerable time discussing and arguing the pros and cons of the seniority system but in the end made only one modest change in the seniority rule. The Democratic Committee on Committees would nominate the chairmen of the committees and the nominees would not necessarily be the most senior members of the committees. In practice this altered nothing. The chairmen who were nominated continued to be the members who had the most seniority. Real change in the seniority system would have to wait. While the committee was absorbed in the debate on the seniority system, however, Frank Thompson slipped through two reforms which would have a far-reaching impact on the power structure. His proposals limited subcommittee chairmanships to one per member and permitted each subcommittee chairman to hire one professional staff member. Members of the Hansen Committee paid scant attention to the impact of these proposals because they had nothing at stake.

Congressman Olin Teague of Texas was the only committee member who chaired two subcommittees, and he was chairman of a full committee as well. Members, diverted by the attack on full committee chairmen, routinely incorporated the recommendations on subcommittee chairmen into the final bill.

These proposals were not as inconsequential as they may have seemed at the time. As a result of the Legislative Reorganization Act of 1970, sixteen members were forced to choose between their subcommittee chairmanships. Positions which could be used to build power and status became vacant. The members who gained from these openings were the members who had launched the reform movement—the more liberal and younger Congressmen from the North and West. The new chairmen had spent an average of 7.3 years in the House, while the old chairmen had averaged 17.8 years of service. Ten of the new chairmen were from the North and West, and six came from the South and Border states. Half of the old chairmen had been from the South. Liberals took over the subcommittees on the Banking and Currency, Judiciary, and Foreign Affairs Committees. The transitions did not always go smoothly. The full chairmen still possessed considerable power, which they could—and sometimes did—use to thwart the new subcommittee chairmen. They controlled the subcommittee budgets. They approved hearings and scheduled floor debate on subcommittee bills. They referred legislation to the subcommittees. The Legislative Reorganization Act of 1970, however, was a start. A few hairline cracks had been chiseled into the power structure. Members who had been left out had found an opening. If they were politically astute, they could use what they had gained to hammer away at the power structure from inside.

This is precisely what they did. Liberals steered a "Subcommittee Bill of Rights" through the Democratic caucus in 1973, which solidified and strengthened their earlier gains. They succeeded for the same reasons as they had previously. Members were diverted elsewhere. While the caucus was considering the Subcommittee Bill of Rights, proposals to open up committee meetings and to require automatic votes on committee chairmen were also before it. These issues were believed more important. Committee chairmen were busy fighting off what they saw as direct attacks on their prerogatives while liberals were outflanking them by mounting indirect assaults on their power. The Subcommittee Bill of Rights guaranteed (1) votes on nominees for subcommittee chairmanships in order of seniority, (2) fixed subcommittee jurisdictions, (3) referral of all appropriate legislation, and (4) adequate budgets and staffing. Power was being decentralized, and new members were acquiring influence and status. These power bases would go far to undermine the authority of the committee chairmen. The liberals became power brokers themselves. They emerged as people to be reckoned with in their own right. In summing up the liberal attack on the seniority system, Norman Ornstein and David Rohde wrote, "Like so many battles over seemingly great principles, the fight over the seniority system has been as rooted in political self interest as genuine moral outrage. While its operation is admittedly arbitrary and often inequitable, the seniority system would not have emerged as a standard liberal issue if congressional liberals had been getting a fair share of choice committee chairmanships."[10]

Although the liberals failed to defeat the seniority system, they did something better. They made the seniority system work to their own advantage. As soon as they moved into the power structure, they cemented their positions there. The requirement that subcommittee chairmanships be filled on the basis of seniority accomplished this. The result, ironically enough, was a further institutionalization of the seniority system. The liberals have muted their attacks on the seniority system in recent years as they have begun to gain by it. In the end the status quo was more or less preserved. Congressman Tom Foley of Washington, a liberal who moved up quickly to become chairman of the Agriculture Committee, said, "One result of this spreading out of the action was that a large number of people became interested in rank and privileges. The institution of seniority was strengthened although modified."

The Senate developed differently and more harmoniously. By accident rather than design, the power structure of the Senate, unlike that of the House, has worked consistently in the interests of a majority of Senators. Moreover, Senators acquire a certain amount of prestige simply because they are members of the world's most exclusive club. When Senator Mike Mansfield was Majority Leader, he liked to visualize a Senate that was composed of 100 coequals, and while he never succeeded in realizing this vision, his lip service to the ideal managed to smooth over some of the differences in power and status among individual

Senators. Although Senators, despite Mansfield's best effort, are not a group of equals, they have sources of power and status which are independent of the Senate. Their power and status are not as intimately tied to their position within the Senate as Congressmen's power and status are linked to their rank within the House. Senators therefore have been spared the painful neccessity of challenging the status quo and confronting the existing power structure.

The seniority system was well established in the Senate long before Joe Cannon's playing-for-keeps brand of politics led to the adoption of the seniority rule there. The Senate initially experimented with various ways of selecting committee members and chairmen. Sometimes they were elected by ballot, with the member receiving the most votes being named chairman, and sometimes they were appointed by the Presiding Officer or the President pro Tempore. Those who became chairmen were not always those with the most seniority. Andrew Jackson was named chairman of the powerful Military Affairs Committee by the President pro Tempore in 1828 although he was a freshman and had less seniority than other members of the committee. Henry Clay was elected to chair the prestigious Foreign Relations Committee in 1834 although he was only the third-ranking member of the committee.

Neither of these methods, however, was really satisfactory. Voting on chairmen and committee members was cumbersome and time-consuming. Selection by the Presiding Officer or President pro Tempore provided no assurance that the majority party would control the committees if the Presiding Officer or President pro Tempore happened to be a member of the minority party. Such was the case in 1833.

The seniority rule offered an easy resolution of these difficulties. More than anything, it was an expedient. The seniority rule was adopted without opposition or discussion during the first ten days of the second session of the 29th Congress, December 7 to 17, 1846. After defeating a motion to have committees appointed by the Vice President, the Senate began to select the committee chairmen by ballots. Six chairmen were selected before a lengthy debate ensued over the procedure for selecting the remaining chairmen and all committee members. The Democratic floor leader then presented motions that arranged the names of committee members in order of seniority and safeguarded the majority party's right to chairmanships which became vacant.

The seniority system in the Senate, like the seniority system in the House, had its origins in the need to preserve and maintain power, but it was the power of the majority party rather than the power of individuals. The two-party system was well established in the Senate by 1846. If the committees were to be the result of political bartering among the senators, they could fall under the control of the minority party. The best protection was the presentation of slates naming members of the majority party in order of their seniority and thereby increasing their party loyalty. Presented at one time and voted on altogether, the slates diminished the likelihood of minority party control.

The seniority system emerged in the Senate before the Senators began to aspire to careers in Congress. Prior to the Civil War few Senators sought reelection. Comparison between the two houses is difficult because of the differences in terms of office, but turnover appears to have been more rapid in the Senate than in the House in the early Congresses. As already stated, five of the original twenty-six Senators resigned even before their terms expired. The Senate was in constant turmoil. Resignations, short-term appointments, elected replacements, and more resignations were the order of the day. After the Civil War and Reconstruction the Senate grew in influence and stature. The executive branch was in eclipse, and Senators controlled the state parties and federal patronage. The federal government's increasing involvement in tariff and monetary policy added to the importance of a Senate seat as it did a House seat. The Senate was a good place for a politican to be, and a career there became more attractive. By the time the number of Senators who sought and won reelection started to climb, a system was already in place to reward Senators who built up seniority. In fact, the seniority system itself was a substantial inducement to Senators to seek reelection. The seniority system encouraged longevity among members. At the turn of the century the Senate had its first six-term veteran.

The composition of the Senate changed during the 1950s and 1960s. Once the will of the Senate had been the will of the Southern Democrats. They made up almost half of the Senate, and they controlled the committees. The proportion of Southern Democrats, however, dropped from 49 percent to 18 percent be-

tween 1947 and 1970. Because of the seniority system they continued to hold a disportionate share of committee chairmanships. These members dominated the Senate, but the seniority
system was not as all-pervasive in the Senate as it was in the
House. A "Keep Out" sign was still posted on the door to the inner club of Senators, who were united not only by their seniority
but also by their common reverence for the Senate as an institution, but the Senate had chanced upon ways of distributing symbols of power and status to the new Senators. And enough power
was redistributed so that the "reform" movements which rippled
through the House in the early 1970s were forestalled. When
Lyndon Johnson became Majority Leader in 1953, he initiated
the practice of insuring that each freshman Senator received one
major committee assignment. This was scarcely an act of charity
on Johnson's part. Quite to the contrary, Johnson, always the
wily politician, used this to increase *his* power by putting the new
Senators squarely in his debt. Nevertheless, the Johnson rule
opened seats on the most prestigious committees to Senators who
had never had an opportunity to serve on them. Even more importantly, members from the North and West who were shut out
of the power structure in the House managed to obtain a number
of subcommittee chairmanships in the Senate. In the House the
number of subcommittees chaired by Congressmen from outside
the South rose from 42 percent in 1963 to 72 percent in 1973.
This was the result of changes brought about by the Hansen
Committee. In the Senate the number of subcommittee chairmen from areas outside of the South went from 59 percent in
1963 to 75 percent in 1973. That happened without a Hansen
Committee, without a Democratic Study Group, without a
group of "young Turks" pushing for change. In some ways the
world's most exclusive club was not so exclusive after all.

Both Congressmen and Senators want to achieve power and
status on the Hill, but the routes they take are not always the
same. The individual Congressman and Senator face different
problems and different degrees of difficulty in their rise within
the Congressional hierarchy. More stumbling blocks are put in
the way of Congressmen. Their paths are longer and more tortu-
ous, and the difficulty they encounter has sharpened the conflicts over power in the House.

The newly elected Congressman arriving in Washington for
the first time must become known. He must somehow distinguish

mise, regulation would continue but with escalating price ceilings. Jackson did not quarrel with that, but he resented the fact that he had not been consulted. The compromise had been reached without his particpation.

Jackson was adamant. Without him there would be no natural gas bill. He was more than willing to scuttle the laboriously reached compromise if Johnston was going to claim credit. Outsiders saw the natural gas fight in ideological terms that pitted producers against consumers in the guise of deregulation versus regulation. Insiders knew better.

In the midst of this stalemate Schlesinger flew the 3,000 miles across the country to plead with Jackson to patch up his differences with Johnston. In that he was only partially successful— Jackson did not go along with Johnston. But Schlesinger got what he really wanted. On February 6, 1978, the *New York Times* headline read "Senate Compromise on Gas Deregulation Expected This Week—Talks Focus on Jackson Plan." The article said, "The discussions are based on a new gas pricing formula advanced on Friday by Senator Henry M. Jackson, Democrat of Washington and chairman of the Senate delegation to the House-Senate conference committee on energy legislation." Pushing Johnston aside, Jackson advanced a proposal which was virtually identical to the compromise he had earlier rejected so vehemently.

This new compromise underlined the fact that the personal conflict between the two was over the images of power and not substantive public policy. It called for the continued regulation of natural gas until 1985, after which deregulation would take place. In effect, the Jackson formula ultimately would affect consumers in much the same way that Johnston's proposal would have.

The process and substance of legislation on Capitol Hill is affected by the continual quest for personal power among members and staffs. In a particularly astute comment about Congress, Woodrow Wilson wrote, "Congress always makes what haste it can to legislate. It is the prime object of its rules to expedite lawmaking. Its customs are fruits of its characteristic diligence in enactment. Be the matters small or great, frivolous or grave, which busy it, its aim is to have laws always a-making. Its temper is strenuously legislative."[1] Wilson goes on to point out, "Legislation unquestionably generates legislation. Every statute may be said to have a long lineage of statutes behind it; and whether that lineage be honorable or of ill repute is as much a question as to each individual statute as it can be with regard to the ancestry of each individual legislator. Every statute in its turn has a numerous progeny, and only time and opportunity can decide whether its offspring will bring it honor or shame. Once begin the dance of legislation, and you must struggle through its mazes as best you can to its breathless end, — if any end there be."[2]

In the enclosed and encapsulated world of Capitol Hill members of Congress and their aides are constantly striving to build their reputations for power through legislation. Legislation is not for the most part specifically directed at constituencies. Broad compromises are necessary to secure the passage of legislation, and these always reduce legislative proposals to their lowest common denominator. Congress will hear from its constituents if it passes legislation that is widely considered to be burdensome. For example, when Congress raised Social Security taxes in 1977, the outcry resulted in serious moves to rescind the action. Generally, however, much of the legislation which Congress passes goes unnoticed by the voters. Members of Congress for the most part do not enact legislation in order to be reelected. Reelection activities are sharply distinguished from legislative activities. Their "home style" has little to do with their "Washington style."[3] Richard F. Fenno pointed out in his study of House members in their districts that the members themselves recognize the chasm that exists between their Washington and district activities. A junior member of Congress said, "I haven't been a congressman yet. The first two years, I spent all of my time getting myself reelected. That last two years I spent getting myself a district so that I could get reelected. So I won't be a congressman until next year."[4] It is only after members of Congress begin to feel secure and settle into their Capitol Hill careers that they begin to pursue seriously legislative activity in order to make their mark and demonstrate their power within the body. Most members of Congress will readily admit, at least to themselves, that their constituencies interfere with their Capitol Hill careers. Morris P. Fiorina argues that the principal linkage between Congressmen and their constituents comes through case work, which essentially involves handling constituent complaints against the bureaucracy, and pork barreling. The Fiorina thesis supports the argument that there is little if any connection between the pursuit of most legislative activity on Capitol Hill and electoral constituencies.[5]

The quest for personal power through legislation involves members and staffs in a multifaceted game and in a multidimensional arena of power. Within Congress there is a micropolitical world composed of hundreds of committees, each of which claims a legislative area as its very own. But committee jurisdictions are not so clear-cut that conflict can be avoided, and fighting for legislative turf is commonplace among committees (see Chapter 3).

The short career of Senate staffer Gregory G. Rushford, who worked for Missouri Senator Thomas Eagleton, is illustrative. Although formally hired by Eagleton's District of Columbia Committee, Rushford became a member of Eagleton's personal investigative staff "to examine waste and inefficiency anywhere in the government." Investigations of government programs, however, inevitably intrude upon someone's legislative turf, as each program has its sponsor on Capitol Hill. Describing his first days on the job, Rushford wrote that "Eagleton and I first set about establishing our turf, which is a tricky business. We had to pick issues that other Senators didn't already consider their own. For instance, military issues were out — they would offend Henry Jackson and Sam Nunn, who had already claimed them. And Lawton Chiles chaired a sister subcommittee that was studying military procurement. Even more important, John McClellan had just granted Eagleton membership on his Defense Appropriations Subcommittee, and it would not be good manners for Eagleton to return the favor by using another subcommittee to investigate the military."[6]

The search for an issue to investigate began. Rushford's first idea was to investigate the $10 billion research and development budget of the Pentagon. "I can't look like I'm on a vendetta against the military," Eagleton told his staffer. "Get me a cripple. Some horrible wasteful weapon no reasonable person could endorse."[7] Even then, Rushford writes, "it was better to hold off for awhile for fear of stirring up resentment on the McClellan subcommittee." Finally, after weeks of testing and rejecting possible areas of investigation, sometimes because they clearly fell within the turf of other Senators, Eagleton decided to focus on the Food for Peace program. The decision being made, Rushford writes, "I carefully laid the groundwork for my investigation

by checking first with Senator Humphrey's staff to see if they had
any objections. Eagleton himself made courtesy calls to Humphrey and Abraham Ribicoff. All this was necessary because
Humphrey is known as 'Mr. Food for Peace' and his feelings were
important, while Ribicoff is chairman of the full Governmental
Affairs Committee under which our investigation was taking
place. After these elaborate hedges against senatorial ill-will,
Eagleton told me to get to work."

The investigation into the Food for Peace Program was
doomed from the start. Wherever Rushford turned, he found
that he was directly or indirectly invading the domain of powerful Senators, including the chairman of the House Appropriations Subcommittee on Agriculture, Mississippi Congressman
James Whitten. However, Eagleton was more worried that the
investigation might antagonize McClellan, who held Eagleton's
future career on the Appropriations Committee in his hand.
"One of my first instructions had been never to displease McClellan," writes Rushford. McClellan was satisfied with the Food for
Peace Program, in part because it bought and exported large
amounts of rice from his state. As chairman of the Appropriations Committee, McClellan controlled the funding for the program; therefore, Rushford's inquiry implicitly invaded McClellan's turf. The undiplomatic way in which the investigation was
handled was an important cause of Rushford's dismissal only a
few weeks later.[8]

Building a reputation for power within Congress begins at
the committee stage, and insofar as it involves legislation, a
member who succeeds in getting a bill with his name on it has
made progress in building his reputation for power. A powerful
House subcommittee chairman pointed out that this was one of
the great advantages of his position. "If the time is ripe, if a bill
is in the area of your jurisdiction, you preempt it, change it
slightly, and put your name on it," he said. The rhetoric of Capitol Hill constantly refers to winners and losers in the legislative
process, not in terms of broad ideological conflict or substantive
issues, but in terms of personalities.

When bills eventually reach the floor, their substance often
seems to be considered secondary in importance to the Capitol
Hill reputations of the members who have sponsored the legislation. For example, Senate Majority Leader Robert Byrd, in discussing an energy bill on the floor, spent as much time lavishing

praise on the Senators responsible for the bill as in discussing its substantive contents. One of those Senators was Floyd Haskell of Colorado, chairman of the Energy Production and Supply Sub-committee. Referring to Haskell and his committee, Byrd told his colleagues, "The work load and contribution of the Energy Production and Supply Subcommittee has been remarkable. No one knows this better than the members of the subcommittee and its distinguished chairman, Senator Floyd Haskell. His con-scientious management of this bill typifies his reputation as a hardworking and effective legislator." Byrd went on, "During the seven long days of legislative hearings, the painstaking sub-committee and committee markup, floor debate, and extensive conference deliberations, Senator Haskell always was personally involved. He participated not only in terms of guiding the bill procedurally, but also substantively." Byrd particularly compli-mented Haskell for his sponsorship of "the provision in this bill which utilizes the Farmers Home Administration to assist private developers in providing housing and related services in areas where coalfields are developed."[9]

While complimenting Haskell, the Senate Majority Leader never lost sight of the fact that Scoop Jackson above all other Senators had to be given primary credit for whatever energy leg-islation emerged from his committee. Before speaking of Has-kell, Byrd had told his colleagues that "I commend in particular Senator Jackson, the distinguished chairman of the Committee on Energy and Natural Resources, for the depth of his under-standing of our energy problems, his incisive analysis of proposed policies, and his exemplary management of a complicated bill in committee, on the Senate floor, and in conference."[10]

Jackson had clearly established his reputation as the domi-nant Senate force in energy policy as a result of his "victory" in the conference on the gas deregulation bill. Jackson emerged as a winner not because his original position was sustained, but be-cause he was the one who engineered the compromise with House forces that broke a major deadlock. Other aspects of the Congressional battle over President Carter's energy program il-lustrate other dimensions of the personal power game in the leg-islative processes of Capitol Hill. Whatever disposition is made of a President's program in Congress, powerful members must end up with their reputations for power intact, or preferably en-hanced. It is not so much the substantive nature of the President's proposals that are important as the way in which they are handled that counts. A classic mistake made by Presidents is to feel that by appealing to the people, that is, to the collective constituencies of Congress, they can be successful on Capitol Hill. The separation of Congress and electoral forces in the legislative sphere, however, dooms this tactic from the start. What Presidents must do is appeal to the key power centers of Congress, including the leadership of the House, more than the Senate, and the chairmen of powerful committees in both bodies. Above all, in order to be successful, Presidents must respect the way things are done on Capitol Hill. Presidents could well heed the advice that Sam Rayburn, that legendary Speaker of the House, gave to a freshman member when he said that "to get along on Capitol Hill one must learn to go along."

The relationship between the governor and the state legislature in Georgia apparently did not prepare President Carter or, more importantly, his chief aides for the intricate world of personal power that exists in Congress. Carter succeeded on Capitol Hill only insofar as members of the Congressional establishment felt their power on the Hill could be enhanced by making the President's proposal their own. This did not necessarily mean complete support for the substantive positions of the President. Rather, certain Congressmen and Senators found they could exercise their personal power by demonstrating their ability to secure passage of the President's legislation. This was particularly true of the President's energy proposals in the House, where Thomas P. "Tip" O'Neill used the energy package to demonstrate his power as Speaker. It was Tip O'Neill who shepherded the President's program through the House maze. A successful reputation for power requires eventual delivery of the goods, and O'Neill, by backing the President's program, was taking a calculated risk because of its controversial provisions.

O'Neill began by announcing that there was strong opposition which would make passage difficult. If Carter's energy policy was to remain intact in the House, he said, it would be up to the leadership. Once allied with the President, O'Neill established the necessary organizational and procedural arrangements to secure eventual passage. The Speaker immediately enlisted the help of the chairmen of the key committees with jurisdiction over energy, particularly Interstate and Foreign Commerce, its Energy and Power Subcommittee, and the Ways and

Means Committee, which had jurisdiction over the tax portions.

By enlisting these chairmen, O'Neill created a situation in which a successful bill would be a credit not only to him but also to powerful chairmen such as Harley Staggers, of the Interstate and Foreign Commerce Committee, John Dingell, of the Energy and Power Subcommittee, and Al Ullman, of Ways and Means. These men were brought together in the form of a confederation of soverign interests represented by a new creation of O'Neill — the ad hoc energy committee. Ullman and Staggers were suspicious of the energy committee but were persuaded, reluctantly, to go along.

O'Neill's ad hoc energy committee was assigned the task of coordinating the various bills as they emerged from the regular standing committees and subcommittees. It could not initiate proposals. It simply considered the recommendations of the standing committees.

In explaining the background of the ad hoc committee, O'Neill stated, "I can remember meeting with the minority leader [John Rhodes of Arizona] . . . and talking with him about an ad hoc energy committee, talking about the fact that it is impossible to put a policy together if we have the legislation going to different committees and being reported as individual bills as in the past. If we did that there would be nitpicking and logrolling. We agreed on a solution: let us have an ad hoc committee. Let us not strip the committees of their rights, but rather send the bill to the standing committees and then have them report to an ad hoc committee."[11]

The creation of an ad hoc committee of forty members, twenty-seven Democrats and thirteen Republicans, composed of the chairmen and some members of the standing committees with jurisdiction over energy, was a stroke of genius. As soon as it became known that the committee would be established, House members, knowing the action would be there in the first session of the 95th Congress in 1977, scrambled to get on it. The committee expanded the number of Congressmen whose reputations would rise or fall in the energy debate. They had a vested interest in resolving the different energy provisions and pushing for a package that would be acceptable to the House. As the energy committee members acted out the script written by the standing committee chairmen, they played to a 435-member house. The chairman of the committee was Thomas Ashley of Ohio, a relatively unknown member of the House despite his twenty-two years of seniority. Before 1977 Ashley was known mainly for his work on the Banking and Merchant Marine Committees. Ashley worked hard on the 1970 Housing Act, which included his provision for a national urban growth policy, sorely needed but mundane compared to a national energy policy. With the creation of the ad hoc energy committee, this unassuming Congressman from Toledo suddenly found himself on the front pages of the country's leading newspapers. As the energy legislation reached the floor, Al Ullman, echoing the sentiments of many, commended Ashley for "a splendid job of pioneering a new procedure in the House of Representatives that enables us now to bring an energy package to the floor that is comprehensible, that is responsible, and that is responsive to the recommendations of the administration."[12] Republican William A. Steiger of Wisconsin, expressing the minority viewpoint, added, "Our distinguished chairman [Ashley], who I must say, has done a superb job under very difficult circumstances, is a gentleman to whom I give great credit in spite of the fact that he runs a hell of a lot better railroad than anybody I see around here [in the House] does. I give him great credit for how he handles himself under these circumstances."[13]

The ad hoc energy committee was successful because it did not intrude into the legislative turf of Interstate and Foreign Commerce, Ways and Means, and the Banking Committee, all of which had primary jurisdiction over the energy package. (By contrast, the ad hoc welfare committee, also set up by O'Neill in the 95th Congress, stumbled into trouble because O'Neill violated the fundamental principle of respect for legislative turf. The ad hoc welfare committee, unlike the energy committee, was given the authority to sift the legislative proposals *before* they went to the standing committees. See pages 94–95.) Ashley was careful to respect the jurisdictions of these committees, and during floor debate on the bill he and the chairmen of the committees stressed that the integrity of the standing committees had been preserved. The proposals that were reported from the ad hoc energy committee were developed and approved by the standing committees. Ullman said that he was pleased to be a part of the process that in producing the energy package preserved the status quo. "We have been able to [develop the energy package] without sacrificing in any way the major jurisdictional responsibilities in the House. We bring here a recommendation from the Ways and Means committee *as we reported it from that committee*, a fine, responsible package."[14]

Senior Republicans on the standing committees with jurisdiction over energy also praised the ad hoc energy committee's respect for their legislative territory. The second-ranking Republican on the Banking Committee, Congressman Gary Brown of Michigan, during the course of an exchange with Ashley, emphasized the "fine programs" that emerged from his committee. Holding in his hand the banking provisions of the energy bill, he turned to Ashley and said, "Let me ask the gentleman this: Who had the jurisdiction over these proposals? Who had real jurisdiction over these proposals? Who had real jurisdiction over all this subject matter?" Ashley replied as if reading from a script, "It was the Committee on Banking, Finance, and Urban Affairs." Brown responded, "Yes, the Committee on Banking, Finance, and Urban Affairs. That is correct, and that is, of course, why the banking provision is a good provision, because we were the most proper forum in the committee with jurisdiction to come out with such a program."[15]

In the end, the energy package which passed the House closely resembled the President's original proposal because the Speaker and powerful members of the House were accommodated and emerged with enhanced reputations. The rest of Carter's programs were not accorded this special treatment, and as a result the President's record in the House was dismal during the first two years. Carter had publicly put energy at the top of his agenda, causing his energy program to overshadow all other White House legislation. O'Neill recognized that if he could demonstrate his ability to lead the House on this one issue by securing the passage of the President's proposal, his reputation for power on Capitol Hill would be secure. Although the Speaker would try to marshal House support for other presidential proposals, he knew that if he succeeded in the major area of energy, his failure to produce other legislation would not be weighed heavily by members of the House in their assessment of him.

While Tip O'Neill and his committee chairmen believed there were advantages in supporting the President's energy package, Senators saw things differently. Senate Majority Leader Robert Byrd chose not to put his power on the line by giving the President his unqualified support. Although Byrd tries to be a strong leader, he never loses sight of the collegial nature of the body. The Majority Leader of the Senate has many of the same powers as the Speaker of the House. It is virtually impossible to bring up legislation without his backing, for instance. However, a prudent Majority Leader will avoid arbitrary decisions. To do otherwise is to risk severe criticism.

Robert Byrd did what he could to salvage an energy program. However, it was not the program of the President that was saved. The Senate, in fact, dashed off in the opposite direction. It voted to deregulate natural gas, while the President wanted regulation continued. And the Senate did not adopt the energy tax portion of the President's legislation, but instead voted Russell Long the authority to work out his own compromise in conference.

The energy bill collided with the power structure of the Senate. Byrd, unlike O'Neill, lacked the incentive and capability to dictate to his colleagues. Scoop Jackson, chairman of the Energy and Natural Resources Committee with jurisdiction over the natural gas portion of the bill, failed to control his committee. Many of the Senators on it had their own ideas about an energy program and were determined to go to the floor with them. Russell Long, whose Finance Committee controlled a major portion of the President's legislation, used the energy bill to demonstrate his independence to his colleagues, the House, and the President.

Long worked hard to have the adjective "wily" routinely affixed to his name. In earning it, he came to control conference committees on tax matters. The demise of Congressman Wilbur Mills, formerly chairman of the House Ways and Means Committee, helped considerably. When Mills left, Long became the man to watch for the lift of a shoulder, a twitch of an eyebrow, or a hearty guffaw which might announce a break in a stalemate. Al Ullman, the new chairman of Ways and Means, was a well-intentioned liberal who simply could not match his predecessor's grasp of the tax code (few could). The energy tax conference with official Washington looking on was an ideal setting for Long to strut his expertise. It was ideal for another purpose too. Long began an early meeting with White House aides by saying, "For those of you who do not know who I am, I'm Russell Long, chairman of the Senate Finance Committee." The energy tax conference was a place where Long could demonstrate to the newcomers at 1600 Pennsylvania Avenue that he was not to be taken for granted.

It was in this setting of the Senate Finance Committee versus the House Ways and Means Committee, the Senate versus the House, that the "wily" Louisiana Senator began his maneuvering on the energy tax proposals. The rhetoric of the debate, of course, spoke of issues, which are the loose change of politics. Long emphasized that the President's program was inadequate because it failed to provide incentives for the production of energy. The American people, he said, would not accept additional taxes that failed to solve an energy problem that could only be resolved through the development of new energy sources. The day that Tip O'Neill scheduled final committee action in the House on the President's bill, Russell Long proclaimed that the White House plan was an "unmitigated disaster." Most members of his Finance Committee agreed. Many undoubtedly recognized before concurring that opposition would hurt their careers in the committee and in the Senate.

Characteristically, Long wanted to go to the conference committee with maximum maneuverability. He did not want to be bound by prior Senate actions, and above all did not want to have to follow instructions from his Senate colleagues. That meant steering an energy tax bill through the body that would give him bargaining flexibility. He succeeded. He maneuvered through his own Finance Committee and through the Senate a bill that gave him total freedom to negotiate. Ignoring virtually all of the provisions of the President's proposal, he also paid scant attention to the proposals of various lobbying groups.

Long easily dominated the debate over the energy bill. He persuaded the Senate to defeat motions that would have limited his bargaining. Afterwards, the whiz kids on Kennedy's staff, annoyed by Long's success, drafted a resolution which suggested that the Finance Committee share some of its jurisdiction over taxes with the other committees. Long, they felt, had simply become too imperialistic. While the Kennedy resolution arose out of the energy debate, it would have the important effect of giving Kennedy's Health Subcommittee some say in the tax portions of national health insurance, a pet project of the Massachusetts Senator.

Long's major victory remained intact. The Senate approved, 52–35, a bill providing tax credits of $40 billion, each one of which was in effect a provision that Long could trade off in the upcoming conference. Al Ullman and the House conferees were not so fortunate in their bargaining position. Under House rules they were bound by the provisions of the House-passed bill and were not free to trade them off in conference. They could make compromises, but only within the framework of the House bill. Moreover, a number of House liberals helped persuade Tip O'Neill to appoint his ad hoc energy committee chairman Thomas Ashley to the energy tax conference to monitor Ullman lest he cede too much to Long. This further reduced the maneuverability of the Ways and Means Committee chairman.

Thus, as the conference opened, Long was the man to watch. White House aides, industry lobbyists, consumer representatives, and reporters waited for Long's signal that the time had arrived for serious bargaining. At another conference, the cue was the announcement that Long expected to attend a birthday party that evening. Obviously Long intended the work of the conference to be completed before-hand. Several hours later the conference resolved the remaining differences and Long went off to his party. In the end, Long refused to accept the key tax proposals of the President, and nothing the House or the White House could do caused Long to change his mind. Just as Tip O'Neill chose to demonstrate his power in the House by passing the energy legislation, Russell Long decided to flaunt his power in the Senate by opposing it.

Off Capitol Hill energy legislation seemed to be dominated by special interests, and to reflect the ideological views of party and regions. President Carter reflected this view when he accused the Senate of capitulating to special interest groups that opposed his program.

Within Congress the energy legislation appeared to be determined by the internal balance of forces between the House and the Senate, and among the leadership, members, and crucial committees of both bodies. Carter was unwilling to go along to get along. The President was accused of imposing arbitrary deadlines on the Hill, of failing to consult adequately beforehand with key Congressional leaders, particularly Russell Long. On Capitol Hill aides scoffed at legislation which they felt was poorly drafted and incompletely documented. White House lobbyists failed to consider the important Congressional norm of expertise in developing and drafting legislation.

The fate of the energy program on Capitol Hill shows that even legislation given top priority by the White House is caught up in the drive for power and status within Congress. As members of Congress seek to build their careers through legislative achievements, constant conflict ensues over legislative territory among committees (see Chapter 3). Each time a bill which is likely to be popular is sent to Congress from the White House, a scramble is set off among members who are eager to claim it for their own. Legislation drafted by Congressmen themselves is often subjected to the imperialistic designs of colleagues. Congressman Jim Corman of California, chairman of a Ways and Means Subcommittee on Welfare and the ad hoc welfare committee, was irked by Carter's wobbling on welfare reform. Two top White House aides had publicly stated that welfare reform would be an impossibility in 1978, causing dismay on the part of Corman, who saw the move as a threat to his committee. When Carter finally sent Corman a handwritten letter that said, "I have every hope and expectation that the welfare reform proposals will be passed by the Congress this year," the California Congressman immediately distributed copies to the press as evidence that the President had not dropped plans for the bill. This allowed his subcommittee to continue work on what promised to be a major piece of legislation. Corman set an April 1 target date for completion of work on the bill, but soon found that he would not have the cooperation of the Ways and Means Committee chairman Al Ullman or of other powerful members of the House and the Senate that would be needed for passage. Corman pressed on, but the atmosphere surrounding the work of his welfare committee was one of gloom. As Carter turned his attention elsewhere, the White House dropped its plans for welfare reform. Corman was denied the opportunity, which he had so earnestly sought, to reap credit for welfare revision.

Other Congressmen and Senators saw similar advantages to themselves in developing legislation that would incorporate the President's proposals in areas such as education, urban redevelopment, health care, and executive reorganization. In the summer of 1976 Sam Nunn, believing that Jimmy Carter would be elected and would attempt to keep his campaign promise to establish a separate Department of Education, introduced his own version of a bill to create a new Cabinet level Department of Education. The legislation was hastily drafted, and neither

Nunn nor his aides expected that the bill would pass. That was not the point. The real purpose, an aide explained, was to establish Nunn's interest in the area. Years later, if Carter sent a Department of Education bill to Capitol Hill, Nunn would be ready. He would be able to point to his long-standing interest in a Department of Education, an interest clearly demonstrated by his 1976 bill.

Nunn's gamble paid off. The creation of a separate cabinet level Department of Education was a major goal of the Carter administration. Nunn was a principal sponsor of legislation to create the department when it was introduced in 1978 and again in 1979. Both times Nunn presided over many Governmental Affairs Committee hearings on the bill along with the committee chairman, Abe Ribicoff, who was the number one sponsor of the legislation. Nunn insisted that the bills include a provision for an independent inspector general and, as a spokesman for the Armed Services Committee, he sought to provide for the smooth transition to the new department of the Overseas Schools that were administered by the Defense Department.

Members of Congress seek recognition as the primary spokesmen on Capitol Hill for different policy areas. Senator Richard Lugar of Indiana, once known as Richard Nixon's favorite mayor, buttressed his staff in the urban area as he set about becoming the major Republican spokesman for urban policy in the Senate. This position had been held by Senator Edward Brooke of Massachusetts, whose tacit approval was required first. Brooke agreed as long as he retained his position as the Republican spokesman on housing issues. Brooke's defeat in 1978 cleared the way for Lugar to expand his jurisdiction.

In the second session of the 95th Congress retiring Democratic Representative Jim Mann of South Carolina, who chaired the House Judiciary subcommittee handling the revision of the criminal code, diligently sought to pass legislation in the House with his name on it so that he could leave his mark. He failed, which transferred the opportunity to claim credit in the House for the revision of the criminal code to Robert F. Drinan, who became chairman of the Criminal Justice Subcommittee in the 96th Congress. Congressman Augustus Hawkins of California used his chairmanship of the Employment Opportunity Subcommittee of Education and Labor to sponsor what later became known as the "Humphrey-Hawkins bill." As a tribute to the late Senator Humphrey the House passed a much watered-down version of the bill in 1978 by a vote of 257–152. Its passage represented an outstanding achievement for the California Congressman. Congressman George Danielson of California, chairman of the Administrative Law and Governmental Relations Subcommittee of Judiciary, gained fame for his efforts on behalf of lobbying control legislation. His committee reported the Public Lobbying Act of 1978, which repealed the 1946 federal lobbying law, known primarily for its loopholes.

As members of Congress build their reputations on the Hill as effective legislators, they are weighed and judged by internal standards and norms. Is a member a "hard worker," an "effective legislator" who is capable of developing and guiding legislation through from beginning to end? Is he intelligent, "a craftsman"producing "good bills" that are carefully drafted? Members seeking to build their careers through legislation strive for such accolades from their colleagues. In order to do this they use committee and personal staffs to represent them in the legislative process.

Congressman Paul Rogers of Florida built his Congressional reputation for power and influence by developing and passing health legislation. The center of Rogers's Congressional district was Palm Beach County, which stretches from the rococo mansions of Palm Beach forty miles straight west to the migrant shacks scattered at the edges of the sugar cane fields in Belle Glade. It is a county of great wealth and staggering poverty that relies heavily on tourism and agriculture. It is not and never has been a medical center. For many years the only major hospital in the district stoutly refused to accept any federal aid in order to avoid compliance with civil rights legislation. Rogers chose to concentrate on health policy, not because it was of vital interest to his constituents, but because through luck and chance it was an area into which he could move and make his mark. Rogers has admitted that few of his constituents were interested in health legislation except in the most general way. Even fewer of the residents of Palm Beach County were aware of his prominence in this field. Nevertheless Rogers set out with singular intensity to establish himself as the major force in health legislation in the country and succeeded overwhelmingly. Among his colleagues in the House he was recognized as the leading figure in health policy on the Hill, the Mr. Health of Congress. Over a

three-year period Rogers was directly responsible for such legis-
lation as the Health Research and Health Services Act, the
Health Information and Disease Prevention Act, the Health Re-
venue Sharing and Nurse Training Act, the Developmentally
Disabled Assistance Act, the Comprehensive Alcohol Abuse and
Alcoholism Prevention, Treatment, and Rehabilitation Act, the
national Foreign Flu and Immunization program, the Safe
Drinking Water Act, the Health Professions Education Act, the
Clean Air Act, the Rural Clinic Service Act, the Medicare and
Medicaid Antifraud and Abuse Act, the Arthritis, Diabetes, and
Digestive Diseases Act, the Emergency Medical Services Act, the
Indian Health Care Improvement Act, and the Health Mainte-
nance and Organization Act. Few members of Congress on ei-
ther side of Capitol Hill can boast legislative achievements of this
scope and depth.

Rogers achieved his position in health policy by mastering
the field himself and by gathering around him a capable committee staff. Together they used the subcommittee to hold extensive hearings and develop health legislation. Rogers had close
and cordial relations with the medical community, since legislation he sponsored channeled millions of dollars into medical research, preventive medicine, and medical education, all of
which are widely supported by the medical profession. Rogers's
bills were generally passed by overwhelming majorities in the
House. The fact that he was able to do this was a reflection of his
skill as a politician. Rogers himself is genial and easygoing. The
most flamboyant thing about him is his penchant for black pat-
ent leather Gucci loafers and belts. In a state where politicians
routinely list in their biographies the year they moved to Florida,
the Rogers family arrived when most of the land south of Orlan-
do was still mangrove swamps and palmetto palms. South Florida is a place of transients, of refugees from the North seeking a
new life in crackerbox houses, but the Rogers family have always
known who they were and where they fit in. Strong passion and
intense emotion seem to have been foreign to Rogers. Instead,
his political style was that of the tactician who works quietly and
steadily to fashion a majority. At the University of Florida in the
early 1940s Rogers was a national debating champion. He remained rational and orderly, marshaling facts and arguments,
one piled upon the other, building the inescapable logic of his
position.

In 1973 Rogers sponsored an emergency medical services bill which would provide grants to communities to equip ambulances, train ambulance personnel, and set up communication systems between ambulance drivers and doctors in hospital emergency rooms. Health-care experts estimated that 60,000 to 100,000 lives a year would be saved at the nominal cost of $185 million over a three-year period. Few could oppose such legislation, and not many did. But on its way to becoming a law the bill got tangled up in a fight between Congress and President Richard Nixon over the announced closing of eight Public Health Service hospitals. When the bill arrived on his desk, Nixon who had called for emergency medical services legislation in his State of the Union address nine months before, vetoed it. The day that the House would vote on whether to override the veto Rogers's aides were in a frenzy. Their slim two-thirds majority of the day before was slipping away under pressure from the White House, and each phone call uncovered another yes vote which overnight had become a no vote. Rogers, however, sat in his private office calmly talking to a reporter from a local newspaper. Only a trace of a fleeting frown, as another "Damn!" and the sound of a phone being slammed into its receiver filtered through the door, betrayed his awareness that anything extraordinary was occurring. An aide arrived with the names of wavering Congressmen who might be called. Rogers dialed the numbers and recited to each in turn all of the reasons why the legislation should pass — the number of lives that would be saved, the small amount of money involved, the lengthy list of groups who supported it — and mentioned, as if it mattered not at all, "We'd like to have you with us on this if possible."

On that occasion Rogers lost, although not by much. The final tally was five votes short of the necessary two-thirds. His aides were despondent. They would have been the ones who first defeated Nixon. Rogers's wife Becky had bottles of champagne in the refrigerator at home for the celebration. But Rogers, noticing an aide slumped at his desk, simply said, "We picked up a few votes that time, and next time it will pass — that's the way it is done," and walked on through to his office. There he began dictating thank-you notes to his colleagues who had voted to override the veto.

Rogers's career demonstrates that the legislative activities of Congressmen often have little, if anything, to do with their constituents. It wasn't on the basis of his health legislation that Rogers was reelected. Rogers's seat was a family sinecure since the district was created. His father Dwight was the first Congressman from the district, and Rogers was elected to fill out the remainder of the term when his father died shortly after being elected to his sixth term in 1954. Rogers's personal popularity was unrivaled. He was unopposed in both the primary and general elections in 1976, when he received 91 percent of the vote. When he was offered the chairmanship of the Merchant Marine and Fisheries Committee, which is more directly related to his constituents' interests, he refused in order to retain his chairmanship of the Health and Environment Subcommittee.

Rogers and his staff tended to seize immediately on new issues, hold hearings, and develop legislation. When *The Cloning of a Man*, the alleged story of a rich industrialist who created a cloned son, was published as a nonfiction book in 1978, Rogers scheduled hearings on cloning. Although many Congressmen tried to edge into the health area, only Dan Rostenkowski of Illinois, chairman of the Health Subcommittee of Ways and Means, managed to do so and then only in the area of national health insurance. Rogers's constant activity deterred competition.

Long before the issue of the protection of the rights of human research subjects received widespread recognition in the medical community and in certain segments of the public, Rogers held a hearing and sponsored legislation on the subject. The year was 1973. Kennedy had already acted in the Senate to guarantee the rights of human subjects. Rogers set the tone of his hearings, which illustrates the politically noncontroversial dimension of health legislation, in the following way:

> The overall question of the ethical conduct of conducting experiments with human subjects received worldwide attention following World War II and was addressed at the Nuremburg trials. Since then there have been several national and international agreements passed.
>
> I think there can be no question as to the need for experiments as part of the scientific progress which gives our medical storehouse new and valuable drugs and methods for the betterment of man.
>
> The question most frequently posed in light of reoccurring stories about the misuse of human subjects is how we can best strengthen existing laws to insure that these misuses do not occur.

> During recent months hearings have documented that our system of surveillance on medical trials using humans has many shortcomings.[16]

Rogers established that the Senate bill embodied in H.R. 10403, then before the committee, was not necessarily satisfactory. "I am not at all sure that the provisions of H.R. 10403, as well meaning as they are, can fully guarantee our goal of protecting individuals who participate in medical research," he said.[17] Rogers's opening remarks suggesting an expanded role for the Congressman in this area epitomize the effective legislator. "If after the hearings are concluded we feel that the scope of legislation presented here is not broad enough, then it may be necessary for us to expand its scope beyond HEW to cover all other departments and agencies which are involved in human experiment. Yet, we may possibly have to move beyond this," he said.[18] As the Protection of Human Subjects Act moved through the House, Rogers's unique stamp was set upon it.

The legislation that Rogers generated in the health sphere spawned additional legislation at a geometric rate. As each bill created new programs, Rogers's committee was required to oversee their implementation and administration. As the flaws in legislation emerged, Rogers and his staff had to correct them through amendments. Much of the important legislation approved by the Health and Environment Subcommittee consists of amendments to Rogers's own legislation. In the face of the inevitable turnovers in the top echelons of Cabinet departments and administrative agencies, Congressmen such as Rogers become the real secretaries and administrators of their own programs. For some Congressmen, who build their careers through committees, this means informal oversight, investigations, and authorization hearings. For others, who build their careers through legislation, this means more bills and amendments to legislation already enacted.

As Rogers reviewed the performance of the National Institutes of Health under the National Cancer Act, which he sponsored, he built on what had gone before in the form of amendments to the original act. As his committee considered these amendments, Rogers demonstrated his role in health policy. While Rogers praised the program, he expressed concern about many aspects of it. At the time Nixon had tried impounding

funds appropriated under the act, but Rogers succeeded in securing their release. He noted the lack of health manpower, one
of his long-time interests, was impeding implementation. And so
was bureaucratic red tape. "We find the program bogged down
in paperwork which we had hoped would be cut," he said. "We
find a grant lag growing because of NIH procedures and we find
new and innovative programs being slowed down or even halted
because of a lack of people. We do not have enough slots in the
clinical center and that applies, I think, across the board to every
Institute." Rogers said, "This committee and indeed the Congress, takes great pride in the National Cancer Act, but this is
only the beginning." He pointed out that over 100,000 lives a
year can be saved with adequate and timely cancer treatment,
and that Americans should recognize that many forms of cancer
can be cured. The Congressman then proceeded to embark upon
two days of hearings with an extraordinary list of witnesses testifying on various aspects of cancer research, and the need for the
expansion of the National Cancer Institute, which was Rogers's
purpose to begin with.[19] With great care, Rogers marshaled expert witnesses to back his legislative proposals. Cancer experts
and leaders of the medical community appeared along with top
HEW personnel to support the Congressman.

Congressmen who build their careers through legislative
achievements always seek close and cordial relations with the administrative departments and agencies that implement their programs. In Rogers's case this meant that support by the Secretary
of HEW and the heads of its bureaus and agencies was often a
major help on Capitol Hill. Below the political appointees in the
career civil service effective Congressmen such as Rogers maintain a mutually reinforcing network. For example, Rogers, in
working with the Public Health Service, prevented President
Nixon from closing a number of public health hospitals throughout the country.

The opposition of the administration, even to a Congressman
as powerful as Paul Rogers, is always a major obstacle to the passage of legislation, although it can be surmounted. When the
Secretary of HEW opposed legislation Rogers sponsored to expand health services programs in 1975, it did not prevent the
eventual passage of the bill that embodied most of the provisions
Rogers wanted. When Rogers backed health insurance for the
unemployed, however, the combined opposition of the Depart-

ments of Health, Education, and Welfare and of Labor helped to defeat it. But such opposition is unusual. The Congressman and his staff forestalled opposition by garnering support behind the scenes before holding hearings and introducing legislation. Rogers's effectiveness stemmed to a degree from his carefulness.

The style, scope, and content of Rogers's legislative activity is illustrated by a glance at some of the activities of his subcommittee since 1975.[20] In February of that year hearings were held on health manpower programs. Witnesses included Secretary of HEW Caspar Weinberger and his assistant secretary for health, who made a general assessment of manpower needs. Other witnesses included a professor of medicine and the director of a health policy program at the University of California Medical School in San Francisco; the president of the Pennsylvania College of Pediatric Medicine and vice chairman of the Federation of Associations of the Schools of the Health Professions; past presidents of the American Board of Medical Specialties; the vice president of the American Hospital Association; the speaker of the House of Delegates of the AMA; the president of the Association of American Medical Colleges; and the president of the Council of Medical Specialties Societies. All of the testimony generally favored Rogers's proposal to extend federal assistance to health manpower training programs. Later in the year hearings were held on amendments to the Public Health Service Act and on health insurance for the unemployed. As the second session of the 94th Congress began in 1976, the subcommittee tackled amendments to the 1970 Comprehensive Alcohol Abuse and Alcoholism Prevention, Treatment, and Rehabilitation Act. In the opening weeks of the session, the committee again heard from a broad cross section of the medical community, all backing Rogers. In the 95th Congress the committee considered various amendments to the Safe Drinking Water Act of 1974.

Rogers began concentrating on health legislation when he became ranking member of the House Subcommittee on Health chaired by John Jarman of Oklahoma. The death of Dwight Rogers at a relatively early age from heart disease had stimulated an interest in health issues, and with his rise on the Health Subcommittee he was able to do something about it. Jarman, soon to retire, was more than willing to let Rogers become the de facto chairman. With the death of John Fogarty of Rhode Island, who chaired the Appropriations Subcommittee on Health, a gap had been created. No one had claimed health legislation for his own and Rogers moved to do so in 1968. Eric Redman, writing about this stage of Rogers's career, says, "He needed new ideas for health legislation, and welcomed any visitor with an imaginative proposal."[21] At the time Redman, an aide to Senator Warren Magnuson, was nurturing a proposal for a National Health Service Corps which would provide money for doctors who were willing to practice where a doctor shortage existed. Priority was to be given to povery areas. Rogers agreed to sponsor the legislation in the House.

For Rogers the National Health Service Corps was a potentially important innovation in health care for which he could claim credit in the House. Magnuson's office was aware of Rogers's growing reputation in the health area and worried that he would steal the idea. The two staffs, meeting together, worked out an arrangement that satisfied both men. Magnuson's aides would write the bill, but Rogers would have a chance to make changes before it was introduced. Redman said the arrangement relieved their fear that Rogers might act precipitously if the bill ran into trouble in the Senate. Magnuson's aides, like all staff, feared that their idea might be stolen before their version of the legislation could be introduced and another would claim authorship. To safeguard against such a possibility, they refused to circulate a draft of the NHSC bill until they were ready to solicit cosponsors. Magnuson's staff was anxious to secure the support of Ralph Yarborough, chairman of the Committee on Labor and Public Welfare and its Health Subcommittee. The bill would inevitably be referred to Yarborough's committee, and without his support the legislation would never get out of committee. The chief counsel of the Health Subcommittee insisted that the bill go through the committee and not be introduced as a floor amendment as Magnuson's staff hoped. As aides to Magnuson and Yarborough clashed, tension between the Magnuson and Rogers staffs also escalated. Rogers's aides were threatening to go ahead. They had a bill which was ready to be introduced, and they saw no reason to delay in the House simply because the bill was becoming ensnarled in jurisdictional disputes in the Senate. Magnuson's staff insisted this would violate their agreement, which was designed to give equal credit to Magnuson and Rogers.

The bill, however, soon encountered difficulties in the House too, although of a different kind. It was an election year, and Congressmen were leery of any bill that, rightly or wrongly, seemed to some to hint of socialized medicine. Rogers did not want to risk defeat by pushing legislation which could arouse the American Medical Association against it. Instead, he held back. As soon as the election was over, however, Rogers quickly set hearings for the end of November. The rest of the year he worked toward passage, and the Emergency Health Personnel Act of 1970, as the bill was known, became the first in a long list of legislative achievements.

In 1978 Rogers was at the peak of his career. After twenty-four years in Congress he was near the top of the seniority rankings. At the relatively young age of fifty-seven and with no serious reelection worries, he could expect, eventually, to inherit the chairmanship of the Interstate and Foreign Commerce Committee. Someday he might even become the dean of the House. Not long before, he had moved into a corner office of the Rayburn Building which overlooked the Capitol dome. National magazines ran profiles with titles like "Your Health Is His Business." The walls of his office were lined floor to ceiling with photographs of him and a whole series of Presidents at bill signing ceremonies in the White House rose garden. The official pens used to sign those bills into laws were also framed along with the copies of the laws.

But at that peak all things were not going well. The trouble was national health insurance. After decades of debate national health insurance was beginning to look like an idea whose time had come. Rogers's Senate counterpart, Edward Kennedy of Massachusetts, had been introducing various national health insurance proposals for some time and was pushing more strongly than ever for its passage. President Carter was sympathetic, and the rising cost of doctor bills and hospitalization was creating public support. Even the American Medical Association was beginning to accept the idea that some form of national health insurance was inevitable.

Rogers, however, had never been comfortable with the national health insurance concept. He recognized the need for catastrophic national health insurance, which would prevent a single disabling disease or hospitalization from wiping out a lifetime of savings and plunging a family into bankruptcy. But even this was more than he felt he could actively support. And if it had to come, Rogers believed that private insurance carriers should play a role. The idea of mandatory national health insurance administered and underwritten by the federal government on the order of Medicare and Medicaid made him profoundly uneasy. For years he had tiptoed around the edges of the issue, never introducing proposals of his own, brushing sideways against the idea rather than confronting it head on.

In 1978 he found he could no longer avoid the subject. Further delay would weaken his authority. Already Dan Rostenkowski of Illinois, the third-ranking member of Ways and Means and chairman of its Health Subcommittee, was elbowing into the national health insurance debate. Rostenkowski was a politician of the old school who learned to play politics, as kids learn to play stickball, on the back streets of Chicago's heavily ethnic wards. Under the tutelage of Mayor Richard Daley, Rostenkowski came to Congress as a bright young man of thirty in 1958, just four years after Paul Rogers had come at the same age. Rostenkowski had the misfortune of manning the telephones at the 1968 Chicago convention when President Lyndon Johnson, watching at home on television, saw Congressman Carl Albert losing control of the delegates and called the platform screaming orders to seize his gavel. Albert never forgave Rostenkowski for his part in that, and two years later Rostenkowski was ousted from his post as chairman of the Democratic caucus. Rostenkowski spent the next six years in limbo. To Albert he was political anathema, and to the new bright young men he was a tired old has-been, a relic of ward politics and the Daley machine. In 1976, however, Rostenkowski began his political comeback. His political savvy and acumen, picked up so many years ago in Chicago, helped to elect Congressman Jim Wright of Texas to the post of Majority Leader by one vote. Suddenly Rostenkowski seemed to have the old zest, and national health insurance was as good a place as any to resume his career.

The year before, in November, his Health Subcommittee had held a series of hearings on national health insurance proposals. The next month Rogers's subcommittee held identical hearings on the same national health insurance bills. The Democratic Study Group set up a task force to resolve the jurisdictional dispute between the two committees. After a year of study the task force recommended the establishment of an ad hoc committee on health to handle national health insurance legislation. This, however, resolved nothing. Rostenkowski continued to edge into the national health insurance debate, and Rogers, handicapped by no substantive proposals of his own, fought to keep his command of health legislation.

In June 1978 Rogers abruptly announced his retirement. The Democratic Party back in his district was stunned, but no less so than his own staff. His closest aides, who had been with him for years, were told of his decision only one day before the official announcement. Rogers said he had concluded that almost a quarter century in the House was long enough. His only career was that of a Congressman, and while he came from an old, well-established family, it was not a family of great wealth. The time had come for him to provide for his own family's financial security and to be a father to his thirteen-year-old daughter while there were still a few years left. All that was no doubt true, but it is equally true that Rogers left with his reputation for power intact. Another term and that might not have been the case.

Like Rogers, Edward Kennedy of Massachusetts has built his career on legislative achievements. When Kennedy, the pudgy baby brother of the President and of the Attorney General, was elected in 1962, he was generally dismissed. Only thirty years old and just three years out of the University of Virginia Law School, Kennedy had previous experience consisting of one year as the assistant district attorney in Suffolk County, Massachusetts. Even his brother John joked, "Give Teddy a job, elect him to the Senate." Kennedy did not win that election by much, and the only reason he won at all, in the opinion of most, was the Kennedy name. The Kennedy name, however, was not enough to win over his new colleagues. John Kennedy had served, but not well. The Senate always seemed of passing interest to him, and in the years immediately preceding his 1960 election he compiled one of the worst attendance records in the Senate. Teddy Kennedy was just another Kennedy as far as the Senators were concerned, and they were less impressed by that fact than the voters back in Massachusetts had been.

A surprise awaited, however. Kennedy was acquainted with the Senate establishment. He knew what he had to do to become recognized. As soon as he arrived, he called Senator James Eastland, the chairman of the Judiciary Committee. That ritual call began a cordial relationship which lasted until Eastland's retirement in 1978. Ideologically, Eastland and Kennedy could not have been further apart on most issues. However, Kennedy's respect for the Senate norms of hard work, courtesy, and reverence for the institution bridged the ideological gap between them.

The Kennedy name and the celebrity status which automatically attaches itself to a member of the Kennedy family prevent the kind of ready acceptance and easy familiarity which would unlock the doors of the inner club. The publicity and scandal that cling to Kennedy keep him forever an outsider. But while Kennedy stood out from the start, he gained a reputation for power and status through hard work. And enough of Camelot lingers that Kennedy can attract a top-flight staff and volunteer experts. With their help Kennedy proceeded to master one legislative area after another. By using his subcommittee chairmanships effectively, he dominated the Senate in a variety of areas.

Until the 1970s Kennedy waivered in his devotion to Senate business. From the beginning, however, Kennedy insisted that if he stayed in the Senate, he would be a power to contend with. His early decision to concentrate on the Judiciary Committee indicated this, although later on it was through his Health Subcommittee of the Labor and Public Welfare Committee that he became recognized as a leader in a major policy area.

Kennedy knew that publicity alone would not gain the Senate's respect. On the contrary, Senate insiders would look askance on the kinds of publicity that Kennedy attracted. (He was once forced to issue a press release to deny an affair with a prominent New York socialite.) As he embarked on his Senate career, Kennedy periodically claimed issues for his own and reactivated dormant committees as he took over their chairmanships. Most importantly, he developed a large, expert, and politically astute staff. Specialization characterized the Kennedy style, and that meant specialized activity in many spheres. His committees frenetically held hearing after hearing, churning out legislation and reports. Kennedy immersed himself in the Senate process. Ten years later he emerged with the reputation for power which he had sought.

Kennedy's career illustrates the way the quest for personal power generates legislation. Legislation is the product of internal pressure to prove oneself. Every committee chairman knows that when he goes before the Rules Committee to justify his committee's budget, he will be quizzed on the number of bills his committee reported, the laws enacted, and the pages of testimony taken in the previous Congress. Kennedy has always provided satisfactory answers.

At one point Kennedy sought a position in the leadership, and he was elected Majority Whip in 1969, defeating Russell Long, who was grappling with personal problems. Two years later, however, he in turn was defeated by Robert Byrd of West Virginia, who went on to become Majority Leader. At the time of his defeat Kennedy was coping with the aftermath of Chappaquiddick and vigorously campaigning for reelection. Long had been distracted by his personal affairs. In turn, Kennedy's personal affairs were taking precedent over his duties as Majority Whip. Since then Kennedy has turned instinct for the legislative game toward the passage of his own legislation.

Despite Kennedy's early presidential ambitions, which aimed his political style toward a broad national constituency, he did not ignore the Senate. He became chairman of the Subcommittee on Refugees and Escapees in 1965, a committee that was seemingly obscure and had been for a long time completely dormant. He turned the committee into an active investigative unit with a large staff that conducted extensive hearings, issued reports, and made recommendations on dealing with the refugee problem. Kennedy did not use the committee primarily to develop and sponsor legislation, but to enhance his reputation as a Senate activist. He knew that a subcommittee chairman has almost complete discretion in shaping the committee's mandates and mode of operation. At the same time that he used the committee effectively to elevate his status within the Senate, by making the major focus of the committee the issue of Vietnam refugees he gained a national platform on Vietnam.

Kennedy's aggressive use of the Subcommittee on Refugees and Escapees, especially when taken in combination with the activity and staff of his other subcommittees—Administrative Practice and Procedure and the Health Subcommittee—caused more than a little jealousy on the part of some of his Senate colleagues. Howard Cannon of Nevada, chairman of the Senate Committee on Rules and Administration, became highly irritated with the Massachusetts Senator when Kennedy's Administrative Practice and Procedure Subcommittee invaded the turf of Cannon's Aviation Subcommittee of Commerce. The Nevada Senator used his position as the head of the Rules Committee, which reviews and authorizes budgets for Senate committees, to question Kennedy's imperialistic designs in budget hearings conducted in 1975. Kennedy's Refugees and Escapees Subcommittee was a target of Cannon's criticism, as well as the Administrative Practice and Procedure Subcommittee. (See pages 63–73 for a discussion of the dispute that arose between Cannon and Kennedy over the issue of whose committee had primary responsibility to develop legislation affecting the airlines.)

At the time Kennedy, along with other Senators, including Scoop Jackson, were under attack by a series of *Washington Post* articles for the improper use of committee staff for personal business. Although Cannon asked each of the Senators mentioned in the article to clarify their use of staff, he took a particularly adversary position only with Kennedy who came with a request for a modest budget increase of 6 percent, to $220,000, for his Refugees Subcommittee. "We have been extremely active," Kennedy said in defense of his committee.[22] He attacked as inaccurate the *Washington Post* articles, which charged that the committee had held only two days of hearings in the past year. "We had six hearings last year," said Kennedy, and "we published two reports." He added, "I, for one, feel that one of the things that the *Washington Post* article did not do, and that is do any kind of evaluation of the performance of the various committees." Cannon suggested to Kennedy that the Immigration and Naturalization Subcommittee of the Judiciary Committee could easily handle the problems investigated by the Refugees Subcommittee. He then asked Kennedy to clarify exactly what his subcommittee did. "You had six hearings last year," said Cannon. "Where were those hearings held? In what relation?" "They were held, I believe here," responded Kennedy. "Were they one-day hearings?" asked Cannon, and "what was the subject matter?" "Some of them [the hearings] were ongoing," Kennedy countered, adding that "they were all held here and some of them were more than the one day."[23] As Cannon continued to press Kennedy, he asked the Massachusetts Senator, "Did the committee make any legislative proposals?" Kennedy responded, "No, we published the report on our findings. We are not a legislative committee." "Well," said Cannon, "the Judiciary Committee is a legislative committee." "That is right," said Kennedy. "Did the Judiciary Committee offer any legislative [proposals stemming from the work of the Refugees subcommittee]?" asked Cannon. "This

[Refugees] committee did not propose any," Kennedy retorted. But he told Cannon, "Some of the recommendations that have been made . . . have been adopted [in the form of legislation] by the Senate."[24]

Michigan Republican Robert Griffin joined Cannon in attacking Kennedy's use of the Refugees Subcommittee. "Being on the Foreign Relations Committee," said the Michigan Republican, "I could not help but listen to the responses to Senator Cannon's questions. It may well be the Foreign Relations Committee should have been looking into some of the matters in the Cambodian, Vietnam [areas] relating to refugees, but it is difficult for me to understand why the [Refugees] Subcommittee and Judiciary Committee would be doing some of the things that your subcommittee is doing."[25] He added, "I say that as a member of the Foreign Relations Committee." Kennedy told Griffin, "We have had a very good working relationship with the Foreign Relations [Committee]."[26] Griffin pressed on:

Senator Griffin.   I do not think that is the point.

Senator Kennedy.   I know, but—

Senator Griffin.   You could just take off into any direction you want to go as long as the committee that does have jurisdiction does not object.

We are sort of interested in preventing any overlapping or duplication.

Senator Kennedy.   The Foreign Relations Committee does not have one thing to do with the conditions of a refugee who is either an escapee or refugee from communist tyranny and adjustment of status here in the United States.

Senator Griffin.   One of the questions is, does your subcommittee have anything to do with it?

Senator Kennedy.   Certainly does.

Senator Griffin.   We have an Immigration and Naturalization Subcommittee on the Judiciary Committee that would seem to be the only jurisdictional tie that you could establish.

This is a little bit puzzling.

Is the *Washington Post* story accurate when it says no bills were referred to this particular subcommittee [the Refugees Subcommittee] during the 93rd Congress?

Senator Kennedy.   Yes, that is correct, Mr. Chairman. As I mentioned before, probably before you came in here, it is an investigatory committee, just like twelve other subcommittees are of the United States Senate.[27]

After the exchanges between Cannon and Griffin on the one hand and Kennedy on the other, even Strom Thurmond, who would later help Kennedy defend his Administrative Practice and Procedure subcommittee against even more severe criticism, said with some relief, "I am not on the Refugees [Subcommittee]," in response to an inquiry from Griffin.

While Kennedy used the Refugees Subcommittee to investigate and to garner staff, he aggressively sought to gain recognition as an effective legislator in other areas.

In 1971 Kennedy began to build his reputation in the health area. His presidential ambitions set aside and the leadership foreclosed, Kennedy at last settled down and worked seriously at his job as senior Senator from Massachusetts.

For Congressmen who choose to make their mark on Capitol Hill through legislation, chance plays its part. Legislative reputations are won or lost primarily within the jurisdiction of the committees or subcommittees a member happens to chair. Legislative careers then depend upon the availability of positions on committees, particularly subcommittee chairmanships, and the whims of the party committees on committees that allocates the slots. The vagaries of election defeats and retirements randomly open up chairmanships. A member who happens to be in the right place at the right time can be catapulted into prominence. Kennedy's succession to the chairmanship of the Health Subcommittee was the result of such a chance occurrence. The previous chairman, Senator Ralph Yarborough of Texas, was defeated by Lloyd Bentsen in a vicious primary fight which brought out the worst in all factions of the Texas Democratic Party. Kennedy was in the right place, and the time was becoming right for a federal role in health care.

Yarborough had sensed this, and under his chairmanship the subcommittee was to continue the active legacy of Lister Hill of Alabama, who had chaired both the Labor and Public Welfare Committee and its Health Subcommittee for fourteen years. He was also chairman of the Appropriations Subcommittee for Health and Welfare. Hill, the son of a distinguished surgeon, was named after Lord Lister, a famous British physician. He was an enthusiastic New Dealer, but whatever his personal predilections, the 1950s and 1960s were not ready for the kind of federal intervention which would come later. Nevertheless, Hill was an active chairman. On his retirement, the *New York Times* said that "Lister Hill has done more for the health of Americans in modern times than any man outside the medical profession." The editorial continued, "He has been a tireless protagonist of generous research budgets for the National Institutes of Health. He was co-author of the Hill-Burton Act, which over the past twenty-one years has made possible the building of thousands of new hospitals and clinics. More recently he has worked on legislation to aid the mentally retarded and to build more medical schools."[28] Hill had established his committees, including the Health Subcommittee, as the focal point for the development of the nation's health legislation. His mantle would fall first to Yarborough and then to Kennedy. In the first year of Yarborough's chairmanship the subcommittee passed nine major health bills.

Kennedy pushed for a more active role in the delivery of health services, medical research, and the prevention and treatment of disease. For a variety of reasons health policy was assuming increased importance on Capitol Hill. Although the medical profession as a whole steadfastly resisted anything that smacked of socialized medicine, some groups within the medical profession favored government support for medical research and medical schools. Members of Congress were acutely aware of the impact that rising medical costs were having on the public. And public attention was focusing on the death rate from such killers as cancer and heart disease. More funds for medical research seemed to be needed. An increasing role for government in health care was an idea whose time was clearly coming if, indeed, it had not already arrived. And there was Kennedy, neatly and fortuitously positioned, to take advantage of it.

Kennedy's first success in this new area for help predated his assumption of the chairmanship of the Health Subcommittee. In the 91st Congress Kennedy, working closely with Yarborough, passed legislation which authorized almost $1 billion over a five-year period to build community mental health centers. This bill failed to become law because a conference committee was never convened to work out the differences in the Senate and House versions. The Senate passage alone, however, was an important accomplishment. Kennedy sponsored other legislation in the 91st Congress, including what was to become his major legislative interest in coming years—national health insurance. Kennedy along with a bipartisan group of Senators sponsored the Health Security Act and convened subcommittee hearings on the legislation.

Without Yarborough's defeat Kennedy would not have taken over the Health Subcommittee when he did. Even with it, his selection as chairman was not automatic. Harrison Williams, who assumed the chairmanship of the full committee, could have chaired the Health Subcommittee as well. But Kennedy's increasing visibility in health policy made him the logical choice to succeed Yarborough there, and Williams did not contest his claim.

By 1972 Kennedy was the Mr. Health of the Senate. As soon as he gained the chairmanship of the Health Subcommittee, he increased its activities geometrically from what they had been in prior years. An aggressive and talented staff, working behind the scenes, used the subcommittee to boost the Senator's reputation. Kennedy's way was clear now, and he and his staff saw the advantages of moving vigorously into the health field.

The activities of the Health Subcommittee during Kennedy's first two years were extraordinary by any standard. Kennedy sponsored, at least in the Senate, the Conquest of Cancer Act, health manpower legislation, the Lead-base Paint Poisoning Act, the National Heart, Vessel, Lung, and Blood Act, the Communicable Disease Control Amendment Act, the Emergency Health Personnel Act, and various bills to help train physicians and other professional public health workers, to establish health maintenance organizations, and to provide health services for domestic and agricultural workers. The Kennedy bills involved the government in health care in previously unprecedented ways.

From the start Kennedy pushed for comprehensive national health insurance. There was not the slightest chance that such legislation would pass the Senate, let alone the Congress, in 1970, but Kennedy knew that. He also had the instinctive feeling that someday it would. Major programs such as Medicare or national health insurance require years, sometimes decades, of slow, quiet germination. By beginning early and never letting go, Kennedy would have a definitive role to play when the time came. The passage of national health insurance would cap his Senate career as nothing else could. He would take his place in history among such Senate greats as Robert Wagner of New York, author of the Wagner National Labor Relations Act of

1935, or Robert Taft of Ohio, author of the Taft-Hartley Act of 1947 that amended the Wagner Act.

Kennedy's extensive activity in the 92nd Congress was a sign of what was to come. His committee held thirty-two separate hearings in the 93rd Congress in 1973 and 1974, a significant increase even from the high level of activity in the 92nd Congress. Kennedy's legislative successes also accelerated, as Congress passed the Lead-base Paint Poisoning Act, federal aid to health maintenance organizations, and other proposals for subsidizing various health programs.

Kennedy was soon looking for new areas to move into. Unlike Rogers, who was content to be known for his work in the health area, Kennedy was eager to dominate as many policy areas as possible. His success merely whetted his ambition. Kennedy was the chairman of the Subcommittee on Administrative Practice and Procedure under the Judiciary Committee. The committee had been taken over by Kennedy in 1969. Its broad mandate allowed him to roam into areas that especially interested him, such as antitrust policy. He became principal sponsor of an amendment to the Freedom of Information Act that opened up secret government files to individuals and newspaper reporters. He also held extensive hearings and developed legislation to expand public participation in administrative proceedings so administrative agencies would be forced to take into account public as well as private interests in their decisions. All of this was well and good, but it was not the kind of riveting issue that Kennedy was seeking. Airline deregulation, however, which his staff began talking about in the early 1970s, could be.

Kennedy was on firm ground in health as far as the Senate went. No one else was particularly interested in health policy, and Kennedy was free to roam wherever he pleased. Airline deregulation was another matter. The Senate already had a subcommittee on Aviation which fell under the Commerce Committee and was chaired by Senator Howard Cannon of Nevada. Cannon had a deep and abiding interest in aviation. He was an airline buff and proud of his position as a general in the Air Force reserves. He served on the Aeronautical and Space Sciences Committee as well. If the Senate were to take up airline deregulation, Cannon's subcommittee was the logical starting point. Kennedy's staff, however, were not interested in logic or rationality. They interpreted their subcommittee mandate in the

broadest possible way. The subcommittee's jurisdiction over administrative practices and procedures became a license to investigate any administrative agency. And when regulatory reform
surfaced as an issue in the mid-1970s, the staff saw an immediate
opportunity. Airline deregulation was chosen, and the Kennedy
juggernaut, ignoring Cannon's claim to anything that had to do
with aviation, simply rolled ahead.

The key Kennedy staffers on the airline deregulation issue
were Professor Stephen Breyer of the Harvard Law School, who
is generally credited by the staffs of both Kennedy and Cannon
with the initial impetus behind deregulation of airline fares and
route allocation and Phil Bakes, who became general counsel of
the Administrative Practice and Procedure Subcommittee at the
time when Breyer, on leave from Harvard, was beginning to
work on the legislation in earnest. The essential entrepreneurial
nature of legislative activity on Capitol Hill is best exemplified by
these two Kennedy staffers who almost singlehandedly, operating as surrogates of Kennedy, succeeded in bringing airline deregulation to the attention of the Senate. Without astute and aggressive work on the part of Kennedy's staff, it is unlikely that
deregulation would have been taken seriously on Capitol Hill
and probably equally unlikely that regulatory reform would have
captured the attention of the Ford and Carter administrations.

David Boies, who helped to floor-manage the airline deregulation bill for Kennedy in 1978, pointed out, "There was no constituency for it in the beginning. Kennedy did not act because of
outside pressures. None of the members of the Senate and staff
who have been leaders in pushing for the legislation have acted
on the basis of constituent pressures. Most constituent pressures,
in fact, have been against it. The constituencies were generated
by the congressional supporters of the legislation — Kennedy and
others going out and convincing people of the necessity for the
bill."

Kennedy's staff knew that the airlines as a whole were against
deregulation at the very beginning. The industry had never lived
in a competitive environment, and had grown comfortable with
the regulatory status quo. It knew how to adapt to regulation
and generally had succeeded in the regulatory environment.
Many interest groups would be affected by deregulation: the airlines, airline unions, shippers, small communities threatened by
curtailed air service, and passengers. The Kennedy staff knew

that it was up to them to try to convince these constituencies that airline deregulation was a good idea. However, while outside forces always have some impact on Congress, legislation ultimately succeeds or fails as a result of internal power struggles. Kennedy and his staff wanted the bill, and the credit for it, although they knew that in the end they would have to share recognition with Cannon.

The staff prepared for a major set of hearings. Before Cannon's subcommittee had quite grasped what was happening, the Subcommittee on Administrative Practice and Procedure embarked upon its investigation of the regulatory policies of the Civil Aeronautics Board. In November 1974 the committee led off with hearings on airline charter fares. The purpose of the hearings was to examine whether or not the minimum transatlantic charter fares set by the Civil Aeronautics Board were in the public interest. Under the guise of investigating CAB procedures the committee in fact was delving into substantive policy. Eventually this would lead to new legislation and to the major CAB decisions in the Carter administration that significantly reduced government regulation of airline routes and fares. Kennedy's staff screened the committee witnesses to insure individuals and groups who opposed the rigid CAB policy of limiting competition by discouraging low-fare charter flights. Of the seventeen witnesses who appeared over the two days of hearings, only five supported the CAB. Representatives of TWA, the Department of Transportation, and the chairman of the Civil Aeronautics Board backed the present policy. Arrayed against the CAB were representatives of charter carriers, the Justice Department, the FCC, Ralph Nader's Aviation Consumer Action Project, and travel agencies. Freddie Laker, the irrepressible president of Laker Airlines, came from England to describe his repeated inability to get CAB approval for his low-cost, no-frills "Skytrain" from New York to London. Laker finally won, but it took another three years before the first Skytrain flew out of Kennedy Airport on its way to London.

None of this pleased Cannon, perched helplessly on the sidelines, in the least. The Kennedy staff had explained their intentions to Mike Pertschuk, chief counsel of the Commerce Committee, and he in turn informed Bob Ginther, the staff director of the Aviation Subcommittee. Pertschuk, who got along well with the Kennedy staff, tried to ease their way with the Cannon staff. But Pertschuk could not disguise the basic fact that Kennedy was usurping Cannon on a matter of substantial interest to the aviation industry. Ginther received Breyer coolly. Ginther's initial reaction was that the Administrative Practice and Procedure Subcommittee was moving into an area where it had no right to be. His impression was that Kennedy was simply searching for something for his new subcommittee to do. Ginther was right. The Kennedy staff had toyed with energy but discarded energy in favor of airline deregulation. As far as Ginther was concerned, the Administrative Practice and Procedure Subcommittee could keep on looking. But Breyer was not so easily discouraged. "Steve had a mission," Ginther recalled. Breyer's expertise and passionate dedication persuaded Kennedy to go ahead.

After several conversations with Breyer, Ginther believed that Kennedy was determined to take up deregulation and informed Commerce Committee Chairman Magnuson and Cannon. Magnuson was not particularly concerned, but Cannon was. "Maggie," Ginther said, "doesn't get upset about turf but Cannon got very upset. Cannon is a classic turf protector." Ginther drafted a letter which Magnuson and Cannon signed and sent to Kennedy. The letter politely asked that the hearings be delayed while international airline fares were being negotiated. The underlying message of the letter, however, was not so polite. "Quit messing in business you don't understand" is how Ginther put it. Breyer and Kennedy were rankled by the letter, but it achieved its purpose. The hearings were postponed for several weeks. But Breyer and Kennedy were deterred only temporarily. The next time the hearings were set, they ignored Cannon and Ginther. Instead, they sought out the press. Cannon, they said, was attempting to stop a potentially explosive hearing into the CAB. Ginther was not surprised when he read the leaks in the paper. "They overreacted, which is a characterisitc of the administrative practice committee mentality," he said. "They play a tough game over there."

The Administrative Practice and Procedure Subcommittee was lucky. Its investigations had uncovered an incipient scandal. The chief of the Bureau of Enforcement at the Civil Aeronautics Board was implicated in alleged political payoffs by the airlines. There were indications that he had suppressed investigations into the illegal practices at the behest of senior officials. The chairman was implicated in the cover-up. Shortly before the hearings began, the bureau chief committed suicide. At the hearings themselves the general counsel, in the midst of fending off increasingly tough questions from the committee, fainted. The hearings were splashed over the front pages of the newspapers. "The CAB at the time was an abomination that played right into their hands," said Ginther. "Kennedy was just plain lucky in timing."

The antipathy between Kennedy and Cannon lingered. Cannon's pique showed in the Rules Committee's review of the budget of the Administrative Practice and Procedure Subcommittee in 1975. Cannon had squirmed while Kennedy captured headlines for his CAB investigation. Now it was Kennedy's turn to be uneasy. He had just been sharply questioned by Rules Committee members Cannon and Griffin on his Refugees Subcommittee, and now they turned their criticisms to the Administrative Practice and Procedure Subcommittee.

Kennedy, in presenting his subcommittee budget, began by recounting the achievements of the subcommittee over the past year. In a long list of committee activities Kennedy did not specifically mention his investigation of the Civil Aeronautics Board. He did, however, make the remark that "we are interested in the whole problem of economic regulation and the oversight of that."[29] This immediately prompted Cannon to ask, "By the way, while you are referring to that, would you point out under Rule 25 [which states the jurisdictions of Senate committees] where the subcommittee's jurisdiction falls in that regard?" Kennedy pointed out that the Judiciary Committee has general antitrust jurisdiction and jurisdiction over administrative procedures that encompasses regulatory agencies. Cannon was not satisfied. He told Kennedy, "I think this is another area where we have needless overlapping jurisdiction." Then, turning to the point of his first question, Cannon said, "I would point out in one [area] specifically, on the Commerce Committee I happen to chair the Aviation Subcommittee, and the Commerce Committee, by the rules, is given complete jurisdiction over civil aeronautics, over all matters which shall be referred to all proposed legislation, messages, petitions, memoranda, and other matters relating to . . . civil aeronautics . . . [and] space administration." Warming up to the attack, Cannon continued, "Now, it seems to me that that committee, that subcommittee under the Commerce Com-

mittee, has complete jurisdiction to matters relating to civil aviation. I have had considerable complaints from the regulatory
agency involved and also from members of the air carriers involved because of a voluminous amount of information they have
been required to supply to the Administrative Practice Subcommittee when the basic committee is pursuing many of those
areas, and it seems to me that it is quite a needless overlap of jurisdiction, or attempted overlap of jurisdiction." Cannon concluded, "I for one feel that the committee is getting in an area
where it has no jurisdiction in that particular."[30]

Kennedy told Cannon that he felt the Administrative Practice and Procedure Subcommittee did have proper jurisdiction
to investigate, but that he had indicated at the outset of his hearings that Cannon's Aviation Subcommittee had exclusive jurisdiction over any legislation that would emerge. Cannon was not
placated, however, and told Kennedy that the Aviation Subcommittee "has held hearings on those very things [under investigation by Kennedy's committee], held hearings with the Board
[CAB] on the question of fares, on the question of regulation, on
the question of routes, and has been consistently on the Board
about its failure or its imposition of a temporary moritorium on
the route expansion." The clear implication of Cannon's remarks was that the Kennedy committee was needlessly duplicat-
ing work. Kennedy, chastised, told Cannon, "We, I think, have
tried to keep your staff people completely informed of where we
have been moving on it [the CAB investigation], so there would
not be any conflict." Cannon replied, "I must say we have been
informed, if only by the press." At that remark, those in the
hearing room burst into laughter. But it was not a laughing matter for Cannon, who continued, "We have been informed by the
press, by the regulatory agencies, by the Board, and by probably
80 percent of the carriers who resent the fact that they have to go
in two different directions at the same time."[31]

Several months after the hearings on the airline charter fares
the Administrative Practice and Procedure Subcommittee announced new hearings on rate and route decisions. Again the
subcommittee was using the administrative code over which it legitimately claimed jurisdiction as a license to rummage through
an agency's files at will. Again a long list of witnesses who sub-
stantiated the need for reform appeared. The industry defended
regulation, while administration officials, including representa-

tives of the Department of Transportation, the Federal Transportation Commission, the antitrust division of Justice, and the Council of Economic Advisers, argued for reform. A number of economists also testified on the economic merits of regulatory reform. The president of Air California explained why intrastate rates were far lower than interstate rates regulated by the CAB. Eastern Airlines defended its shuttle rates along the northeast corridor on logistical grounds. Representatives of World Airways, North Central Airlines, Continental Airlines, Allegheny Airlines, United Airlines, and Pan American objected to the route moritorium that prevented new entries into major air routes. At the same time, these major carriers stressed that deregulation would have serious unsettling economic consequences for the airline industry.

As the hearings continued on for six days, Ralph Nader alleged that the Civil Aeronautics Board failed to consider consumer interests in its policies and in enforcement. He also pointed out the incestuous ties between the Civil Aeronautics Board and the major carriers, which, he claimed, led to an overrepresentation of airline executives on the board. Representatives of the CAB appeared again, defending themselves and their policies. However, the hearings documented widespread dissatisfaction throughout the airline industry with the CAB. Once this was shown, of course, the only thing to do was to change the CAB in order to eliminate the complaints. The logical people to do this were those who had studied the problems— Kennedy and his staff. By the end of the second set of hearings, the Senate and the aviation industry looked to Kennedy for a solution.

A short time before, Kennedy had been an interloper in aviation issues. Now, suddenly, through a combination of diligent staff work, manipulation of the press, and sheer good fortune, Kennedy was the established spokesman on the most important issues that affected the airline industry. Cannon had been neatly circumvented. Any legislation, of course, would eventually have to go through the Aviation Subcommittee. But with the inadequacies of the CAB so thoroughly documented and the press captivated by the hint of scandal and scenting a good story, Cannon would have to go along.

In April 1976, five months after Kennedy adjourned the last of his hearings on the CAB, the Aviation Subcommittee embarked upon its own extensive hearings. Before the subcommit-

tee were three bills—the Kennedy bill running close to 100 pages
and providing for a gradual deregulation over a four-year period, the Ford administration bill, and the CAB bill. Substantively
the bills differed little. All three would phase in deregulation.
But it was Kennedy who in the end would be able to claim credit
for the bill that emerged from the committee.

Kennedy was the lead-off witness on April 6. He reviewed the
general need for deregulation of the airlines and outlined the
provisions of his legislation. Kennedy was followed by administration officials, who testified on the Ford bill. Many of the same
witnesses who previously appeared before the Kennedy subcommittee returned to testify before the Cannon committee. The
Aviation Subcommittee called few new witnesses and added little
to the hearing record compiled by the Administrative Practice
and Procedure Subcommittee during its three months of hearings. The Kennedy staff had been so thorough that the Cannon
staff had little choice but to repeat what had gone before. Cannon was merely following where Kennedy had led.

Despite his irritation with Kennedy, Cannon was willing to be
open-minded about deregulation. As he listened to the witnesses,
his initial skepticism began to wane. More and more he became
convinced that the existing policy of airline regulation was inef-
fectual. Cannon was also politically astute enough to realize that
some kind of deregulation bill was likely to pass sooner or later
and it would be in his political self-interest to be on the winning
side. He set out to salvage what he could.

Ginther had organized the Aviation Subcommittee hearings
in the hopes that they would educate Cannon on deregulation.
Ginther by now had been convinced that the present system
needed to be changed, and he set about persuading his boss. The
hearings succeeded. Shortly after they ended, Cannon delivered
a speech, written by Ginther, that called for significant deregulation.

Ginther set about drafting a bill which Cannon would introduce in the fall of 1976. He still did not trust Phil Bakes, his
counterpart at the Administrative Practice and Procedure Subcommittee, but he told Bakes that he agreed with him on the
need for some deregulation. Bakes wasn't particularly trusting of
Ginther either. In Bakes's view Ginther was nothing more than
an industry spokesman. In Ginther's view Bakes was a near
crazy. But self-interest drew them together. Neither would get

very far without the other. By this time they needed each other. Ginther and Cannon were more cautious than Bakes and Kennedy had been. Cannon had inched away from his previous stance that regulation per se was good. Kennedy was willing to concede that his legislation was impractical. Bakes and Ginther tossed ideas back and forth. Finally they managed to agree on a series of basic principles which would be embodied in any final bill. Once Ginther and Bakes were in agreement, they had to prevail upon Cannon and Kennedy to cooperate. Their personal differences aside, the two Senators were good allies. Kennedy represented the Senate liberals, and Cannon personified the Senate conservatives. Together they could unite forces that would otherwise clash. The staffs of Kennedy and Cannon worked toward that end. Ginther had to convince Cannon that Kennedy would be useful. With the bills now in his committee Cannon was inclined, as Ginther commented, to say to hell with Kennedy. He had seized the issue from Cannon. Now Cannon wanted it back. Kennedy, who knew the way to a politician's heart as well as any member of the Senate, set about mollifying Cannon. He made sure that Cannon was singled out as often as possible for his leadership in airline deregulation legislation. The private telephone line in Cannon's office often found Kennedy on the other end, and with words of praise for Cannon's conduct of the Aviation Subcommittee hearings. Kennedy would assure Cannon that he was doing a great job. Press releases out of Kennedy's office and the Administrative Practice and Procedure Subcommittee mentioned Cannon's contribution to CAB reform. Ginther, bemused by the Kennedy treatment, said, "Kennedy began a year long process of stroking [Cannon] so brilliantly that in the end a camaraderie developed between the two. Kennedy was remarkable."

Finally Cannon, Kennedy, Ginther, and Bakes sat down together. The two aides outlined the legislation as they now saw it. The compromise, they said in the parlance of the Hill, was something they could all live with. The two Senators agreed, and their staffs proceeded to turn the agreed-upon principles of airline deregulation into legislative language. The Cannon-Kennedy bill was introduced in Februrary 1977. Significantly, Cannon's name appeared first. If the bill was ever to be reported, Cannon, not Kennedy, would be responsible. The Kennedy staff was ready to admit that "without the active, vigorous support of Cannon the bill would never have been enacted." And, as Ginther emphasized, it was Cannon who was "in the trenches" during the unprecedented 20 days of markup sessions in which the bill was reviewed and amended line by line.

Cannon, now chairman of the full Commerce Committee, introduced the bill on the floor. His praise of Kennedy's initial support for airline deregulation came easily. By this time Cannon had nearly forgotten his previous animosity toward Kennedy. Wooed and stroked by Kennedy, Cannon now saw the two of them as full and equal partners in the development of airline deregulation legislation. Stressing the importance of "his" legislation, Cannon said, "I bring to the Senate today one of the most significant pieces of legislation in the past several decades. Important not so much by itself, but because it represents one of the only opportunities this body has had in recent years to vote for less government regulation and for more free enterprise for a major U.S. industry."[32]

Ignoring the years of hearings held by the Administrative Practice and Procedure Subcommittee, Cannon said, "The Air Transportation Regulatory Reform Act of 1978 was developed through a slow and thoughtful debate in the Committee on Commerce, Science and Transportation. The committee met more than twenty times to mark up a bill before voting 13–3 to send this legislation to the Senate." Cannon finally received the praise of his colleagues for which he had yearned as one after another paid tribute to his skill in bringing the bill to the floor. James B. Pearson, the ranking Republican member on the Commerce Committee who managed the bill for the minority, said, "I particularly pay tribute to my distinguished colleague, Senator Cannon of Nevada, the chairman of our committee, for his patience and perseverance through these two years and the leadership he has exhibited in being one of the chief architects of bringing this measure to the floor of the Senate."

Kennedy started his remarks with the kind of florid statement that is typical of Senate debate. "We shall have the opportunity to vote on legislation which will change the entire face of the domestic aviation regulatory process," he said. "We will have the chance to tell the American public that we believe competition to be better than regulation, that businessmen and women can make better decisions about the conduct of their businesses than bureaucrats, and that four decades of federal control over an industry does not guarantee four more decades without change." But he quickly went on to a more politically important point. "Only slightly more than four years ago," he pointed out, "the Subcommittee on Administrative Practice and Procedure looked at the performance of the Civil Aeronautics Board and discovered that the Board's procedures were unfair to some industry groups, inadequate to protect the interests of the traveling public, inefficient, and biased in favor of existing major carriers. Underlying our report on the CAB, issued in 1975, was the firm conviction of the subcommittee members that the existing federal aviation act needed substantial overhaul if both the industry and the public were to be best served."

Kennedy said that the need for regulatory reform "has been tested and proven over the last three years by dozens of days of hearings before my subcommittee as well as the aviation subcommittees of the Senate and House." Kennedy observed that the pending bill, S. 2493, was the work of many different Senators. "Above all," Kennedy said, "S. 2493 is the result of the effort and skill of the chairman of the Commerce Committee. He has chaired dozens of days of hearings on aviation reform legislation; he has participated in lengthy subcommittee and committee markups on the bill; and he has brought his experience and sensitivity from six years as Aviation Subcommittee chairman to the drafting of a well-balanced, comprehensive bill. I commend him and the members of his staff, as well, for an excellent job."

The airline deregulation bill passed the Senate essentially unchanged. Only one substantive amendment, which was offered by Kennedy with Cannon's support, was added. That required the authorization of new airline service unless it was inconsistent "with the public convenience and necessity." Thus the burden of proof would fall on the opponents of applications for new airline routes. The Kennedy amendment reversed the original language of the bill to provide easier entry into airline markets. The amendment came up in committee at the end of a long series of markup sessions. Cannon, despite his support, felt he had pushed his committee as far as it could reasonably go. Cannon wanted to report out a bill as soon as possible, and when the amendment was defeated, he left its fate to the floor, where Kennedy resurrected it.

Senate bill 2493 passed 83–9 and by unanimous consent was renamed the Cannon-Kennedy-Pearson Air Transportation Reform Act of 1978.

Insiders who observe the legislative process will readily agree with the Kennedy aide who said, "It is a miracle that anything ever gets done." When it does get done, it is because the power incentive has asserted itself. If Cannon had failed to see a personal advantage in airline deregulation, the bill would have died in committee. If Kennedy had not agreed that it was in his self-interest to charm Cannon, the legislation would never have reached the floor. Such incentives are highly personal, and legislation reflects delicate maneuvering among members and staff to protect and enhance their power and status within their respective houses. As the Senate was completing action on the airline deregulation bill, the staff of Kennedy's Antitrust and Monopoly Subcommittee was preparing to move into trucking deregulation, which, like airline deregulation, fell within the jurisdiction of Cannon's Commerce Committee. At the close of the 95th Congress the Kennedy staff was investigating the antitrust implications of the operations of the trucking industry under government regulation. At the opening of the 96th Congress, Kennedy, now the chairman of the Judiciary Committee, held a carefully staged press conference to announce that the Antitrust Subcommittee would consider a Kennedy deregulation bill.

This time Kennedy did not surprise Cannon, and the Commerce Committee chairman claimed exclusive jurisdiction over trucking deregulation. Cannon announced that he was preparing his own deregulation hearings. Cannon promised to take the jurisdictional dispute to the Senate floor if Kennedy persisted. Several months after the opening of the 96th Congress Kennedy appeared to back off. His staff said that Kennedy all along had merely sought to spur action on trucking deregulation. In effect, the Cannon hearings were a victory for Kennedy.

The stories of Congressman Paul Rogers and Senator Edward Kennedy, both of whom built their Capitol Hill reputations on the basis of legislative achievement, are typical of those members who seek success through legislative endeavors.

Members and their staffs seek to pass legislation that will redound to their credit. The enormous increase in the legislative activity of Congress—the holding of hearings, the issuing of reports, and the drafting of bills—reflects the quest for power through the passage of legislation. Legislation is always linked to members and, for those knowledgeable in the ways of the Hill, to the aides who smooth the way behind the scenes.

The desire to shape reputations through legislation has significantly shaped Congress. Legislation is an entrepreneurial activity. It reflects constituents only as it fulfills the entrepreneurial desires of Congress. Congressmen can mobilize a vast array of political interest groups who can help lobby their ideas through Congress, but they are the instruments of power rather than the source of legislation. The most successful legislative careers are built in such relatively noncontroversial areas as health legislation because it is easiest to assemble support behind such bills. In order to pass legislation, however, Congressmen and Senators must finally organize political forces within and not without Congress. These political forces consist of individuals in positions of power—the leadership in both bodies and the chairmen of standing committees and subcommittees. In many ways Congress is the last bastion of the free enterprise system. The result is often innovative public policy, as the ideas which are spewed out are extraordinarily diverse.

The idea, however, is only the beginning. Legislation must wend its way through a variety of committees on its way to passage, and these committees and subcommittees fight over jurisdiction in the same way that members fight over legislation. Committees are the means through which individuals realize their aspirations to make their legislative mark and through which power goals unrelated to legislation are achieved. In the end, Plato's couplet is an apt description of much of what goes on in the committee rooms and legislative chambers of Congress:

> The politician makes his own little laws
> And sits attentive to his own applause.

3
Committees, Power, and Status

THE GREAT COMMITTEES of Congress—the House Appropriations and Ways and Means Committees, the Senate Foreign Relations and Judiciary Committees, and the predecessors of the Armed Services Committees of both bodies—date to the early days of the Republic. These committees are among the most prestigious on Capitol Hill, for the responsibilities that have been delegated to them reflect the most important powers given to Congress by the Constitution. Achieving the chairmanship or ranking-member status on one of these committees automatically signals a high degree of success. Prestige and status are automatically accorded the members who hold such positions. True power, however, rests in the exercise of it. On these and other committees chairmen must constantly demonstrate their power to their colleagues if they are to preserve their reputations for power. The most effective demonstrations of power are those undertaken within Congress itself—power over other committees, over the leadership and Congressional party apparatus, and over the "other body." The arena of conflict is Capitol Hill itself as members and committees seek to establish and reestablish their reputations for power.

It is the committees of Congress and not constituents that are the major force behind legislation. The following exchange between Texas Senator John Tower and Rhode Island Senator John Pastore during a debate over antitrust legislation in the 94th Congress makes the point vividly.

Mr. Tower.   There is no popular demand for this legislation.
Mr. Pastore.   How do you know? Did you talk to the people of the state of New York? Did you talk to the people of the state of

Pennsylvania? Who did you talk to? A few oil men down there in
Texas?

Mr. Tower.   Whom did *you* talk to? How many people have
communicated with *you* demanding this legislation?

Mr. Pastore.   Who are you trying to kid?

Mr. Tower.   Who has demanded it?

Mr. Pastore.   Who has demanded it?

Mr. Tower.   Yes.

Mr. Pastore.   Why, the committees of this Congress!

In short, the passage of legislation is a game for insiders; and
constituents, "the folks back home," in Congressional parlance,
are quintessential outsiders.

The more than 250 committees of Capitol Hill are the em-
bodiment not only of Congress but also of the ambitions of those
who chair them, those who aspire to become their chairmen, and
those who are the ranking minority members. While senior
members of Congress who have achieved ranking minority positions on important committees, such as Senator Jacob Javits of
New York, the ranking Republican on the Foreign Relations
Committee and formerly on Human Resources, have used their
staff to help build considerable reputations for power, the arena
of power within which minority members can function is very
limited. Committee power rests almost entirely in the hands of
the chairmen. They control the staff, and through the staff the
legislative and investigative activities of the committee. Within
his sphere of jurisdiction the chairman is a supreme power.
Hearings cannot be held without his approval, and legislation
cannot be marked up without being scheduled by him and his
staff. Committee chairmen oversee jurisdictional disputes within
their committees and determine which bills will be placed on the
committee agenda. If a committee member lacks his own subcommittee, the chairman determines whether or not any hearings will be held on his legislation.

Besides their formal powers, chairmen of committees and
subcommittees possess symbolic powers which lead to enormous
control over the workings of Congress. Members who try to oppose chairmen find the power structure closing ranks against
them. Senator Charles Percy of Illinois found himself in such a
position in the 94th Congress when he attempted to get the
Government Operations Committee to take up his regulatory reform legislation. Percy, the ranking minority member of the

committee, had long worked closely—too closely in the opinion
of some Democrats on the committee—with its chairman, Abraham Ribicoff of Connecticut, in running Government Operations. As a result, Ribicoff was sympathetic to his pleas. Ribicoff
tentatively scheduled a markup for Percy's regulatory reform bill
and Senator Ed Muskie's sunset legislation, which were similar in
intent but different in approach, on the same day. Muskie and
the staff of his Intergovernmental Relations Subcommittee were
outraged. The sunset bill was their pet project. It required the
authorizing committees to review periodically administrative
programs under their jurisdiction. Unless the committees voted
to continue the programs, the "sun would set" on them and they
would die. The bill had gone through lengthy hearings and several revisions, and they wanted the committee to consider it
alone and on its own merits and not in conjunction with Percy's
regulatory reform bill. Percy's bill, they argued, was not ready to
be marked up. In fact, the Intergovernmental Relations Subcommittee had insured that the bill would not be ready by refusing to hold hearings on it. Behind the scenes, Muskie's staff lobbied the staff of other committee members. The Percy bill, they
reminded staff members, had not been reported out of their subcommittee. It would not be fair to consider it. It would be an affront to Muskie as chairman of the subcommittee. Moreover, if it
were to be taken up, being a subcommittee chairman would be
meaningless. It was not only Muskie's power as subcommittee
chairman that was at stake, it was the power of all subcommittee
chairmen, and most members of the committee chaired their
own subcommittees. That argument, helped along by the linger-
ing resentment against the relationship between Percy and Ribicoff, won out. When the committee met for the scheduled
markup, a compromise was reached. The Government Operations Committee would mark up the sunset legislation at a later
date and the Intergovernmental Relations Subcommittee would
hold hearings on Percy's bill.

The committee chairmen are assumed to be the most powerful members of Congress. This expectation adds to the pressure
on the chairmen continually to reaffirm their power and the
power of their committees. No chairman worthy of the position
will permit the jurisdiction of his committee to be reduced, legislation to be stolen from him, or his staff to be reduced. And being the chairman of a prestigious committee does not guarantee

immunity from attack by Congressional colleagues seeking to augment their own power.

The early establishment of committees created the forum for later political combat on Capitol Hill. It was in the House of Representatives that committees were first created.[1] They provided a model for Senate committees, which were formed later. The 1st Congress saw the establishment of the Rules Committee. By the 4th Congress the Commerce, Manufactures, and Agriculture Committee was created, along with the Ways and Means Committee. Manufactures and Agriculture were spun off into separate committees in the 16th Congress, while Ways and Means spawned the Appropriations, Banking and Currency, and Pacific Railroad Committees in 1865. In the period between 1805 and 1815 committees were created on Public Lands, the District of Columbia, Post Offices and Post Roads, and the Judiciary, as well as on Pensions and Revolutionary Claims, and Public Expenditures. In the 14th Congress separate committees were created with jurisdication over expenditures in the Departments of State, the Treasury, War, and the Navy, and committees were added to oversee the expenditures of the Post Office and those for public buildings. In the 17th Congress separate committees were added on Military Affairs, Naval Affairs, and Foreign Affairs. The Education and Labor Committee was established in the 40th Congress, and divided into separate committees on Education and Labor in the 48th Congress.

As executive departments were created, corresponding Congressional committees were sooner or later established. A committee with jurisdiction over expenditures in the Department of Justice was created in the 43rd Congress, and for the Department of Agriculture in the 51st Congress. The Ways and Means and Appropriations Committees were by the end of the nineteenth century considered to be the most important in the House.

Five committees were created between 1789 and 1893 that dealt exclusively with internal House affairs—Elections, Accounts, Mileage, Rules, and Ventilation and Acoustics.

Unlike the House, the Senate tended to work through ad hoc select committees, establishing only four standing committees in the period from 1789 to 1816. In 1816 eleven new standing committees were created—Foreign Relations, Finance, Commerce and Manufactures, Military Affairs, the Militia, Naval Affairs, Public Lands, Claims, the Judiciary, the Post Office and

Post Roads, and Pensions. These committees paralleled similar committees that had previously been established by the House.

During the first half of the nineteenth century Senators acquired no vested interests in their standing committees, as the membership rotated from one Congress to another. As Senators in the latter part of the nineteenth century began to regard the Senate as a career in itself, committees were seen as bases for the exercise of power in the body. The number of standing committees expanded, and by 1889 had increased to forty-two. By the early years of the twentieth century there were seventy-four standing committees. During this period of expansion chairmanships were eagerly sought primarily because they provided office space and federal clerks.

In the latter nineteenth century committees began to become important as adjuncts of internal power. Committee seats reflected greater continuity of members, who saw "their" committees as important repositories of power on Capitol Hill. The Speaker appointed the standing committees, but, as Woodrow Wilson pointed out in his 1885 work *Congressional Government,* "by custom, seniority in congressional service determines the bestowal of the principal chairmanships."[2] As Congress began to spawn an ever increasing number of committees in the twentieth century, efforts were periodically made to reduce their number. Significantly, all of these efforts failed. Moreover, subcommittees proliferated. For example, in the Senate in the period from 1947 through 1976 subcommittees expanded from 49 to 109. A similar increase occurred in the House. The major reason for the dispersion of committees is that they are of central importance in developing reputations for power on Capitol Hill.

Woodrow Wilson first emphasized the power of committees on Capitol Hill. He described the beginnings of the institutionalization of the House and the Senate as it was reflected in the growing dominance of powerful committees. Moreover, although not as sharply refined as it would be later on, a committee hierarchy of power and status existed. The top committees included those which were not directly involved in legislation but which had important power within Congress, the House Rules Committee and the Appropriations Committees of both bodies. Wilson quotes one member as exclaiming that the principal forces in the House were "the Brahmins of the Committee of Ways and Means—not the brains but the Brahmins of the

House; the white-button mandarins of the Appropriations Committee; the dignified oligarchy called the Committee on Rules; [and] the Speaker of the House. . . ."[3]

Since the Speaker exercised tight control over the floor action, Wilson found that the new member was forced to seek a committee base for his quest for personal power. If a new Congressman had the audacity to introduce his own bill, he discovered that the rules of the House, which embodied its power structure, prevented even a few remarks in behalf of his legislation on the floor: "The rap of Mr. Speaker's gavel is sharp, immediate, and preemptory. He is curtly informed that no debate is in order; the bill can only be referred to the appropriate committee."[4] This constituted the new member's "first lesson in committee government, and the master's rod smarts; but the sooner he learns the prerogatives and powers of the standing committees, the sooner will he penetrate to the mysteries of the rules and avoid the pain of further contact with their thorny side."[5]

This institutionalization of the House and the Senate reflected a Congress whose attention was turning inward as members increasingly sought to carve out their political careers there. In a statement that is as true as the 1980s approach as it was in the 1880s, Woodrow Wilson wrote:

> The privileges of the standing committees are the beginning and end of the rules. Both the House of Representatives and the Senate conduct their business by what may figuratively but not inaccurately be called an odd device of disintegration. The House virtually both deliberates and legislates in small sections. . . . the work is parcelled out, most of it to the forty-seven standing committees which constitute the regular organization of the House, some of it to select committees appointed for special and temporary purposes.[6]

The multiplication of committees produces internal power struggles on many levels. At the subcommittee level vacant chairmanships are frequently in doubt, as senior committee members vie for subcommittees that bring with them large staffs and legislative jurisdictions which can be used to develop reputations for power. In fact, in the House subcommittees may be more important to a member's internal power than a major standing committee. In 1977 Michigan Congressman John Din-

gell and Florida Congressman Paul Rogers renounced the chairmanship of the Merchant Marine and Fisheries Committee in
order to retain their powerful subcommittee chairmanships of
Energy and Power, and Health and the Environment, respectively. Dingell and Rogers each felt he had more power as chairman
of a subcommittee than he would have as chairman of the constituent and pressure group oriented Merchant Marine and Fisheries Committee. Both had worked hard to make their subcommittees and by extension themselves into powerful forces, and
they were not inclined to relinquish them.

The withdrawal of Dingell and Rogers opened the chairmanship of the Merchant Marine and Fisheries Committee for John
Murphy of New York, who gave up his chairmanship of the
Commerce Subcommittee on Consumer Protection. In line to
take over the subcommittee was Virginia Congressman David
Satterfield, who was the most senior Democrat on the Interstate
and Foreign Commerce Committee without his own subcommittee. Sensing dissatisfaction among committee Democrats over
the low-keyed Satterfield, Bob Eckhardt of Texas challenged
him and won the subcommittee's chairmanship on a secret ballot, 17–12. The prize of subcommittee chairmanships is such
that members are encouraged to challenge the seniority rule and
compete against a more senior member of a committee for va-
cancies. When Paul Rogers announced his retirement in 1978,
Congressman Henry A. Waxman declared his candidacy for the
chairmanship of the Health Subcommittee. The chairmanship
would normally be given to Richardson Preyer of North Carolina, who had more seniority and was backed strongly by the
Democratic leadership team of Speaker Tip O'Neill, Majority
Leader Jim Wright, and Rules Committee Chairman Richard
Bolling. Waxman, a strong supporter of Rogers, launched a
concerted campaign for the chairmanship. As representative of
California's 24th "Hollywood District," Waxman received many
contributions from movie stars. Facing only weak opposition in
his district, Waxman formed his own political action committee
to channel some of his donations to other Congressmen, including nine members of the Commerce Committee who would
vote on the chairmanship of the Health Subcommittee. This was
sharply criticized by the House leadership. Richard Bolling accused Waxman of violating the spirit of House reform by challenging a more senior member of Preyer's stature and reputa-

tion. Undaunted, Waxman continued to garner support within and without Congress. He gained the backing of fellow California Congressman Phillip Burton, who saw the Waxman campaign as an opportunity to demonstrate his power by helping to defeat the leadership's candidate. Waxman's unconventional tactics succeeded. The tally in the Interstate and Foreign Commerce Committee was 15 for Waxman and 12 for Preyer. Seven members of the committee who received campaign contributions from Waxman voted for him.

Junior members increasingly are unwilling to let chairmanships be won by default. Like Waxman, Congressman Bob Eckhardt of Texas defeated a more senior member, John Murphy of New York, for the chairmanship of a key Commerce Subcommittee. Eckhardt was backed in his quest for the chairmanship of the Oversight and Investigations Subcommittee by Waxman, Toby Moffett of Connecticut, and Andrew Maguire of New Jersey. These young Congressmen forced Eckhardt to promise that he would consult with them on the committee agenda and operations. One of Eckhardt's supporters, Toby Moffett, had previously shocked the House by capturing the chairmanship of the Environment, Energy, and Natural Resources Subcommittee of Government Operations.

In the Senate, subcommittees are important in slightly different ways. While a Senator would be unlikely to choose the chairmanship of a subcommittee over a committee, he typically is determined to chair the biggest and most powerful subcommittee he can find. At the start of the 95th Congress the members of the Judiciary Committee were engaged in playing just such a game of musical chairs. When it ended, no one wanted to be left out. Ted Kennedy was in line for chairmanship of the prestigious Antitrust and Monopoly Subcommittee of the Judiciary Committee which had been left vacant by the death of Philip Hart of Michigan. Birch Bayh, however, had been serving as acting chairman since the Michigan Senator withdrew because of illness. A Bayh-Kennedy fight was averted when Bayh decided to chair the new Constitution Subcommittee (Senators cannot chair more than one subcommittee of a major standing committee).

By taking over the Antitrust and Monopoly Subcommittee Kennedy acquired a staff of twenty-eight and a far-reaching jurisdiction. For both of these reasons he quickly dropped his chairmanship of the Administrative Practice and Procedure Subcommittee, which had a far smaller staff and a more limited jurisdiction. The subcommittee offered a sneak preview of what would happen when Kennedy took over the full committee in the 96th Congress. Kennedy was an aggressive subcommittee chairman. He was an even more assertive chairman. He moved at once to consolidate the committee under his control. Rumors circulated that Kennedy was scheming to abolish subcommittees altogether. Such a move would violate the traditions of the committee and the spirit of committee reorganization that had taken place in 1977 which was partially designed to reapportion committee and subcommittee chairmanships. Kennedy aides hinted that the new chairman would control top level staff appointments to subcommittees, and would refuse subcommittee chairmanships to freshmen. Kennedy quickly realized that such radical changes would destroy his long-standing good relations with both the Democrats and Republicans on the committee. Kennedy tightened his control without major organizational changes. He reduced the number of subcommittees from ten to seven, and placed close allies in the chairmanships of his former subcommittees. His close friend, John Culver of Iowa, became chairman of the Administrative Practice and Procedure Subcommittee, and the liberal Howard M. Metzenbaum of Ohio assumed the chairmanship of the Antitrust Subcommittee. The new freshmen Democrats, Max Baucus of Montana and Howell Heflin of Alabama, received their own new subcommittees, and Joseph Biden of Delaware finally achieved a long sought goal when a new Criminal Justice Subcommittee was created for him. Although subcommittees continued, Kennedy left no doubt that he would keep a close watch on the subcommittees and retain control of major legislation by keeping it within the province of the full committee.

The balance of power in the Senate is always delicate. A single shift, the movement of only one Senator to another committee, is felt throughout the entire body. The power relationships carefully constructed over time are set awry. Although the seniority rule is not always respected, especially in the House, it does mute the constant conflict over committee assignments at the beginning of legislative sessions. Senior committee members are automatically considered first for choice subcommittee chairmanships. When a committee chairman leaves, his slot is automatically filled by the member next in line. McClellan's death during the second session of the 95th Congress, for example, opened up the chairmanship of the top-ranked Appropriations Committee, and Warren Magnuson of Washington, the second-ranking member, automatically moved up to the chairmanship, giving up the chairmanship of the Commerce Committee. (Cannon, second in seniority on Commerce, became its chairman.) Magnuson, of course, could choose between the two committees. Appropriations in the Senate is not considered to be a College of Cardinals as it is in the House, but it is still the most powerful committee in the body. Therefore, given the opportunity to assume the chairmanship of Appropriations, no Senator striving for power would decline it, and no Senator has ever done so.

Conflict over committee assignments starts in the earliest stages of Capitol Hill careers, when newcomers attempt to stake out their claims to the most powerful committees. The brash and aggressive Bella Abzug, for example, on arriving on Capitol Hill as a freshman in January of 1971, coveted a position on the powerful Armed Services Committee. That January 22, Congresswoman Abzug wrote in her diary that she sought support for her bid for the Armed Services Committee at a dinner for the New York delegation, and that everyone with the exception of powerful Congressman John Rooney "seemed to approve." The diary entry continues:

> I concluded my speech by saying, "I'm looking forward to your unanimous support in my bid for a seat on the committee, and that includes you, too, John."
> "Agriculture for you," he piped up. "You start at the bottom. You stay at the bottom;"
> "John," I said, "I can't believe you would be so mean to a still unseated member of this delegation."
> "Like I said," he went on, "you start at the bottom. You stay at the bottom — with your seat. And you got a pretty good seat."[7]

Congressman Rooney's observation that Agriculture was at the bottom and Armed Services near the top of committee rankings in the House was shared by all Congressmen who had been on the Hill for any length of time. Agriculture is basically a constituent oriented committee whose members are largely drawn from agricultural states. Its commodities subcommittees are selected to serve narrow agricultural interests in different Congressional districts throughout the country. Armed Services is not primarily a constituent committee. Powerful members can, if they are at the top of the committee in seniority and have their own subcommittees, do favors for their constituents by attempting to channel defense funds or military bases into their districts. Chairmen of Armed Services have unabashedly channeled Department of Defense funds into their districts. Among the most notorious chairmen in this respect was L. Mendel Rivers of the first district of South Carolina that encompassed Charleston. He represented the district for thirty years until his death in 1970, and he was chairman of Armed Services from 1965 until 1970. Thirty-five percent of the payrolls in his district came from defense industries or military installations, and his district contained eleven major Navy bases and installations. But the internal power and prestige of the Armed Services Committee results from its history as a representative of the role of the House in exercising its constitutional war powers, and from the prominence of the Department of Defense in the post-World War II era. It is because of the internal recognition of the committee's power in the broad sense that members desire it.

Abzug too recognized the prestige of Armed Services, noting that "the House Armed Services Committee is not just another committee. I recall its chairman, Mendel Rivers, who died just before the session opened, once saying, 'This is the most important committee in Congress. It is the only *official* voice the military has in the House of Representatives.'"[8] But she also recognized the realities of being a freshman on Capitol Hill. As she pointed out, "The tradition down here is that new members, like myself, take what they get. They don't make a lot of noise; they don't ask for anything unreasonable; and they humbly go through the proper channels."[9]

Abzug finally received assignments on the Government Operations and Public Works Committees, and as a freshman she immediately evaluated these assignments in terms of their potential for building her internal power on the Hill. She noted, "Government Operations is a committee that could have extensive power, but its chairman, Chet Holifield, is not interested in challenging the system. Its most useful function, as far as I am concerned, is that it has investigatory powers over parts of the government. Potentially, it could investigate the military, the

CIA, the FBI, the Treasury Department, anything it wants, and it can make all those guys pay for the way they have been tyrannizing the lives of the people in this country. At the moment, I'm angling for a seat on the Military Operations subcommittee of Government Operations, because that's where I'll be, well, let's say 'more useful.' "[10] In short, Abzug saw Government Operations as a base from which to develop a reputation for power. She perceived at once the importance of power symbols within the House. She cleverly saw that the Public Works Committee, exercising jurisdiction over pork barrel projects, could be used to serve district interests but more importantly its members could use their position to exert internal power because of widespread interest in the committee's legislation. Abzug wrote, "Public Works is also potentially powerful because it's the pork barrel committee of Congress . . . and since a lot of people from the South and West and Midwest and Southwest want to get on this committee, it's possible if I don't like it that I'll be able to trade it for another assignment in the next session."[11] Abzug clearly saw her career in the House of Representatives in terms of building her power on Capitol Hill through assignments to top-ranked committees. If she were unsuccessful, she would use other committee posts to gain visibility and move up in the House.

This jockeying for committee slots is the inevitable result of a committee hierarchy. Some committees are universally considered to have more power and status than others. Congressmen agree, for instance, that the Appropriations and Ways and Means Committees stand at the very top. The elevated position of these committees stems from the constitutional prerogative of the House to originate appropriations and revenue-raising legislation. They are, in effect, symbolic of the constitutional power and responsibilities of the House, and they act as ambassadors of the House to the Senate and the executive branch.

The chairmen of Ways and Means and Appropriations rival the leadership of the House in influence within the body. And the ranking minority members of these committees exert leadership within their Congressional party. Barber Conable of New York, for example, willingly relinquished his chairmanship of the Republican Policy Committee in the 95th Congress in order to become the ranking Republican member of the Ways and Means Committee. (Party rules prevented his holding both positions.) Conable quickly plunged into his Ways and Means

Committee work, and soon rivaled Illinois Republican John Anderson, chairman of the House Republican Conference and a top-ranking member of the Rules Committee, for recognition as spokesman for the party. Reflecting on his new position, Conable said: "As ranking member of Ways and Means, people listen to me when I talk. What is power? All it is, is influence. As long as people listen when I talk I've got some influence."[12]

The House Rules Committee, which stands near the top of the committee hierarchy, is also sought after by members who wish internal power, although its clout is no longer what it once was. In its heyday the committee had life-or-death power over legislation. The committee's power was also by extension the power of its individual members. In 1965, for instance, the then chairman, James Delaney of New York, managed singlehandedly to kill federal aid to education. Its very power made the Rules Committee a natural target for the "reforms" of young House members in the mid-1970s. The resurgent Democratic caucus of the 94th Congress tried to bring the Rules Committee under the control of rank-and-file members by reducing it to a tool of the Speaker. Such "reforms," however, were only partially successful, and the Rules Committee remains, even with less independence and a reduced reputation for power, an important base for building influence within the House. In recent years such diverse members as Richard Bolling of Missouri and Gillis Long of Louisiana have used the Rules Committee for precisely this purpose. When he became Chairman of Rules in 1979 Bolling let it be known by his statements and actions that he planned to use his position to exert strong leadership.

Long has built his reputation as a quietly effectual, rising young Congressman who knows how to get things done through his work on the Rules Committee. Virtually unknown outside of his district and off Capitol Hill, Long is considered a man to watch by Congressional observers. Long has had more than a helping hand from the voters back home in this enterprise. His seat, the state's eighth Congressional district, has been passed around from one member of the Long family to another since 1960 and at one time was the home district of the celebrated Huey Long. In 1960 Earl Long, the Kingfish's brother, fresh from the governor's office, won the Democratic primary. Long died before the general election, and his opponent went to

Washington instead. In 1962 Gillis Long, Earl's cousin, won the seat only to be beaten two years later by another cousin, Speedy O. Long, an archconservative who appealed to the strong anti-civil rights mood of his largely rural northern Louisiana constituency. Speedy retired in 1972 and was succeeded, predictably enough, by Gillis. Long won the general election in 1976 with 94 percent of the vote after being unopposed in the primary. Thus Long has been spared the necessity of devoting the initial years of his House career, as many members from less secure seats must, to getting reelected. He has been able to devote his time and attention to establishing his place among the House leaders-to-be. Despite Long's relatively junior status in the House, he was selected by Richard Bolling to manage his unsuccessful campaign for Majority Leader in 1977. Long has clear ambitions for the leadership someday himself.

Long won a significant victory in this regard in 1977 when he was given the chairmanship of a new subcommittee of the Rules Committee with potentially extraordinary powers. The Rules Committee press release announcing this action played up its significance. "In precedent breaking action," the press release announced, the House Rules Committee "voted to create the first permanent subcommittee in its 188-year history." Gillis Long was unanimously elected to chair the new Subcommittee on Rules and Organization of the House. It acquired authority over House rules, committee procedures and jurisdictions. Rules Committee chairman James Delaney noted that "the responsibilities and sensitive political nature of this subcommittee require the talents of a chairman who is both strong and impartial." Long said that his role would be that of "a negotiator, a seeker of common solutions to uncommon problems." He would not be a power broker, he said, but a moderator among the diverse interests of the House. This was Long's first subcommittee chairmanship, and it promised to launch a successful career toward House leadership.

The Senate, a "body of equals," has no committees that have been used like the House Rules Committee to dominate the body, but it does have prestigious committees, analogous to the House Appropriations and Ways and Means Committees, which reflect its constitutional role. Both the Foreign Relations and Judiciary Committees are eagerly sought after for this reason.

Foreign Relations represents the constitutional role of the

Senate in foreign policy, particularly its powers to ratify treaties and to advise and consent on ambassadorial appointments. It is the penumbra effect of the treaty-making power of the Senate that gives the Foreign Relations Committee its clout. Under such distinguished chairmen as Henry Cabot Lodge, Sr., who led the successful opposition to the Treaty of Versailles in 1919, and Senator J. William Fulbright, who helped to focus public discontent with the Vietnam war in the late 1960s, the Foreign Relations Committee has exerted extraordinary influence over foreign policy. Since World War II, even under the chairmanship of Fulbright, the power of the committee over foreign policy has declined as the President's has grown. But this external diminution of the committee's power has not appeared to reduce its prestige in the Senate. When Frank Church took over the committee after the retirement of John Sparkman of Alabama in 1978, he was determined to bolster the committee's reputation outside the Senate. He hired a new staff director from the Pentagon to provide an expertise in defense policy that the committee lacked and to strengthen the staff in other policy areas. Church well remembered his embarrassment when the Armed Services Committee conducted more thorough hearings on the SALT I agreements in 1972 than the Foreign Relations Committee did. He wanted to make certain that his committee would be at the forefront of the hearings to be held on the SALT II agreements, which promised to be a major initial test of the committee. Church also sought to consolidate subcommittees and centralize control in the full committee. He was only partially successful. He eliminated his own Foreign Economic Policy Subcommittee, and the Foreign Assistance Subcommittee that had been chaired by Hubert Humphrey.

The Senate Judiciary Committee reflects the constitutional role of the Senate to advise and consent on judicial appointments. Other Senate committees perform similar roles in the appointments of "public ministers," which from the early days of the Republic has been interpreted to mean the secretaries of Cabinet departments. More recently, Congress has extended this to include many other executive-branch appointments. The Judiciary Committee alone, however, oversees appointments to the Supreme Court, which provides it with checks over both the executive and judicial branches. This role in the constitutional scheme of checks and balances inevitably enhances its reputation for power in the Senate. Moreover, Judiciary at least indirectly oversees the process of senatorial approval of presidential appointments to the lower federal courts, which traditionally fall within the province of individual Senators from the states where the courts sit. At this level, the Judiciary Committee is principally a conduit for the requests of Senators. Although the committee customarily acquiesces to the demands of senatorial colleagues, Senators are still forced to seek committee approval of their recommendations, thus further boosting the power of committee members.

While Foreign Relations and Judiciary are top-ranked Senate committees, the Appropriations Committee remains the most prestigious of committee assignments. Although somewhat overshadowed by its House counterpart, the Appropriations Committee is the most influential within the Senate. All legislation eventually comes within its jurisdiction as all expenditures authorized by the standing committees must be approved by the Appropriations Committee.

As members of the House and the Senate constantly strive to advance their careers on Capitol Hill by securing slots on the most powerful committees, inevitable frustrations occur due to the limited number of seats. When Congressman Harley Staggers of West Virginia, chairman of the Interstate and Foreign Commerce Committee, unexpectedly announced in 1978 that he would seek reelection to a sixteenth Congressional term, veteran California Congressman John Moss, who had risen to second in seniority on the committee, issued an announcement of his own: he would not run again. Blunt and sometimes irascible, Moss had proved to be a capable and aggressive chairman of his Oversight and Investigations Subcommittee. But the same doggedness which won him the fear and respect of dozens of federal bureaucrats also irritated many of his colleagues. A decade earlier Moss had been passed over for the position of deputy Whip, the first of the many rungs in the long climb up the ladder toward the Speakership. Denied a spot in the leadership, Moss focused his ambitions on the Interstate and Foreign Commerce Committee, which he had joined as a freshman in 1953. Now after twelve terms in Congress, his ambitions were again thwarted. There was no hope in the immediate future that Moss would become committee chairman, and there was no telling how long Staggers would stay. Moss decided that time had come for him at last to retire.

Just as Congressmen and Senators scramble for assignment to committees with the highest power and status, so, too, committees themselves compete for ever more influence and prestige. Committees are constantly striving to expand their legislative turf in order to gain more power and thus status. The larger a committee's jurisdiction, the more potential power it has. The conflict is constant and unremitting. In the process Congress's attention is often diverted from collective deliberation of the important issues of the day. After President Carter's energy plan was sent to Capitol Hill in 1977, it became a pawn in the power game played not only by the House leadership and powerful members on both sides of Capitol Hill but also by the committees. This was at the root of conflict between Russell Long and other Senators, including Kennedy, because Long had carefully garnered most of the energy proposals under the umbrella of his Finance Committee's jurisdiction, leaving very little residual turf for other Senators.

Similar power plays also went on behind the scenes in the House. Chairmen of two subcommittees of the Science and Technology Committee sought to upstage Congressman John Dingell of Michigan who, as chairman of the Energy and Power Subcommittee, had dominated this area. Well before President Carter sent his budget proposals for the Department of Energy to Capitol Hill in 1978, Walter Flowers of Alabama and Mike McCormack of Washington scheduled hearings before their respective subcommittees on Fossil and Nuclear Energy Research and on Advanced Energy Technology. Dingell simultaneously claimed jurisdiction over the same part of the budget. The strategy of the Science subcommittee chairmen was to beat Dingell in making recommendations to the Appropriations Committee. If the Appropriations Committee were to consider their proposals first, their territorial claim would have passed an important first hurdle in the House power structure.

The energy debates of the 95th Congress brought up the issue of government regulation and promotion of coal-slurry pipelines, which immediately invoked a jurisdictional fight among three House committees for control over the legislation: Interior, Interstate and Foreign Commerce, and Public Works. Each committee saw coal-slurry pipelines as properly within its jurisdiction. The pipelines would cross public lands, and therefore the House Interior Committee claimed jurisdiction. The pipelines also would cross railroad property, which falls under the jurisdiction of Interstate and Foreign Commerce. Pipelines, being a form of transportation, also relate to the Public Works Committee's jurisdiction over "measures relating to the construction or maintenance of roads and post roads" and public works in general, including those for the benefit of navigation.

The constant committee fights over legislative jurisdiction are supplemented by fights to preserve or expand the administrative departments and agencies under their jurisdiction. The Department of Energy bill quickly passed the Senate because it added to the jurisdiction of the Energy Committee chaired by Henry Jackson, who also happened to be a senior member of the Governmental Affairs Committee considering the bill. Previous committee reorganizations, such as the transfer of jurisdiction over the Federal Power Commission from the Commerce Committee to the Energy Committee, helped smooth the path, although on some issues delicate maneuvering still occurred. Behind the scenes, the Governmental Affairs Committee, chaired by Senator Abe Ribicoff of Connecticut, had to make certain that the new Energy Department would not upset existing committee jurisdictions. The transfer of agencies to the new Energy Department would automatically shift jurisdiction over them to Jackson's committee. For example, the staff of Senator James Sasser's Civil Service and General Services Subcommittee maneuvered to protect its jurisdiction by clarifying the fact that the new department would not have authority over the construction of new government buildings. This guaranteed the continuation of the status quo for Sasser's committee and for the General Services Administration. (See Chapter 4 on staff further elaboration of this incident.)

Conflict between Jackson and his staff on the one hand and Ribicoff and his staff on the other was a major factor in shaping the final structure of the Department of Energy. Since Jackson would have control over the new department, he favored a strongly centralized department headed by a powerful secretary. Jackson also had strong professional and personal ties to James Schlesinger, whom President Carter had already tapped to be the first Secretary of Energy. Ribicoff unwittingly acknowledged that the real energy czar would not be Schlesinger, but "Secretary" Jackson, as Ribicoff at one point inadvertently called the Senator from Washington during the markups on the bill. Ribicoff and his staff along with other influential Senators on the committee preferred a looser structure with more decentralized authority for the department and were not inclined to give hasty approval to the administration's bill. Their reluctance was not solely a reflection of philosophical differences. Several months before, the administration had sent to the Hill legislation which gave the President basic authority to reorganize the government. The Senate had routinely approved the legislation, but Congressman Jack Brooks of Texas, chairman of the Government Operations Committee of the House, had stalled. As a result Brooks had garnered substantial publicity and been courted by the White House. The attention left members of the Senate Governmental Affairs Committee and their staffs with the nagging suspicion that they had given without getting. Now they had a second chance. Jackson's staff naturally fought attempts to emasculate the department. In the end Ribicoff won, but Jackson's efforts managed to reduce the independent authority given to the Energy Regulatory Board, formerly the Federal Power Commission, that was set up in the new department. The organization of the federal bureaucracy is more determined by internal Congressional politics and by committee infighting than by the wishes of the White House or by standards for managerial efficiency.

Committee fights to preserve administrative jurisdiction are illustrated by conflict on Capitol Hill over President Carter's proposal to take the food stamp program out of the Agriculture Department and replace it with direct cash payments administered by the Department of Health, Education, and Welfare. Predictably, Herman Talmadge of Georgia, the chairman of the Senate Agriculture Committee, and the House Agriculture chairman, Tom Foley, publicly attacked Joseph Califano, Secretary of HEW, for his bureaucratic imperialism which would impinge on the Agriculture Department and reduce the jurisdiction of the Agriculture Committees on Capitol Hill.

The controversial food stamp program was also caught up in intense Congressional infighting among House committees. When House Speaker Tip O'Neill hoped to follow with an ad hoc welfare committee his successful deployment of the ad hoc energy committee to smooth jurisdictional squabbles over the energy package among House committees, he was disappointed. Like ad hoc energy, ad hoc welfare represented the relevant power domains of Agriculture (seven members), Education and Labor (seven members), and Ways and Means (fourteen members). When a motion was made in the ad hoc welfare committee to abolish the food stamp program, the members from Education and Labor voted 6-1 in favor, the representatives from the Agriculture Committee voted 5-2 to continue food stamps, and the Ways and Means representatives voted 8-6 for elimination of food stamps. Agriculture considered food stamps exclusively to be within its jurisdiction, so that its delegates to the ad hoc committee guarded their interests. The Agriculture Committee was not about to allow an ad hoc panel to invade its jurisdiction and eliminate a program that is an integral part of the Agriculture Department and a significant portion of its budget. Al Ullman saw the matter differently. He felt food stamps should fall within the jurisdiction of the Ways and Means Committee. His committee considered food stamps to be involved in welfare reform, and the elimination of the program would ease the way for his committee to consider it as part of a total welfare program later.

Special committees, such as the ad hoc energy committee, collide head on with the entrenched interests of the standing committees. They are considered upstarts, interlopers, the enemy. The most vivid example of this in recent years is the running feud between the Senate Armed Services Committee and the Intelligence Committee. The clash between the two committees was inevitable. The very creation of the Intelligence Committee was viewed by senior members of the Armed Services Committee, particularly its chairman, Senator John Stennis, a gentleman of impeccable personal integrity but questionable objectivity toward the military, as a personal affront. And in a sense it was. The Intelligence Committee grew out of an investigation into abuses by the various intelligence agencies, including the CIA and FBI, conducted by Senator Frank Church. The continuing revelations had been splashed across the front pages of newspapers off and on for months. A "something must be done" atmosphere had been created. But the reason that the Senate felt something had to be done was that the Armed Services Committee, which was responsible for overseeing the intelligence agencies, had done nothing for years. The Armed Services Committee had permitted the CIA to go its own way until at last they wandered into a kudzu patch from which even their old friends on the Armed Services Committee could not extract them.

Incidentally, the power and prestige of committee chairmen and the ability of the chairmen to capitalize on them are such that special conditions were imposed on Frank Church before he was named to head the investigation. Church, who had a hankering for the presidency, pledged that he would not become a formal candidate while he was chairman of the select committee which investigated intelligence operations. Thus he would not be able to use his chairmanship to further his presidential ambitions. This was important in a body where half a dozen of his colleagues harbored similar ambitions.

As debate on the proposed committee began, Senator Abraham Ribicoff urged his colleagues to put aside their petty concerns for power and status. The Senate, he said, should not allow "the jurisdictions of its own committees to overshadow the national interest."[13] The national interest, however, is an amorphous concept, and one's perception of it depends on where one stands. As far as John Stennis was concerned, the national interest required his Armed Services Committee to retain control over military intelligence. What was good for the Armed Services Committee was good for the country.

Stennis was not the only one who saw things this way. The Subcommittee on Defense of the Appropriations Committee also has a special interest in intelligence. The members of that committee similarly believed that the national interest hinged on preserving the current committee jurisdictions. Stennis, ranking Democratic member of the subcommittee, turned to Milton Young of North Dakota, the ranking Republican member, for help. Young was also the ranking Republican member of the Appropriations Subcommittee on Intelligence Operations. In speaking out, he represented the positions of both subcommittees. Young said, "I think it is fair to say that almost every Senator who has served on [the Intelligence Operations Subcommittee] felt that, because of the very sensitive information we must deal with, it should be a small committee. Most members would be very reluctant or would even decline to serve on a committee with a much larger membership and an unlimited staff."

In fact, the Intelligence Committee had already been trimmed somewhat to meet just those objections. Originally the proposed

Intelligence Committee was to consist of seventeen members who would be appointed from the Senate at large. But as the resolution emerged from the Rules Committee, the Intelligence Committee would be composed of fifteen members, eight of whom would come from the Armed Services, Appropriations, Judiciary, and Foreign Relations Committees. By guaranteeing representation on the Intelligence Committee for the committees which would lose jurisdictions, Senator Howard Cannon, sponsor of the substitute resolution, hoped to pick up support. Clearly, it was not enough.

The entire debate over S. Res. 400 came down to conflicting committee jurisdictions and the reluctance of the powerful Armed Services Committee and the Appropriations Defense Subcommittee to relinquish any part of their power. The members of the Armed Services Committee had won a victory of sorts in securing representation on the new panel, and in the provision for rotating membership and a limited term for the chairman, which would prevent any vested interest from being firmly established in the committee and its jurisdiction. They had gotten a lot but not enough. John Stennis, Sam Nunn, and the hardline Republicans on Armed Services insisted that legislative and budgetary power over the military intelligence agencies remain exclusively within their committee. They offered such an amendment.

Stennis cast the argument in global terms. The very role of the United States as a world power was at stake in the battle over committee jurisdiction. The Senate had created a special system, he said, to develop and oversee intelligence activities, and any threat to the traditional approach would jeopardize the security of the nation. Those who administered this system were bound to honor "a kind of general understanding" which had been in effect since the CIA came into existence. They could be trusted because they were primarily the last members of the inner club which had once dominated the Senate, the venerable chairmen of Appropriations, Armed Services, and Foreign Relations. "It has been," said Stennis, "a special setup." The proposed Intelligence Committee would not just enlarge this group but also would change its very makeup. The Senators appointed to the Intelligence Committee would be, as Ribicoff had said, "a cross section of the Senate, especially the younger men of the Senate." Stennis had no desire to share his power, but if he had to, he wanted at least to share power with those of his own ilk. The Intelligence Committee was one more sign that the last days of the club were at hand.

Stennis was willing to grant the new Intelligence Committee oversight of the CIA, since oversight power alone is essentially meaningless. But, he argued, power over legislation, authorizations, and appropriations had to remain in the traditional committees. Those committees, particularly Armed Services, had the necessary expertise, continuity, and background to deal with intelligence. Moreover, the Senate had to be able to do effective battle when it met the House in conference. The new Intelligence Committee would disrupt the Senate, creating an unwieldy two-tier budgetary system. In effect, Senate power would be reduced in dealing with the House, something no true Senator should support. Stennis concluded, "I hope that this little amendment [retaining exclusive legislative and budgetary jurisdiction over military intelligence agencies within the Armed Services Committee] — and it is small — for the protection of this part of the intelligence program will be passed."

The lengthy and often acrimonious debate over the creation of the Senate Select Intelligence Committee centered upon the effects this committee would have on the internal power structure of the body. The Senators who had the greatest stake in the existing power structure opposed those whose interests would be unaffected or enhanced by the new committee. Very little time was spent on the need for effective oversight over the intelligence community, or on the abuses by intelligence agencies uncovered by a special committee created to investigate the intelligence agencies that was headed by Frank Church. Every Senator speaking in favor of the resolution felt compelled to address himself to the question of the reductions in power the new committee would mean to the senior chairmen of the most prestigious committees in the Senate — Appropriations, Armed Services, Foreign Relations, and Judiciary.

Senator Charles Percy of Illinois tried to counter Stennis's objections in part by pointing out that "the Senator from Mississippi and the members of the Armed Services Committee are among the most overworked Senators in the Senate." He went on, "What the Senator from Illinois would hope would happen is that a tremendous burden of responsibility for a lot of follow-through on intelligence would now be taken over and assumed by the Select Committee on Intelligence Activities, providing to the members of the Armed Services Committee an assurance that the details of these programs have been looked to."

Majority Whip Robert Byrd, who supported the new committee, pointed out,

> It is a most difficult task to shift jurisdiction in the Senate to allow for the changing priorities which the national interest demands. It is not that our present committee structure did not want, or try, to prevent abuses in the intelligence community—the fact is that the intelligence activities of our government have grown so large and so complex that the substantive committees, with all of their other heavy responsibilities, could not hope to give the necessary time and develop the specialized expertise needed to constantly monitor and effectively control the intelligence community.

Senator Ted Kennedy, then fourth in seniority on Judiciary, supported the cut in the jurisdiction of Judiciary. He addressed his colleagues "as a member of Judiciary":

> . . . as a member of the Senate Committee on the Judiciary, I had the occasion to hear testimony and to join debate over whether any new permanent Senate intelligence oversight committee should have jurisdiction to oversee the intelligence activities of the Federal Bureau of Investigation. I came away convinced that while the Judiciary Committee must maintain its historic jurisdiction over every aspect of the Bureau's operations, the new committee should nevertheless be vested with authority over the FBI's intelligence activities.[14]

Senator John Pastore of Rhode Island, himself a member of the Appropriations Defense and Intelligence Operations Subcommittees, had little personal interest at stake because of his low seniority on Appropriations. Even so, his attention was directed to the ongoing conflict over committee jurisdictions: "My regret at the moment is that apparently we have drifted into the sensitive question of committee jurisdiction, " he said. But, Pastore told his colleagues, other issues were at stake. "We must remember, Mr. President, that what we are dealing with here now is not the composition of the committees today or the sensitivities of the various members. What we are dealing with here today is the matter of how do we resolve this very important question [of oversight of the intelligence community] that now confronts the Congress of the United States in a way that is for the public benefit."

Not all of the conflict over the proposed Select Intelligence Committee centered on committee jurisdictions. Senator Robert Taft raised another internal issue—who would be qualified to be a member of the new committee. Taft, who actively engaged in the debate over the creation of the intelligence panel, finally voted against it. He offered an amendment to S. Res. 400 designed to decide whether or not the new committee would be designated a "minor" committee, Senators could add minor committees on to their regular assignments to two "major" standing committees, although certain Senators such as Cannon and Jackson had been "grandfathered" and were permitted three major committees. Minor committees included any permanent select or special committee, any joint committee (with the exception of the Joint Committee on the Library and Printing), and the District of Columbia, Post Office and Civil Service, Rules and Administration, and Veterans Affairs committees. Senators were not permitted to add on to their two standing committee memberships more than one minor committee. Under S. Res. 400 members of the Select Committee on Intelligence would not have to give up any other committee assignments. Thus Senators could serve on the new committee, a second minor committee, and their standing committees. Taft's amendment, which was defeated, would have required Senators to give up their membership on minor committees if they served on the Intelligence Committee. Taft declared that his amendment would prevent the new intelligence panel from becoming inferior even to the minor committees, which Taft described as "dogs." Arguing for his amendment, Taft stated:

> Mr. President, members, particularly those with the greatest abilities, may tend to seek to avoid such a committee assignment [on the Select Intelligence Committee] because it is an uncompensated add-on to their primary committee responsibilities. Can we afford to have this committee regarded by the membership as one of the "dogs," so to speak, as far as committee assignments are concerned?[15]

Every Senator knows, said Taft, that minor committees do not always receive the attention from their members which they might deserve. Taft's amendment was defeated because no Senator would give up membership, and therefore seniority, even on a minor committee in order to serve on one with an eight-year limitation and a revolving chairmanship elected by the majority caucus at the beginning of each Congress.

Although the Senate weakened the power of its Select Intelligence Committee in order to placate the major committees whose interests were threatened and to assure the others that this would not become a new power center, the apprehensions of the opponents were not unfounded. Hawaiian Senator Daniel K. Inouye, the first chairman, immediately adopted the mantle of "Mr. Intelligence" of the Senate. Birch Bayh, elected chairman in the 95th Congress, sent out tentative feelers seeking support for a change that would make the temporary chairmanship of the committee permanent.

In the Senate of the past, many of the senior members of the body that backed Stennis in his efforts to protect the Armed Services Committee jurisdiction would have formed the nucleus of a ruling "Senate establishment." A reverence for the institution and its traditions would have prevented the creation of a committee that impinged upon the jurisdictions of the Senate's most prestigious committees. Senior Senators such as John Stennis, Howard Cannon, Russell Long, Herman Talmadge, John McClellan, and James O. Eastland would have been able to assure the passage of the Stennis amendment to uphold the status quo. And all of these Senators did in fact back the Stennis resolution, but it failed 31–63. The vote reflected a general recognition in the body, not that there should be more effective oversight of the intelligence community, but that the Senate's power structure should be more open than in the past. The vote illustrated the waning of the traditional Senate establishment.

The origin of and debate over the Senate intelligence panel is a microcosm of the broader world of Capitol Hill. Within Congress issues are always encrusted with power conflicts among members and committees. The creation of any new committee is a threat to the old order. The Budget Committees of both the House and the Senate, viewed by outsiders as a Congressional counter to presidential imperiousness, in fact originated in power struggles in both bodies. The committees were seen by some members as a boost to their personal power, and the legislation creating them was an addition to these members' reputations for power on Capitol Hill. The fight over the House Budget Committee, like that over the Senate Intelligence Committee, ended up weakening it by providing a rotating membership and almost guaranteeing control by vested Congressional interests. Ten of the twenty-five members of the House Budget Committee would come from the Appropriations and Ways and Means Committees. To control the committee, they would have to win over only three other members. Moreover, assignments were restricted so that no member would serve on the committee more than four years in any ten-year period. The Budget Committee in the Senate escaped the fate of its counterpart in the House, but in the process the Senate set the stage for a major power struggle between Russell Long, chairman of the Finance Committee, who represented the old order and the established way of doing things, and Edmund Muskie, the upstart chairman of the Budget Committee, who had his own ideas about how things should be done.[16]

Muskie was at a turning point in his career when the Budget Committee was set up in 1974. At the age of sixty, after nearly three terms in the Senate he had come closer to achieving power outside the Senate than in it. Muskie had narrowly missed being elected Vice President of the United States in 1968. After an abortive try for the presidency in 1972, he appeared to renounce national ambitions and settle down as the senior Senator from Maine. His Senate career, however, was stalled. His counterparts in the Senate, the Democratic members of the class of 1958, with the exception of Senator Phil Hart of Michigan, whose lack of personal ambition was notable, were already in positions of power. Howard Cannon, Vance Hartke, Harrison Williams, Frank Moss, and Gale McGee chaired full committees of varying degrees of importance. Robert Byrd was Majority Whip. By contrast, Muskie was still limited to subcommittee chairmanships. The most powerful of these was the Air and Water Pollution Subcommittee of Public Works, which Muskie had used to pass major environmental legislation. By 1974, though, the basic legislation in this area had been enacted and the environmental protection movement which culminated in the nationwide observance of Earth Day in 1970 had peaked. He had few options. His well-known prickly temper ruled out any leadership positions. He could take over Government Operations from Sam Ervin, who was retiring, and become the chairman of a middle-ranking committee. He could wait until Jennings Randolph retired and become chairman of the Public Works Committee, which had a more substantive jurisdiction but was another middle-ranked committee. He could become chairman of the Budget Committee, which he had helped create, and try to make something of the committee. Muskie chose to give up his seat on the Foreign Relations Committee to chair the new Budget Committee. It was a gamble, but Muskie intended to win. A Senator in the midst of his career does not ordinarily give up a seat on a prestigious committee to languish as the chairman of a second-rate committee. Muskie went for broke. And in the process he trod where Presidents had frequently feared to. In seeking to increase his power through the Budget Committee, he ran head on into Russell Long.

Long in his twenty-six years in the Senate had had his ups and downs, but in 1974 he had surmounted his personal problems and was happily ensconced as the chairman of the Finance Committee. At fifty-six, with no reelection worries, Long looked forward to a lengthy career as one of the most powerful members—perhaps the one most powerful member—of the United States Senate. Then the Budget and Impoundment Control Act was passed, and the Budget Committee with Ed Muskie as chairman was established. Long viewed the Budget Committee in much the same way that Stennis saw the Intelligence Committee. It was a slap in the face. The Budget Committee, like the Intelligence Committee, was set up to do what the existing committees failed to do. In this case it was the failure of the Appropriations and Finance Committees to work in tandem and wield together disparate revenue-raising and appropriating measures into a logical and consistent budget.

Long undoubtedly would have chafed anyway, but Muskie's attitude didn't help. The budget process was superimposed on the existing appropriations and revenue-raising process. Muskie chose to interpret this to mean that the Budget Committee would oversee the work of the Appropriations and Finance Committees. Part of the Budget Act called for the Budget Committee to keep a score card on the appropriation and revenue-raising bills wending their way through committees and to warn the Senate when the agreed-upon overall budget figures were threatened. Muskie, like a Yankee schoolmaster, frequently took the floor to remind his colleagues of this fact and to chasten their spendthrift ways. Muskie could be aggressive because he had the backing of his committee. The members of the Budget Committee were just beginning their Senate careers in most cases. The

If Muskie was for a proposal, regardless of how much it would cost, the Budget Committee and the Senator from Maine would find a way to support it. A Senate Budget Committee press release quoted Muskie to the effect that he supported the individual tax rebate, which would have cost the government far more than the business tax credits. The Finance chairman told his colleagues, "If the Budget Committee is against something, particularly its chairman, it looks like the world is going to come to an end if we spend five cents, if he is opposed to it. But if he is for it, you can spend eleven billion dollars and that will help everything. We will all be better off."

The Senator from Maine, said Long, was a little bit like a Texas poker player:

> I think a little bit of the situation of one of our Louisiana fellows who went to West Texas. He was telling about his experience out there. He got into a poker game with some pretty tough hombres. After they dealt some cards around, he bet quite a bit.
>
> He said, "I think I will win. I have a full house. I have aces over kings, and I will win."
>
> The other fellow said, "No, old friend, I am sorry, you lose."
>
> He said, "Why? You don't have anything in your hand."
>
> He said, "I know, but that is what they call a phloogie. Look at that sign up there."
>
> It said, "A phloogie beats anything."
>
> "So I win."
>
> So he takes all the money off the table.
>
> I asked this fellow, "I guess you quit playing after that, didn't you?"
>
> He said, "No, I played a little while longer. This time I got the same kind of hand. No two cards looked alike and no more than two cards in the same suit, so I bet everything I had left. I showed my hand and the fellow said, "That is too bad, you lose."
>
> I said, "How can I lose? It says right there, 'A phloogie beats anything.' "
>
> He said, "Yes, but look at the sign behind you. That one says, 'Only one phloogie to the night.' "[20]

As Long finished, the Senate chamber burst into laughter. Long went on, "That is about how my dear friend from Maine handles this budget situation. If he is for something, if we are going to go another twenty billion dollars in the red, that is all right, it will all work out just fine and it would be irresponsible not to spend the twenty billion dollars. If he is against it and it costs five cents, that is going to bring the country into national bankruptcy. We understand that is how it works and we have learned to adjust ourselves to all that."

Seeking to discredit Muskie, the entire budget process, and the power of the Budget Committee over it, Long was anticipating the long-term struggle between his committee and Muskie. Moreover, knowing that he had the votes for his proposal, he pointed out to Kennedy, Bumpers, and Muskie that a motion to recommit a bill to the Finance Committee was improper under the circumstances. "If the Senator wants to strike some part of the bill, he ought to seek to amend it when the time comes, and not seek to make the [floor] manager and the committee redraft the bill to make it read the way he wants it to read and to work from there." With the vast majority of the Senate on his side, Long was safe in arguing that the Senate "should reject this motion [to recommit] and go ahead and amend the bill, however the Senate wants, in the orderly, proper, legislative process. Having done so, then the Senate can work its own wisdom and vote up or down on its final work when it has properly amended."

While the barbs flying between Muskie and Long were sharp before the roll call, they became even sharper as Senators were scurrying to leave the chamber after the vote. Muskie shouted, "Mr. President, if I might have the attention of our colleagues for about thirty seconds." Rapping his gavel and raising his voice, the Presiding Officer asked the Senate to be in order. Muskie then attempted to continue his lecture of the Senate and more particularly Long on the budget process, and the violation of it that had just occurred. Muskie disingenuously told his colleagues that the vote might well require a return of the budget resolution to his committee, thus jeopardizing the tight time schedule for the development and consideration of budget resolutions. The entire budget process would be threatened. Muskie continued, "When I say this I am not being critical of any Senator's vote on the issue we have just considered. But there are budget implications, and I think Senators ought to know what they are. That is all I wanted to say while a number of Senators are in the chamber."

Long exploded. Refusing to be interrupted by Muskie, he stated that the Senator from Maine was, to say the least, inconsistent if not misleading. He was tired, said Long, of being admonished by the chairman of the Budget Committee about proper procedures and particularly about tax legislation. "We recall the experience that we had when we were voting on the Tax Reform Act last year," he said. "We were admonished, admonished, and admonished that the Tax Reform Act was going to bankrupt the country, because we were told that it was unrealistic to assume that Congress would ever dare to bring an end to those temporary tax cuts including the thirty-five dollar tax credit. The reason it was unrealistic so soon was that the chairman of the Budget Committee led the charge to knock out the part that would balance the bill, so that having led the charge to knock out the part that would bring to an end the temporary tax cuts, he made it unrealistic to assume that that would be a balanced bill." Refusing to yield to Muskie, Long intensified his attack on the chairman of the Budget Committee as well as some of its members, who had, he said, by meddling in tax-reform legislation, produced severe budget imbalances. The new budget process simply did not work, said Long, and in the case of the Tax Reform Act it was the Finance Committee and its chairman that saved the day by correcting the mistakes of the Budget Committee. Long went on: "So the budget balancing, after all that conversation about ending the budget process [by Muskie] was done in the same old traditional fashion, by the conferees from the Senate, the senior members of the Finance Committee, going to conference with their counterparts from the House Ways and Means Committee to try to work things out the best they could, to meet all the budgetary problems one might anticipate and consider."

When Long finally agreed to yield, Muskie retorted,

> I do not know what I did to enrage the Senator from Louisiana. All I did was state a simple fact, and as I see it, I have a duty as chairman of the Budget Committee to state facts. I do not try to restrain anyone from offering an amendment, but let the facts speak for themselves. I do not intend to get into another hassle with the chairman of the Finance Committee over what we did last year. I think the Senator has confused his history a little bit, but that is his prerogative.

Muskie then repeated at length his former arguments about the need to keep the integrity of the new budget process intact, with the Budget Committee as its guardian. As Muskie concluded his statement, he reiterated that what Long had just engineered in the Senate was "the old method. That is the old method that I remember so well. When spending bills come to the floor—"

At this point Long leaped to his feet.

Mr. Long.   Mr. President, who has the floor?

Mr. Muskie.   Spending bills come to the floor, and the Senator says, "This is all right, this is within the budget."

Mr. Long.   How did we write the budget? Bill by bill by bill.

Mr. Muskie.   I am sorry I cannot finish my thought.

Mr. Long.   Mr. President, I would like to finish my statement: Then the Senator can have the floor as far as I am concerned. I just want to finish my part of it. . . .

Everyone knows the budget resolution for 1978 is not binding until we vote the second resolution. I have managed tax bills before. I have managed big tax bills before. I have seen Senators put amendment after amendment on the bills, to where someone would wonder whether we were going to absolutely run out of all the money the printing press could print before we finished amending the bill. By the time the bill went to conference and the differences were worked out between the Senate and the House, the bills have come out with a balance everyone thought we could live with, including the Administration.

So I am not concerned to the degree the Senator from Maine is worried that every time we vote for an amendment someone does not agree with, that is going to destroy the country. . . .

But I remember last year, when the chairman of the Budget Committee led a fight to break the budget, we found that it is possible to work out the overall package to bring it within whatever target we may want to insist on here.

I, of course, welcome the right of the Senator to advise us amendment by amendment with regard to what he thinks this would do with regard to 1978 or any year. But I point out that the Senator has been known to support a lot of things that could break the budget, because he favored the amendment. . . .

Mr. Curtis [Carl C. Curtis of Nebraska, ranking Republican on Finance].   Mr. President, will the Senator yield?

Mr. Long.   I yield.

Mr. Curtis.   I have great respect for the Budget Committee. I think it is made up of eminent gentlemen, dedicated to their task. But after all, they have a very big job. . . .

Why do we have a Budget Committee? There was a time when the taxing committees were the appropriating committees. The job got too big so they divided it [by creating appropriations committees]. Both groups carried on their work without any co-ordination or without the coordination they should have. Here we have vested in one committee the responsibility of bringing our budget under control.

Every time we have a tax bill there is a catastrophe about every amendment which the Finance Committee seems to have worked on for months.

Even if the bill objecting to the Finance Committee prevailed it would not be a drop in the bucket on bringing this budget into balance. . . .

[In attempting to balance the budget] we did not get any help from that mighty force that heads the Budget Committee. . . .

I hope the Budget Committee will come to the rescue of our country and that they will attack the job that the country expects from them, to cut down on expenditures from the Treasury. . . .

Mr. Muskie.   Mr. President, as I have frequently said, and I think it should be repeated at this time, first, I want to assure the distinguished chairman of the Finance Committee and the ranking Republican [Curtis] that try as they may, they will not succeed in intimidating me from doing my job. We have only one discipline in the Budget Committee. I would be amazed if the Senator from Louisiana did not understand that. As a matter of fact, I think he understands it all too well. That is why he responded with such outrage to what I said earlier. We have only one discipline, the discipline of information. And if I do not have that responsibility, I do not have any.

Second, the Senator and his colleagues can rail against me as much as they like for using the budget process to serve my own ends. The record will show that I have voted in committee and out to hold down spending on things I was interested in and I will continue to do so.

I believe the record will be an accurate reflection against the charges that the chairman of the Finance Committee has made this afternoon.

Mr. Long.   Will the Senator yield?

Mr. Muskie.   I want to finish. It will not require thirty seconds.

The third point I make is I cannot see the Finance Committee, its chairman and ranking member, are any different from any other Senator. They would like to see the budget discipline applied to all the others but not to them. That is why the budget process was created in the first place, because on our separate authorizing committees we have a tendency to get committed to particular programs, to particular policies, and we lose the perspective of the whole picture.

We are all fallible on the Budget Committee. We are all members of other committees. We are going to make mistakes, but this mistake we will not make as long as I am chairman. I can be displaced by the Democratic caucus in any caucus, as the Senator from Louisiana well knows.

As long as I am chairman, the Senate is going to get the facts, to the best of my ability. It can accept the facts or not. If the Senator from Louisiana thinks I am going to come to the floor after an action such as we took and say to the Senate, "That has no budget impact," or that these other amendments that are coming up have no budget impact, if the Senator regards that as a proper discharge of the duties of the chairman of the Budget committee, then he is mistaken.

Mr. Long.   Will the Senator yield?

Mr. Muskie.   I yield.

Mr. Long.   Let me say if I wounded the Senator's feelings I want to apologize to the Senator because I love him.

Mr. Muskie.   The Senator has not wounded my feelings.

Mr. Long.   I think the Senator is a great American. I am proud of him. I love him. I am proud to be the Senator's friend, even though sometimes I know I irritate the Senator. He is a great American. Insofar as I may have offended him, I am sorry.[21]

However much Long might love Muskie, it was not friendship that was at stake, but, as Long had noted, power. And Long's personal fondness for Muskie did not extend to permitting him to take over legislation that heretofore had been within the jurisdiction of the Finance Committee.

Long adopted a technique in 1976, which met the formal requirements of the Budget Act while keeping control firmly within the Finance Committee, of delaying the effective dates of budget cuts until the succeeding fiscal year. Under the Budget Act, once the budget resolution is voted by the House and Senate, authorizations must fall within its limits and the ceilings are based upon an estimate of revenues. In effect, this reduces the authority of the Finance Committee to pass tax cuts, since these would decrease the amount of revenues in the budget. Long circumvented the Budget Committee by arguing that since the tax cuts wouldn't occur until the next fiscal year, the budget process was not affected. When the Budget Committee went to work on the budget resolutions for that fiscal year, it would be presented with a fait accompli. Long also tried to make revenue-raising provisions in tax legislation retroactive to the beginning of the fiscal year. This presumably would not upset the budgetary process because it would have the effect of increasing the spending limits of the budget resolution.

Russell Long is routinely referred to in the press as the "wily chairman of the Senate Finance Committee," and he did not win the label "wily" for nothing. In tackling Long, Muskie had taken on the most formidable foe possible, and Long was more than equal to the challenge. In 1978 Muskie, despite his aggressiveness and combativeness, was still on the fringes, still lusting after power that was not quite within his grasp. The Senate committee chairmen had been careful to limit the power of the Budget Committee when the Budget Act was passed. The Budget Committee was given no automatic control over the authorization or appropriations process. The Budget Committee could recommend, but that was all. The power of the Budget Committee chairman was the power of his ability to persuade. A Budget Act which gave formal powers to a newly created Budget Committee would never have passed, out of respect for committee sovereignty. As Muskie lost one battle after another, doubts began to be raised in the minds of more than one colleague and staffer about whether or not Muskie would continue as chairman. A chairmanship without formal power and without a reputation for power would ultimately be the subject of derision on Capitol Hill.

The formal powers and jurisdiction of committees do not exist in a vacuum. The ways that committees are used in the quest for personal power always reflect the personalities and styles of their chairmen. The reputation of a committee can change dramatically with a change of chairman. A dynamic chairman can infuse a lethargic committee with verve and vigor, while a chairman whose interests lie elsewhere can let an active committee sink into somnolence. Congressmen such as Paul Rogers and Senators such as Edward Kennedy built their Capitol Hill reputations through their committees and staffs by using them to initiate, develop, and pass legislation. But there is another way of using committees, in which legislation is incidental. The goal is not the passage of legislation, but direct impact on policy. The key to this is hard work on the part of the Congressman and his staff, the development of specialization and expertise in the area of the committee's jurisdiction, and, above all, a demonstration of these qualities in extensive hearings and reports on policy issues. The hearings and reports are ends in themselves. Legislation may result, but this is entirely unnecessary. In recent decades committees have proliferated, staffs have grown, and hearings and reports have increased, while the number of bills passed has stayed constant and by some measures has actually declined. Power is demonstrated not by the passage of legislation, but by influencing and shaping policy.

Senator Sam Nunn, the boyish junior Senator from Georgia, is an example of a person who has pursued this route to power. The Manpower and Personnel Subcommittee of the Armed Services Committee was created for Nunn in 1974, and his use of the committee and its staff is a model for the way in which members of Congress strive to build their power. As Nunn began to build his Capitol Hill career and reputation through his subcommittee, he did not initially sponsor any important legislation. The manpower authorization bills which moved through his subcommittee were routine, noncontroversial measures whose passage was never in doubt. Nunn was admired and respected because of his diligence and intelligence, not because of legislation which bore his name.

Nunn wanted a position on the Armed Services Committee from the start. In fact, in his 1972 election campaign he promised to try to regain the state's slot on the committee which had been lost with the death of Georgia's senior Senator, Richard Russell. The elderly Senator, who had died in midterm after thirty-eight years in office, served as chairman of Armed Services before relinquishing the chairmanship to become chairman of the Appropriations Committee. Armed Services was a natural spot for Nunn. His great-uncle, Congressman Carl Vinson, like Russell a grand old man of Southern politics, served fifty-one years in the House and was chairman of the House

Armed Services Committee from the time it was created in 1947 until his retirement. One of Nunn's first jobs after graduating from Emory Law School was as counsel to the House Armed Services Committee, and he met his wife, Colleen, while in Paris on business for the committee. Colleen was working for the CIA there.

Nunn was helped by the fact that he was elected to fill out the remainder of Russell's term and, being sworn in immediately, was in a better position than the other twelve incoming Senators to get his choice of committee assignments. After his election, Nunn, accompanied by Vinson and other Georgia supporters, went to Washington to call on Armed Services chairman John Stennis and other key members of the committee, including Henry Jackson. Nunn also visited with Majority Leader Mike Mansfield and Majority Whip Robert Byrd. The trip played an important part in his later appointment to the Armed Services Committee.

Soon after his appointment Nunn got a chance to impress the committee members. In the winter of 1973 Stennis, arriving home late one night, was robbed and shot outside his northwest Washington house. He spent the remainder of that session in the hospital recuperating. The running of the committee fell by default to Senator Stuart Symington of Missouri. And Nunn pitched in to help out. The Armed Services Committee was predisposed to like Nunn. After all, he was the grandnephew of Carl Vinson, he was a Southerner, and he was from Georgia, which has a long history of support for the military. Nunn's hard work during this period convinced the senior members of Armed Services that he was one of them, dedicated to the committee and competent to assume an important share of its responsibilities. Russell, the epitome of the Senate establishment, would have been proud of the man that Georgians picked to replace him. Nunn might wear the latest in polyester suits, but he was essentially cut out of the same cloth as his predecessor. Reflecting on this period, Nunn said, "Symington was looking for an awful lot of help, because he had other responsibilities, and he kind of had responsibility for the committee without total authority, and I pitched in and helped him an awful lot, and was given probably more responsibility that first year because of that unique set of circumstances than I otherwise would have been given. And Senator Stennis, I think, when he got back, had talked to staff, and they knew I

had done a lot of work, and he started giving me a lot more responsibility than would probably have been the case otherwise.
He asked me to go to NATO within two or three months after he
got back up here, and to undertake a study of it, and I took him
seriously, and I did undertake quite a study of that."[22]

Nunn soon became an expert on NATO and, befitting a
member of the Armed Services Committee, an advocate of a
strong military posture that includes both conventional and nuclear deterrents. As soon as he was given the Manpower and Personnel Subcommittee, he sought assurances from the Defense
Department that manpower needs were being met. Above all, he
became an active chairman of the subcommittee, holding hearings on a wide range of manpower issues. During his first year as
subcommittee chairman, Nunn held hearings on increasing the
number of lieutenant colonels and colonels in the Air Force, on
military pay increases and on methods of discharging military
personnel. Witnesses included Secretary of Defense James Schlesinger, chairman of the Joint Chiefs of Staff George Brown, the
secretaries of all three military branches, and other top-level
civilian and military personnel. In 1975 the subcommittee held
hearings on manpower authorizations, which traditionally had
fallen within the province of the full Armed Services Committee.
The hearings lasted seventeen days, and by their conclusion
Nunn was the acknowledged power in Congress on manpower
policy. The authorization hearings, which constituted the bulk
of the subcommittee's work, provided an obvious forum where
Nunn could develop his expertise and stake out his subcommittee's jurisdiction. In addition, Nunn laid claim to other defense policy areas such as NATO. In 1976 the Manpower and
Personnel Subcommittee and the Research and Development
Subcommittee held joint hearings on the future of NATO. Nunn
became an expert on disarmament and the volunteer Army as
well. Working quietly and always deferential to the senior members of the Armed Services Committee, Nunn became the man
to consult on a growing number of issues. And the *New York
Times* began running articles with the theme "Nunn, a Senator
to watch."

More hearings followed. The West Point cheating scandals
catapulted Nunn into national prominence. In the summer of
1976 the Manpower Subcommittee held seven days of hearings
on the allegations of widespread cheating at West Point. The

hearings captured the interest of the full committee, and one day the chairman, John Stennis, made a rare appearance at a subcommittee hearing to join the questioning of witnesses. Stennis's appearance was a real coup for Nunn and a signal that he had arrived at last. The hearings also drew the attention of the national press, and as his fellow Senators opened the morning *Washington Post* and *New York Times*, they saw pictures of Nunn intently questioning still another witness. Back in Georgia his constituents turned on the CBS Evening News to hear Walter Cronkite announce the latest revelations uncovered by Senator Sam Nunn and his Subcommittee on Manpower and Personnel. Nunn reopened his hearings a year later in the fall of 1977. Nunn also garnered attention with hearings on the all-volunteer Army, which he did not entirely favor. In March 1977 his subcommittee held hearings on alternatives to the all-volunteer force and, joined by Barry Goldwater, Nunn investigated the current status of the Army.

Spending for manpower constitutes 60 percent of the budget of the Defense Department. As a result, the activities of the Manpower and Personnel Subcommittee constitute a significant portion of the work of the Armed Services Committee. The authorization hearings chaired by Nunn have been the most extensive of any held by the Armed Services Committee or its subcommittees. Nunn has managed to take over such a crucial area because he has enjoyed the support of Stennis from the very beginning. To an extent Nunn has been Stennis's protege, and he in turn has been appropriately deferential toward the aging Senator from Mississippi. In and out of committee, Nunn addresses Stennis as "Mr. Chairman." Nunn has also been careful not to rankle the senior Democrats on the committee, such as Henry Jackson and Howard Cannon. Nunn early on ingratiated himself with Jackson and ran Jackson's Permanent Subcommittee on Investigations for him while Jackson was campaigning for the Democratic presidential nomination.

Traditionally the Armed Services Committees are composed of conservatives who believe in a strong military posture. A rising member of the Senate Armed Services Committee would be foolhardy to adopt any other stance, for if a career is to be built on a committee dealing with the military, the interests of the armed services must come first. This does not preclude close questioning of Defense Department officials, but the purpose of the questions must be to strengthen, not weaken, the military. As Nunn launched his career on Armed Services, he looked for direction to chairman John Stennis, a staunch defender of the military, and its ranking member Henry Jackson, whose defense policies, frozen fast in the cold war of the 1950s, had yet to thaw in the 1970s. Nunn brilliantly used his subcommittee and position on Armed Services to adopt a stance that was at one and the same time independent and supportive of the military. For instance, he has questioned military costs but never suggested a cut in military manpower.

Nunn has been active on the full Armed Services Committee as well. He has demonstrated interest, expertise, and hard work. He has also carefully operated within the generally accepted philosophy of the committee. When the Armed Services Committee meets, Nunn is there and ready with questions carefully prepared in advance by the two aides who handle his Armed Services work. The hearing on the nomination of Dr. Harold Brown to be Secretary of Defense offered a chance for Nunn to demonstrate his ability and acceptability to the Armed Services Committee.

His questions were far-reaching, and they drew respect from fellow committee members and Brown for his obvious grasp of military matters in general and manpower in particular.[23] Hearings are a chance for committee members to display their expertise. And confirmation hearings are an opportunity to secure policy commitments from nominees before they are swallowed up by the bureaucracy they are supposed to run. In this instance, Nunn hopscotched across his turf, moving from disarmament and the dangers that would proceed from failure to reach agreement on SALT II to the defense capabilities of NATO to the desirability of the all-volunteer Army.

Nunn said, "I hope you keep an open mind on the statistics you have seen about the costs of the volunteer force. I think any good accountant could rip considerable holes in the cost allocation that the Department of Defense makes to the volunteer force now."

Brown replied, "I see that you, Senator Nunn, have learned to question assumptions of studies and we will follow your example." Neatly sidestepping the underlying question, Brown offered hope that he might reexamine the concept of the volunteer Army at some undetermined date.

Nunn, pressing on, asked, "Do you have any thoughts on whether or not manpower costs need to be restrained and second, whether you have any general ideas about the direction you will be going in that area?" In short, Nunn wanted to know if the new Secretary of Defense would be cutting into "his" part of the budget.

Brown said that manpower costs had risen from 45 percent of the budget in 1964 to 60 percent in 1977 and that the trend toward ever-larger costs for manpower would have to be stopped. But Brown added, "I don't have any fixed notions about where to look. I think we have to look everywhere in the personnel costs and to list the places would just be to excite unnecessary apprehension."

Nunn's feisty questioning of Brown on the volunteer Army pleased both chairman John Stennis and Strom Thurmond of South Carolina, the second-ranking Republican on the committee. Shortly afterwards they were even more pleased when Nunn joined them in opposing the nomination of Paul Warnke as director of the U.S. Arms Control and Disarmament Agency and leading negotiator at the SALT II talks.[24] Led by Stennis and Jackson, the conservative members of Armed Services were unanimously opposed to the nomination. (Stennis, Jackson, Cannon, and Nunn among the Democrats voted against the nomination. All of the Republicans opposed it.) Nunn's hostile questioning in committee and subsequent opposition on the floor placed him in the limelight with Jackson as they were the two most outspoken of the Senators opposing Warnke's nomination. Such a coupling was bound to elevate Nunn's status on the Armed Services Committee. Nunn's stature was further enhanced by the fact that he was opposing not only a Democratic President but also a President from his own state on a crucial nomination. If Nunn opposed the nomination and it was defeated, the Georgians in the White House would not soon forget it. If Nunn opposed and lost, he could expect even less from the White House.

Warnke was thought by the conservatives to be too weak a negotiator on arms control, too likely to give away to the Soviet Union on some crucial point. The Senate tradition, however, is to confirm a President's appointments unless they are outright corrupt or flamboyantly incompetent. (Even incompetence is not always enough to prevent confirmation. An argument used by supporters of Nixon nominee Harold Carswell in favor of his confirmation was that the mediocre deserved representation on the Supreme Court.) Hoping to pick up additional votes against the nomination, the conservatives adroitly maneuvered Warnke into defending not only his beliefs but also his honesty. The issue shifted. The question became whether or not Warnke was lying to the United States Senate. Jackson openly accused him of intellectual dishonesty. Nunn pointed out the inconsistencies between Warnke's statements before the Armed Services Committee and previous Senate testimony. During his questioning Nunn said, "Some of your past statements I find very, very inconsistent, almost diametrically opposed to the statement this morning. I find no problem with that. If a man changes his mind, that is fine, but it does bother me that you have changed your mind without acknowledging you have changed your mind, and it bothers me worse if you have changed your mind and don't realize that you have changed your mind." The following exchange occurred:

Mr. Warnke.   Senator, I don't think either of those is the case. This is the sort of statement I could have subscribed to at any point.

Senator Nunn.   Well, it never has been made before the nomination. I have never seen anything like this.

Mr. Warnke.   I believe it has except, of course, that the analysis of the present strategic situation has to be based on the present facts as I know them.

Senator Nunn.   Well, just —

Mr. Warnke.   I say that is the only respect in which that statement would have varied from what I would have said in 1970, 1972, 1976, and now.

Senator Nunn.   In 1976 there was a dialogue with Senator McClure in the Budget committee. I remember it very well because I was there.

Mr. Warnke.   Yes.

Senator Nunn.   I know I am running out of time, but in essence you made it very clear that even if the Soviet Union completes all of their programs that are now being carried on that you would find that there would be no change in the strategic balance, and I can quote that exactly if you want me to.

Senator McClure says to you in response to your statement,

"There would be no change in the strategic balance if the Soviets continue with all of their plans that they now have underway."

Senator McClure says that is an incredible statement.

Mr. Warnke.   That is correct.

Senator Nunn.   Mr. Warnke says, "I did not consider it so, Sir, or I would not have made it."

But now how can you reconcile that with your statement at the bottom of page 9, within twelve months, that you see signs that if the trends continue they are going to have superiority or we are going to be in an unfavorable position? I cannot reconcile those two.[25]

Later in the hearings Nunn remarked, "I am trying to find ways to support you. I don't mind anybody changing their position. I have a great deal of difficulty when we sit here and go through the first strike, third strike situations, and it is exactly on the point you made in the debate, and it is exactly the point a lot of people have been debating with all sincerity for a long time, and I think you have changed your position. I happen to think you have changed it in the right direction. For you not to think you have changed your position leaves me in a state of total bewilderment. I don't know where you are."[26]

Again and again Nunn quizzed Warnke on the discrepancies among his various statements, but none of Warnke's explanations were fully satisfying. Nunn found no way of supporting his nomination. On the floor Nunn urged the Senate to defeat the nomination, saying:

A SALT II agreement is controversial, inherently complex, and difficult. It is going to be extremely difficult to explain. It is hard for me to understand it, frankly.

When I get away from the Strategic Arms discussion for several days I have to go back and reorient my own mind to be able to play this kind of game that is sheer insanity if it is carried to its ultimate, but it is very difficult at best; and when you take a person who is so controversial and you place him in charge of an agreement that is this difficult anyway, then I think the chances of having a SALT II agreement are diminished.[27]

By the time the Senate voted 58–40 to confirm Warnke, Nunn was being heard night after night on the evening news arguing against the confirmation. Although his side was defeated, Nunn did not lose entirely. His vocal opposition against a President from Georgia and with the odds against winning added a few inches to his stature in the Senate.

Nunn's career shows the shrewd use of a subcommittee and active participation in committee work in building power. The keen interest of other Senators in Nunn's subcommittee helped, but under a less astute chairman the subcommittee might easily have languished.

At the same time, an astute chairman can build his power on a committee that has low status and seemingly little significance. The lackluster House Administration Committee became a "frightening base of power"[28] under Wayne Hays, once referred to as "the meanest son-of-a-bitch on the Hill" in *New York* magazine.[29] From 1971, when he became chairman, to 1976, when he was forced to resign by the Elizabeth Ray scandal, Hays used the committee's power over office allowances, travel vouchers, telephone service, and office space to reward his friends and punish his enemies. Hays's willingness to use his chairmanship to thwart members who had managed to displease him—and his easily provoked temper made irritating him easy—was the source of Capitol Hill gossip for years. At one point Hays maneuvered a resolution through the House which gave his committee power to set Congressional allowances and benefits. Thus members were spared the necessity of voting to increase their own allowances and then having to explain their votes to constituents in the next election. This, however, turned into a dubious blessing. Instead of justifying themselves to the voters, they had to justify themselves to Hays. As Hays's power grew, efforts were begun to curb him. The Democratic Steering and Policy Committee voted secretly 13–11 in 1975 to remove him, but the caucus, voting openly, reversed the decision. Hays had done enough favors for enough members to assure their support, and his promise of a meeting room for the newly established freshman caucus swayed enough of the new members to keep his chairmanship. His backers were liberals and conservatives alike. Internal power, not ideology, was the issue. His backers found in him a way to solidify and expand their own power in the body, and freshmen, looking ahead, knew their House careers would be crippled without his support.

An even less consequential committee was the Government Operations Subcommittee with jurisdiction over the General Services Administration. Traditionally the committee routinely ratified GSA's intention to dispose of surplus government property, its chairman merely informing the Congressmen whose districts received the property. (Surplus property is property no longer needed by the federal government which GSA donates to local governments and communities.) Early in his House career Congressman Jack Brooks of Texas became chairman of the subcommittee and everything changed. No longer were surplus property disposals automatic. Brooks made his colleagues come to him to request the property, and Brooks made it known that his approval was not pro forma, but a political favor for which trade-offs could be expected in the future.

Brooks advanced to become chairman of the Government Operations Committee. It was not a position of great importance then, but Brooks bolstered the status of the committee, and the committee in turn boosted his power. When President Carter requested authority to reorganize the federal government subject to Congressional veto, Brooks immediately announced that the President's plan was very likely unconstitutional. Agency reorganization requires an affirmative vote by Congress, Brooks argued, and should not take effect simply because Congress fails to veto a reorganization. And committee chairman Brooks was a key man. The initial Reorganization Act would go through his committee, and subsequent agency reorganization plans would be referred there also. President Carter was not asking for more authority than previous Presidents had received, but this was irrelevant. If Brooks said no, the President might get no authority at all.

The committee's jurisdiction by itself gave Brooks power, and his posture as a stubborn member of Congress, upholding the integrity of the House against incursions from the executive, won admiration on Capitol Hill. While Ribicoff was shepherding the President's proposal through the Senate Governmental Affairs Committee, Jack Brooks was standing firm. Even before the first session of the 95th Congress began, Brooks had been called by Carter to a meeting in Georgia, a recognition by the President-elect of Brooks's Capitol Hill power and a real boost for the Texan's Hill reputation.

Soon after meeting with the President, Brooks began to argue that administrative agencies should not be reorganized without an affirmative vote by both the House and the Senate. Brooks held carefully staged hearings to support his position and subject administration witnesses to sharp questioning. Brooks's opposition made Government Operations members reluctant to introduce the Reorganization Act for the administration. Finally the President invited the Democratic members of the committee to breakfast at the White House to gain their backing. Carter managed to persuade Congressman Dante Fascell of Florida, the third-ranking member of Government Operations, to sponsor the legislation.

Brooks abruptly shifted his position when he sensed widespread opposition to his proposed limits on the President's reorganization powers. Wavering Congressmen were lobbied heavily in and out of the committee rooms by the White House Congressional liaison staff, who insisted that all the administration wanted was what every other President had gotten. The last President to have such reorganization powers, they reminded Democrats, was Richard Nixon. They asked, "Are you going to give us less than you gave Richard Nixon?" Brooks's switch, however, came after he had wrested maximum advantage from his chairmanship. The President had invited him to Georgia to discuss the reorganization bill in the first place and had sought out his support.

Brooks's last-minute switch was engineered so that he remained a central figure in reorganization. Brooks maneuvered privately to compromise with administration officials. When the reorganization legislation finally emerged more or less as the White House wanted, Brooks had metamorphosed into a leading supporter. When the reorganization legislation finally passed the House by an overwhelming margin of 395–22, Brooks was on the winning side. He even argued against an amendment containing the very same provisions he had once sought. Not only did Brooks have his way in the House, but also the bill was now recognized on the Hill as his. The Senate routinely accepted the House version without a roll call or debate. When the President signed the bill, Brooks was at his shoulder looking on.

Committee activity intended to boost power reputations is constant. Once a committee chairmanship is obtained, regardless of the seeming importance of the legislative jurisdiction of the committee, immediate activity must start to increase the visibility of the committee. This requires an extraordinary amount of work and persistence on the part of the committee's staff. Most committees have the potential to engage in wide-ranging activities, including the development of new legislation, overseeing the activities of administrative agencies under their jurisdiction, conducting investigations, and, perhaps most important, reviewing the budgetary requests of executive departments and agencies.

Since the budgets of executive agencies are prepared yearly, appropriations and authorization legislation occupy much of the time of Congressional committees. Subcommittee and committee chairmen must demonstrate initiative, independence, hard work, and an ability to conform to budgetary schedules, including the rigid deadlines of the Congressional budget process. Within the confines of their committee jurisdictions, which usually can be interpreted very broadly, committee chairmen and staff can roam as far as their imaginations, limited by political realities, carry them.

The range of committee hearings during a normal work week of Congress, which usually encompasses Tuesday through Thursday—on Monday and Friday generally members of Congress are traveling to and from their districts—is astounding. Each committee hearing involves an extraordinary amount of advance work by the staff. The chairmen must be scheduled, and the schedules of all Congressmen and Senators are tight. Witnesses must be contacted and scheduled, and this too is a time-consuming and difficult process, particularly as the witnesses' views must be sifted in advance to assure support for the chairman's legislation. Even the scheduling of rooms for a hearing may be difficult for subcommittees which lack regular meeting rooms.

Given the logistical difficulties and the hundreds of hours of staff time that are consumed, the extract from the *Congressional Record—Daily Digest* (see Appendix, p. 241) is an indication of the strong drive to demonstrate power through committee activity. Particularly interesting is the imagination of committee chairmen and staff in finding something for their committees to do. In the House the Subcommittee on Environment, Energy, and Natural Resources held a hearing on crime in federal recreation areas, the Intelligence Subcommittee on Legislation heard testimony on "foreign intelligence electronic surveillance," and the Subcommittee on International Development held a hearing on rethinking United States foreign policy toward the developing world with special reference to Nicaragua. The Subcommittee on Fisheries and Wildlife Conservation and the Environment held a hearing on "Marine Mammal authorization," while the Subcommittee on Oceanography heard testimony on "Sea Grant authorization." The Select Committee on Population conducted "overview hearings on world population." In the Senate subcommittees were equally busy. The Subcommittee on Science, Technology, and Space held hearings on the future of space science and space applications, and on the implementation of the National Science and Technology Policy Act. The Subcommittee on Transportation turned its attention to the federal highway program, while the Subcommittee on Public Assistance held its first hearings on a proposed Better Jobs and Income Act.

Behind the scenes of committee and subcommittee hearings, through reports and legislation, members are striving to gain visibility on Capitol Hill and a reputation for power that comes with being thought of by colleagues as an "effective Senator," a "hardworking and competent legislator," "an active member of an important committee," such as Armed Services or Foreign Relations, and "a member who is making his mark on the committee and in the body."

4

Staff: The Surrogates of Power

WHILE THE CONGRESSMAN who wants power struggles to rise within the committee empires, the Senator who seeks the same thing sets out to build a kingdom of his own. This is not as difficult as it might appear. The number of committees and subcommittees in the Senate more than equals the number of Senators. Everyone has his own bailiwick, and Senators are frequently gifted with a subcommittee early on. Senator James Sasser of Tennessee became chairman of the Governmental Affairs Subcommittee on Civil Service and General Services one month after taking the oath of office. The subcommittee had jurisdiction over the General Services Administration, which builds and maintains federal buildings throughout the country. As the "housekeeper" for the federal government, the General Services Administration's tentacles extend into every state and Congressional district. Sasser also inherited three staff assistants from the previous chairman. Sasser, newly elected to his first public office, hadn't the vaguest notion of the responsibilities of his subcommittee or of what his duties as chairman entailed. Such good fortune would not befall a Congressman. In fact, the jurisdiction of the Senate subcommittee was divided in the House between the full Government Operations Committee, chaired by veteran Congressman Jack Brooks of Texas, with twenty-five years experience, and the Post Office and Civil Service Committee headed by Congressman William Dulski of New York, with eighteen years service. Sasser's experience was a little unusual. The chairman of the subcommittee in the preceding Congress, Senator Sam Nunn of Georgia, resigned his post to pursue other interests, and the chairman of the full committee, Senator Abe Ribicoff of Connecticut, was inclined to create subcommittees for all Democrats on the committee. A Senator normally is expected to put in some time on mundane committee tasks, cooperate with the leadership, and win the good will of the chairman before he is entitled to a subcommittee. Sometimes more than good will is required. In the past, members of the Judiciary Committee were also expected to drop by for a few ritual drinks with the venerable chairman, Senator James Eastland of Mississippi. In the spring of 1973 former Senator John Tunney of California, the most junior Democrat on the committee and the only one without a subcommittee of his own, was seen entering Eastland's office around nine in the morning. He emerged an hour later, somewhat unsteady, but as the new chairman of the Subcommittee on Representation of Citizens' Interest. The length of time and the requirements vary from committee to committee, but all Senators can confidently assume that they will become chairman of at least one subcommittee during their first term.

Committees are crucial to empire building. They lend legitimacy to legislative activity. A Senator is expected to speak out on the issues that fall within the realm of his committee, to introduce bills and make speeches on its subject matter. They provide a platform for hearings that can capture the attention of the press and generally increase a Senator's visibility. A Senator can have impact on a variety of issues, including ones that are outside of his committees' jurisdictions, but it is more difficult. When that happens, it is usually because the issues do not easily fit within the committee structure. Senator Birch Bayh of Indiana, for instance, has specialized in women's issues and won recognition as an advocate of women's rights legislation. These issues overlap the existing committees, so Bayh was able to seize them without invading the turf of other Senators.

Committees, however, are mere symbols of power, not power itself, unless they are accompanied by adequate staff. A good staff is necessary if a Senator wants to wield power through his committees. If he wants to exert influence beyond his committees, a capable staff is essential. Staff and power go together in the Senate. For that reason allowances for staff and access to staff are jealously guarded.

Sasser was fortunate to acquire staff along with his subcommittee, but others are not so lucky. Senator Robert Morgan of North Carolina, for example, recounted the following episode.

"I came in and I was made chairman of the Subcommittee of Small Business [of the Banking, Housing, and Urban Affairs Committee] which pleased me because as attorney general of my state for six years, I was vitally interested in business and consumer protection, which is basically small business and consumer protection," he said. "I told the committee's chief staff member: 'Look, there have to be a lot of possibilities here because realistically we are not going to break up the giant monopolies in this country and the hope and salvation of the free enterprise system are small businesses. Who, on the staff, am I going to be able to work with?' He said, 'I am sorry, Senator, there won't be anybody for you to work with in our system. The chairman has so many people working for him, the ranking member has so many working for him. By the time we get down to you and Senator Biden, there is nobody left.' I told the staff member: 'You go back and tell the chairman I don't want the chairmanship.'"[1] Without staff, Morgan's chairmanship would be largely honorary, a nice title and useful perhaps in campaign literature but without any real clout on the Hill. As a result of that experience, Morgan backed a measure which had been pending in the Senate for a number of years to combine the Small Business Subcommittee of the Banking, Housing, and Urban Affairs Committee, which had the power to report legislation but no staff, with the Select Committee on Small Business, which had a staff but no legislative jurisdiction. Morgan said, "I simply thought that the power to act ought to be where the staff was available."[2]

The quest for the staff acquires real urgency as Senators realize, in the words of the Commission on the Operation of the Senate, that "among the 100 co-equals who are the Senate's principal players, relative power is often a function of and measured by how much staff each Senator controls. . . . Controlling committee employees is a source of power among Senators."[3] The consequences of this are not always pleasant to behold. The offices of new Senators resemble meat markets as the arriving Senators sift through hundreds of resumés and interview dozens of prospective assistants, looking for that just right amorphous combination of brains, talents, and knowledge which can give them the edge. The offices of other Senators are well known to have revolving doors through which aides enter and exit at regular intervals as Senators, thwarted in their drive for power, take out frustrations on long-suffering staff. Stephen Isaacs of the

Washington Post once wrote about "the sight of many Senators scrambling after staff bodies like hunters in pursuit of prey, hungering for the impact that extra staff person, or two, or three, or even dozens can give to them and their political careers."[4]

Staff in this sense, as an adjunct of power and status, is a Senate phenomenon. Congressmen, limited in their number of committee assignments and emphasizing specialization, feel less need for behind-the-scenes staff guidance and advice. A long running joke around the Capitol is that conference committees are composed of House members and Senate staff. Congressman David Obey of Wisconsin said, "What happens in conference is that we go in and talk to Senate staff." A top lobbyist for the AFL-CIO, himself a former Congressman, said, "The most important contacts we have are with the staff. That's where the work is done especially in the Senate. It is very rare for Senators to be able to talk substantively about legislation before their committees." Congressmen pride themselves on running their own show and put down Senators for their heavy reliance on staff coaching. When Congressmen have felt the need to boost staff resources, they have formed informal caucuses such as the New England Caucus and Black Caucus and organized study groups such as the Democratic Study Group and the Environmental Study Conference that employ a central staff and disseminate information to all members equally. In the Senate it is every man for himself, and staff is a continuing preoccupation. In the spring of 1975, for example, the suite of offices in the Russell Office Building occupied by the staff of Senator Lloyd Bentsen of Texas was jampacked with aides. Following his election to the Senate, Bentsen had called in an efficiency expert, and on his recommendation Bentsen had dispensed with traditional office furniture and installed instead modern cubicles expressly designed to utilize every square inch of space. Fourteen legislative aides were squeezed into two rooms, and several part-time aides and college interns worked at a large conference table in the back of one office. The quarters, nevertheless, were so cramped that the staff played a perpetual game of musical chairs. Professional staff members were nervous when they left the office to go to the restrooms several paces down the hall lest their place be usurped by an aide who did not have a permanently assigned work space. Bensten also employed several staff assistants who were on subcommittee payrolls and housed elsewhere. Despite all this, Bentsen felt he needed more staff. He emerged as a prime sponsor of S. Res. 60 that year, which gave additional staff to first and second-term Senators.

The relationship between power and staff is an intricate one. Controlling a large staff cannot in itself make a Senator powerful, but a huge staff by itself is a symbol of a Senator's power. Most Senators who command large staffs do so because they have acquired positions of power. They chair a full committee or several subcommittees and control financial resources which can be used to hire staff. The result of a large staff is information and ideas which cement the power of the Senator in charge. Access to staff is the prerogative of the chairman. Staff know that their first allegiance is to the chairman, although nominally and legally they work for all members of the committee. Access and information are sources of power in Washington, and Senators who control both closely guard them. To break this stranglehold, Senators have sought out committee staff and personal aides of their own. Whether more staff leads to more impact is debatable, but it is a widely shared, deeply believed tenet of Senate life that this is so. And as politicians who know that power often resides in the eye of the beholder, Senators are not about to discount the value of symbols of power in acquiring the real thing.

Former Senator Bill Brock of Tennessee once remarked that the Senate "is not a democratic institution" and that one way of distinguishing those who are more equal from those who are less equal is through staff. In 1977, for example, the Senate created the honorary position of Deputy President pro Tempore for one of its most distinguished and beloved members, Senator Hubert Humphrey of Minnesota. Humphrey had refused, despite considerable urging, to enter the presidential primaries in a last-ditch effort to stop Jimmy Carter's peanut express toward the Democratic presidential nomination. In doing so, he had abandoned his long-cherished dream of winning the presidency. Humphrey had then refused to campaign actively for Majority Leader although his name had been mentioned as a possible candidate. The Senate wanted some form of special recognition for Humphrey that might help to compensate for his recent losses. The post of Deputy President pro Tempore was the result. The position was not entirely honorary. A staff allowance of over

$100,000 went along with it. The President pro Tempore, however, had no staff help. James Eastland had served for years as President pro Tempore and had never seen the need for staff in his largely formal post. He was not about to let his deputy have something he lacked. Before long the Senate decided that the President pro Tempore also needed a staff to help him carry out his ceremonial duties and voted a staff allowance for that office. The unintentional difference in status was corrected.

The link between staff and power is so taken for granted in the Senate that Senators sometimes use the words interchangeably in discussing the two. Senator Lee Metcalf of Montana tacitly acknowledged this situation in a series of free-wheeling interviews with the *Washington Post* in 1975. Metcalf charged that Senator Ed Muskie of Maine resigned his post on the Foreign Relations Committee rather than the Governmental Affairs Committee when he became chairman of the Budget Committee because he was loath to relinquish the large staff which he commanded as chairman of the Governmental Affairs Subcommittee on Intergovernmental Relations. Metcalf said, Muskie was "kind of like that eagle on the coins, the one with all the arrows. He just reaches out and grabs everything in sight." He added, "Muskie has made the biggest power grab of anybody."[5] It should be pointed out in fairness that Muskie claimed his decision was based on other considerations. The point, however, is that Metcalf saw grabbing power and grabbing staff as one and the same. This was not a particularly profound insight on Metcalf's part. Senators who grab staff are able sooner or later to grab power as well. A recurring issue on the Hill is the amount of staff that will be allocated to minority members. A well-staffed minority is obviously more troublesome to the majority. An adequately staffed minority can have impact beyond its numbers. Being the majority, the Democrats, predictably, have resisted pressures for minority staff, while the Republicans, unsurprisingly, have pushed for as much minority staff as they can get. Committee chairmen who presented their budget requests to the Rules Committee when Senator Robert Griffin of Michigan was Minority Whip were sure to be grilled on the number of staff positions set aside for the minority. Senator John Sparkman of Alabama, when he was chairman of the Foreign Relations Committee, once replied smoothly to questions about minority staff, "I have no idea [of the number]. I never ask my staff about their political affiliations." Republicans sometimes try to justify their pushing for more staff in terms of enhancing the national interest by a full and complete debate on the issues. It is difficult, however, to marshal a cogent argument that the well-being of the nation hinges on hiring one or two aides to draft bills, prepare amendments, and write floor statements for Republican Senators. It is the ability of the Republican Party to advance its views and of Republican Senators to challenge Democratic Senators that is enhanced. A Senator without staff is a Senator without impact.

The Senate has become more open in recent decades. While it is not yet a body of 100 equals as former Majority Leader Mike Mansfield liked to say, it has still come a long way from the "self-perpetuating oligarchy with mild, but only mild, overtones of plutocracy" that former Senator Joseph Clark of Pennsylvania called it.[6] The Senate at the beginning of the eighties is somewhere in between. As the inner club has relaxed its control and new Senators have gained positions of power and status, there has been a concomitant increase in staff. Power has been spread out and down, and the result is more staff for more members.

For the last 100 years Congress has followed a consistent and cyclical pattern in staff. Staff has first gone where power has flowed. Those who have power also have funds to hire staff that can buttress and even augment that power. In response, those who lack power have sought staff which would enable them to acquire power. Power has then flowed where staff has gone. Power and staff hang in a delicate balance which rarely reaches an equilibrium, constantly tilting, instead, toward one or the other. Because of this tenuous relationship between power and staff, the Congressional haves and have-nots are constantly maneuvering for more of the one in order to get more of the other. Congress, of course, always justifies its staff increases in lofty terms. Staff increases are merited, so the argument goes, because of an ever-expanding work load or in order to develop legislative expertise. But in fact, Congress continually expands its staffs for internal reasons that have nothing to do with work load or expertise. Moreover, the battles over staff have not been waged so that resources would be allocated more equitably, as some political scientists have alleged. They have been fought in the hopes that staff would be distributed inequitably—the more unevenly the better. In general, the cycle begins when committee chairmen seek more staff for their committees. The committee

chairmen must prepare new budgets and defend their new requests before the Rules Committee at the start of each Congress.
Just as agency heads, department chiefs, and all bureaucratic
empire builders increase their budgets each fiscal year, committee chairmen, who have their own fiefdoms to protect, go in for
larger appropriations and more staff. More often than not, their
requests are met. The committee chairmen build up their empires year after year until members who lack full committees or
major subcommittees and who have nervously watched this process start to demand more personal staff, which will redress the
balance of power. This cycle is most clearly visible in the Senate,
where the links between power and staff are strongest. Each
stage of the cycle occurs first in the Senate and begins in the
House only after it is completed there. The House, in fact, has
occasionally increased its staff simply to keep up with the Senate.

The first committees acquired staff in 1856.[7] They were the
House Ways and Means Committee and the Senate Finance
Committee, which have always been among the most powerful
and prestigious committees in Congress. The Ways and Means
Committee has a special relationship with the House because of
the constitutional requirement that revenue-raising measures
originate there, and the Finance Committee is its tax-writing
counterpart in the Senate. Shortly afterwards, the other committees in both houses began to employ full-time staff assistants.
This staff, mostly clerical and secretarial, was controlled by the
committee chairmen, and while staff was supposed to devote all
its time to committee business, they frequently ended up helping
out in the personal offices of the chairmen. The other members
either paid secretaries from personal funds or did without. They
often answered letters in longhand during floor debates or late at
night in their boarding-house rooms. In fact, committees were
created and maintained, as they sometimes are today, solely to
provide staff to members. During the original debate on personal staff assistants Congressman Newton Blanchard of Louisiana said, "I believe if we adopt this proposition . . . it will result
in a great reform in bringing about the abolition of from 15 to 20
useless committees of this House that are now maintained simply
because of the pressure upon the Speaker for committee chairmanships, which means a clerk to each of the chairmen."[8]

The Senate authorized personal assistants in 1885. Senators
who did not chair committees were allotted the princely sum of

$6 a day when the Senate was not in session to pay clerical help. The House approved personal aides in 1893. Later on, clerks were hired on an annual basis. Everybody, then, both Congressmen who chaired committees and Congressmen who did not, had staff. The committee chairmen relied on their committee staffs. The rest turned to their personal office staffs. This situation, however, was not to last. After the turn of the century the committee chairmen were also authorized to hire personal aides. And so it has gone ever since. Whatever staff one Congressman has, they all go after.

Today's professional staff had its beginnings in the Legislative Reorganization Act of 1946. Before its passage the two Appropriations Committees and the Joint Committee on Internal Revenue Taxation were the only committees that consistently hired well-trained, technically competent staff. The other committees averaged five or six employees in the Senate and two or three employees in the House. Committee staffs, in fact, had not grown appreciably since World War I. There were 190 committee aides in the Senate and 114 committee aides in the House in 1943. Personal staffs were also small. The Legislative Reorganization Act authorized four professional aides for each Congressional committee. Even so, committees were slow to add staff. By 1961, for example, only one House committee and five Senate committees exceeded their original statutory quota. Six House committees and four Senate committees employed fewer than four. There were good reasons for this slow growth, however. Relatively few men in each house held positions of power, and by holding a number of such positions, they controlled a variety of staff slots. There was no need to create new positions. Congress was still a small world in many ways. When Lyndon Johnson became Majority Leader in 1959, for instance, he also chaired the Democratic Conference, the Democratic Policy Committee and the Democratic Steering Committee. In addition, he was chairman of the Aeronautical and Space Sciences Committee, chairman of the Subcommittee on the Departments of State and Justice of the Appropriations Committee, and chairman of the Preparedness Investigating Subcommittee of the Armed Services Committee. Such concentration of power is a thing of the past. When Robert Byrd became Majority Leader in 1977, he still chaired the party committees, but the chairmanships of the other committees and subcommittees had been dispersed among other Senators. The Aeronautical and Space Sciences Committee had been merged with the Commerce Committee chaired by Senator Warren Magnuson of Washington. The Appropriations Subcommittee on the Departments of State and Justice was chaired by Senator John McClellan of Arkansas. And the Armed Services Preparedness Investigating Subcommittee was chaired by Senator John Stennis of Mississippi.

Since 1970 power has been spread out and down in Congress. The current cliché holds that rule by committee has given way to rule by subcommittee. This is debatable. Subcommittees by themselves are symbols of power, not power incarnate. It is true, however, that more people hold more positions of power than at any time in the past. The dispersion of power began with the Legislative Reorganiztion Act of 1970, which limited Senators to a single full-committee chairmanship and to one subcommittee chairmanship on any committee. Grandfather clauses, of course, protected the power of incumbent chairmen, but the impact was still felt immediately. As a result of the act most Senators could expect to become chairman of a committee or subcommittee during their first term. Some even acquired subcommittee chairmanships along with their initial committee assignments. In fact, four of the five Senators elected in 1970 were given subcommittee chairmanships that year. At the same time the recommendations of the first Hansen Committee and the Subcommittee Bill of Rights were opening up committee and subcommittee chairmanships to more Congressmen. Power began to flow in new currents, and along with the power went staff. Between 1966 and 1976 Senate committee staff went from 642 to 1,534; between 1966 and 1976 House committee staff grew from 566 to 1,548. Those were not the only staff additions. Congressmen who lacked subcommittee chairmanships and Senators who did not command large subcommittee staffs set out to boost their personal staffs. There were huge increases. Between 1966 and 1976 the personal staffs swelled from 3,795 to 6,939 in the House and from 1,803 to 3,251 in the Senate.

The cordiality and collegiality of the Hill masks most of the power plays in Congress. Underneath, however, the tension between the haves and have-nots is always present, and in 1975 in the Senate it broke into the open. The Senators who took office in 1970 were different. They were not content to bide their time, waiting placidly for power to pass to them. They wanted power now. They organized a freshman class group, and out of that informal caucus emerged a new idea. Senators would no longer be limited to their personal office staffs and subcommittee aides who had to be coaxed out of the full-committee chairman. Henceforth, all Senators would be given funds to hire their own committee staff aides. These aides, now known as S. Res. 60 staff, were to be a hybrid. They would be hired by the individual Senators themselves and therefore owe their jobs and loyalties to them, but the aides would be equal in every way to the full-committee staff hired by the chairman. This was a generational revolt, pure and simple. The freshmen Senators had had their fill of begging information out of the committee staffs. Senator Sam Nunn of Georgia, who was among that group, said, "When I got here, I learned that I was going to have to kow tow to the Armed Services Committee staff or I wouldn't know anything." If the Senators could have their own committee aides who would have clout with the committee staff of the chairman, they wouldn't have to. Senator Mike Gravel, one of the prime movers of S. Res. 60, explained the need for such staff with the following anecdote:

> I went to the Committee on Armed Services to read a secret document. I was really impressed by the way they threw the door open, gave me the full committee room, sitting in there by myself—a much more palatial room than I am accustomed to enjoying. I sat there with this secret document and I had a few questions.
>
> I called the staff and the head of the staff sat there and counseled me. He gave me the best counsel I ever received. He was frank and candid and helpful. When we got to an area of expertise, he called over another staff person and we sat together and counseled and we were working diligently. Suddenly the expert of the experts—they were all of good will—got up and said, "Senator, I have to leave." I said, "Well, I am pressed on time, too." I was surprised. After all, we come to feel that we are here to be waited on. I was there and he said, "I had better leave. Senator Byrd called me, also, for a briefing and I must leave." So he did not accomodate me on my appointment. He just got up and left.
>
> He left for good reason—because Senator Byrd is on the committee and I am not. Also, Senator Byrd is more senior than I am and there is a likelihood that Senator Byrd may become chairman of the Committee on Armed Services before I become chairman

on the Committee on Armed Services and be the one to sign his
pay check. That is just good thinking. There is nothing wrong
with that. It is understandable. I do not fault it.

The point is that I am pressed for time, too, and I want some
knowledge and I would like it at my convenience — not in that
pecking order, but as if the person works for me; because when
that person works for me, Senator Byrd will come in second, not
first.[9]

Not even the most junior Senator could legitimately claim in
1975 that he lacked the staff to carry out his senatorial duties.
Staff allowances had been increasing rapidly. Between 1971 and
1975 staff allowances increased by 57 percent for the Senators
from the most populated states and by 33 percent for Senators
from the least populated states. Staff budgets ranged from
$751,980 for Senators from heavily populated states down to
$392,298 for Senators from sparsely populated states. The staff
explosion was very real, as Senator Howard Cannon of Nevada,
chairman of the Rules Committee and an opponent of S. Res.
60, pointed out during the debate. "In one of the committees I
serve on," he said, "we have a hard time now getting into the
room where executive sessions are held because so many staff
people are in there. On one or two occasions the chairman has
had to clear the room of the staff people to make room for all the
Senators to try to sit around in an executive session and mark up
a bill."[10] But although the junior Senators might have adequate
staff to carry out their duties in representing their constituents,
they did not have the kind of staff that would enable them to successfully play the power and status game. There is a pecking
order among staff just as there is a hierarchy among Senators.
Some staffs consider themselves more equal than others, and in
1975 the committee staffs and the staffs that worked for the entire Congress thought that they were superior to the personal office staffs and often the Senators. Senator Sam Nunn, who har-
bors a deep-seated distrust of staff, said, "We are in the position
of being deferential to staff because they have a lot of power and
run the subcommittees or committees. They wield power but
they are not a responsible part of the process." Those Senators
who were bent on shaking up the system frequently bumped into
the obstructionism of these staffs. The office of the Architect of
the Capitol refused to give Senator Brock and several other Sen-

ators floor plans of Capitol suites. The Senate Disbursing Office tried to prevent the Joint Committee on Congressional Operations from obtaining records which would reveal which Senators returned parts of their office allowances. And the staff of the Rules Committee, which has been known to strike terror in the hearts of those who are forced to deal with them, threatened the staff of Senator Brock with retaliation if they continued to probe into matters within the Rules Committee's jurisdictions. Senator Brock said, "Boy, do they get mad at some of us. Obviously, they're not going to say anything to me, but things they have said to my staff about, 'If you guys want to push us, you'll get a response. It may not be what you want, but you're going to get one.' "[11] The committee staffs also shut out the personal staffs of Senators. The personal staffs were not told about crucial meetings on legislative strategy or were cut off from important information about bills before committees. When personal staffs managed to be influential, they did so by winning the favor of the committee staffs. They cultivated the committee staffs in the same way that their bosses courted the committee chairmen. Otherwise, they were ignored. When they lost out, as they frequently did, their Senators were the real losers.

Although he couched his chagrin in the rhetoric of all the reform movements that are not reforms at all, Senator Gravel accurately described the situation that existed in 1975. He said, "We are all supposed to be equal in the Senate and the only way we can truly make ourselves equal is, of course, to have equal chance to gain the knowledge and acquire the information that we need to discharge our obligations as Senators in our legislative roles. . . . In a rational democracy, power is dependent upon knowledge. What we talk of here is the ability to acquire knowledge through the use of staff."[12] That ability, of course, was not evenly distributed among the Senators. In fact, Senator Gravel had said previously that he and Senators Quentin Burdick of North Dakota, Gaylord Nelson of Wisconsin, and George McGovern of South Dakota had all quit the Interior Committee in the early 1970s because of Senator Henry Jackson's refusal to allocate some of the staff which he controlled as chairman to other committee members. Earlier Senator Gravel, introducing S. Res. 60, had pointed out in balder terms the demeaning position that the junior Senators were forced into. "The only im-

mediate remedy to this situation [of inadequate committee staff]
is to curry the favor of one's committee chairman in the hopes of
gaining additional staff," he said. "The latter machinations take
place, well hidden from public view under layers of seniority,
Senatorial courtesy, private back scratching and negotiations."

The junior Senators flocked to Senator Gravel's cause, and
the senior Senators, with the exceptions of some Republicans
who had also been shortchanged in staff over the years, closed
ranks against him. Senator Hugh Scott of Pennsylvania, the Minority Leader and a proponent of S. Res. 60, complained that he
had served in the Senate for over sixteen years before he had
committee staff to assist him. When the resolution came before
the Rules Committee for hearings, the senatorial generation gap
was readily apparent. Testifying in favor were Senators George
Hansen of Idaho, Howard Baker of Tennessee, Mike Gravel of
Alaska, Alan Cranston of California, Robert Packwood of Oregon, Richard Schweiker of Pennsylvania, Bill Brock of Tennessee, Floyd Haskell of Colorado, James Abourezk of South
Dakota, Joseph Biden of Delaware, Peter Domenici of New Mexico, and Dewey Bartlett of Oklahoma. All were elected in the
late 1960s or early 1970s. Testifying against were Senators
Howard Cannon of Nevada, William Randolph of West Virginia, Frank Moss of Utah, William Proxmire of Wisconsin, Frank
Church of Idaho, John Sparkman of Alabama, John Pastore of
Rhode Island, and Warren Magnuson of Washington. All were
elected in the 1940s and 1950s. These camps cut across party,
ideological, and regional lines. Both the proponents and the opponents numbered Democrats and Republicans, liberals and
conservatives, Northerners, Southerners, and Midwesterners
among their ranks. They were united by only one thing — the relative amount of power which they possessed. Those who opposed
S. Res. 60 were chairmen of Senate committees or vice chairmen, soon to be chairmen of joint Congressional committees.
Those who favored S. Res. 60 were neither. The opponents had
had time to climb to positions of power. The proponents had
not. The Senate generation gap spanned ten years, and the Senators who took office at either end of that decade lined up with
their colleagues.

Senator Herman Talmadge of Georgia emerged as the primary opponent of S. Res. 60, as Senator Mike Gravel was the pri-

mary proponent. There could not have been two more disparate personalities. Gravel was an outsider. He achieved notoriety in 1971 when he called a meeting of his Subcommittee on Public Buildings and Grounds and read excerpts of the then classified "Pentagon Papers" until he collapsed in tears. Such behavior was not calculated to endear Gravel to the power structure of the United States Senate. Talmadge was the consummate insider. He was a third-term Senator, and as chairman of the Agriculture Committee he controlled a million-dollar-plus budget. Gravel's election to the Senate was a fluke. He managed to scrape together enough votes to beat the aging incumbent Senator Ernest Gruening in the primary and went on to win with less than a majority over desultory competition. Talmadge's election had been a foregone conclusion. His political career started when he was selected at the age of thirty-three to succeed his father as governor of Georgia, and he has been virtually unopposed since he was elected to the Senate in 1956. Talmadge had a sizable staff of the Agriculture Committee at his beck and call. Gravel had no staff to speak of.

It's not surprising then that while Gravel thought more staff was the solution, Talmadge saw too much staff as the problem. Gravel wanted to add staff. Talmadge suggested decreasing staff. During floor consideration of S. Res. 60 Talmadge said, "As I remarked to the distinguished Senator from Tennessee, in my judgement, if we had half the staff on Capitol Hill that we have at the present time and if we did not permit a paper to be read on the floor of the U.S. Senate, our business could be concluded by July 4 and we could adjourn sine die. But the Senator knows that some of these staff members are busy thinking up amendments, thinking up bills, thinking up programs and convincing their Senators to bring them in here on the floor of the Senate, ad infinitum. The more staff we have, the longer we will stay here."[13]

Brock, the distinguished Senator from Tennessee to whom Talmadge had been referring, who with Gravel was a leader in the fight for S. Res. 60, saw things differently. Brock proposed to fight fire with fire. The problem of government bloat would be solved by an increase in Senate staff. "I am going to tell the Senator that the people of Tennessee want me to exercise oversight responsibility and cut down on some of these things that are not necessary up here and I cannot do it without sufficient staff," he said.

Talmadge replied, "I will tell the Senator how to do that."

"I cannot do it unless I get the support to do a proper job," said Brock.

"I will tell the Senator how we can do that, if the Senator will yield," said Talmadge. "If we would fire half the Senate employees we have, fire half the staff and not permit a paper to be read on the floor of the U.S. Senate we could complete your business and adjourn by July 4.

"The Senator from Georgia knows that when you get more staff and more clerks they spend all their time thinking up bills, resolutions, amendments. They write speeches for Senators, and they come in here on the floor with the Senators. Unanimous consents are obtained for so-and-so to sit. He is there prodding, telling the Senator how to spend more money.

"The Senator from Tennessee does not want that. That is not his philosophy. But that is what his resolution does."

"No, it does not," Brock insisted. "That is not the kind of staff we are trying to find. We are going to try to find some areas that we can cut. If they do not justify their salary by finding some areas they can cut, I will fire them."

Talmadge retorted, "The Senator is headed in the wrong direction to do that. If he gets this host and swarm of new employees he wants to bring in here to help him think up new ideas, think up new bills, think up new amendments, think up new speeches, we will have to run 24 hours a day. We would have to change the calendar to 18 months in a year. That is what will happen if we add these several hundred new staff members here. The Senator should realize that and I think he is headed in the wrong direction, and I hope he will consider the error of his ways."

Talmadge, of course, had no need of a "host and swarm of new employees." He had a large staff to serve him, and the staff, by serving him exclusively, helped to maintain Talmadge's reputation as the acknowledged master of agriculture policy in the United States Senate. If S. Res. 60 passed and new staff members were hired, the members of the Agriculture Committee would have, as Talmadge accurately pointed out, a number of legislative assistants who would be busy helping them to "think up new ideas, think up new bills, think up new amendments, think up new speeches" in the area of agriculture. In the process Talmadge's own domination of that legislative area might be challenged and, naturally enough, Talmadge saw no reason to encourage that.

Talmadge, however, was one of the few senior Senators who bothered to actively oppose S. Res. 60 on the floor, and his opposition was futile. The power structure had considered throttling S. Res. 60 in the Rules Committee, but the backers had the votes and were determined to push on. If the Rules Committee would not report the resolution, they threatened, they would go to the floor, overpower the committee, and force the resolution through. As much as the Rules Committee disliked S. Res. 60, they liked that idea even less. The prospect of such a public showdown with the Rules Committee on the losing end was anathema. They reported the resolution. Once it reached the floor, passage was assured. The Senate had come a long way from the heyday of the inner club in the 1950s. Senator Ed Muskie, reminiscing about those days, once said, "I remember when I was a young Senator I was part of the young Senators who tried to change things. . . . We [hit against] very hard rock: Lyndon Johnson. We found ourselves suddenly on the outside looking in with not even an open window to crawl through." The young Senators were no longer in that position. Those days were gone forever. The freshman class club and their allies who pushed through S. Res. 60 comprised a majority of the Senate in 1975. The old guard no longer had the votes to defeat them on the floor, much less to strike back at them in public. S. Res. 60 passed for the same reason that almost all bills and resolutions pass the United States Senate: it was an idea whose time had come. The young Senators controlled the votes, and they wanted some of the power. It was time to open the window and let them through.

In the often heated debate over S. Res. 60 an exchange took place between Mike Gravel and Herman Talmadge that came close to summing up what really goes on in the Senate.

Gravel said, "I do not think the issue is whether we stay here a short while or a long while, whether we stay here 2 months or 3 months or 4 months. I think the issue of final concern should be, 'Are we doing the people's business?' That is what the issue should be; not whether or not we have a bunch of bright young staff that may have the ideals in their bosoms to try to solve some of the problems that besiege us.

"Is there anything wrong with that? I think that is something that the American people want to see happen. It is for us to get out here and say, there is something wrong there and we are going to try to solve it; not say, there is something, forget it, I do not want to focus on the problem.

"What my colleague cries out against is the fact that the people want to be served. That is what my colleague is saying.

"What I am saying is, let us serve the people."

Talmadge said, "I am saying the Senators ought to be serving and not the staff."

As it turned out, Talmadge need not have protested quite so much. Over half of the staff hired immediately after the passage of S. Res. 60 were added to the payrolls of just six committees. Those were the committees which in the past had been most thoroughly dominated by their chairmen: Small Business, Finance, Commerce, Interior, Public Works, and Appropriations.

The issue was clear-cut for both Gravel and Talmadge. For Gravel, more staff meant more impact as a Senator. For Talmadge, increasing staff meant more power devolving on staff. Both were right. Staff is a sword that cuts both ways. Through the adroit use of a large staff a Senator is able to have influence on a wide range of issues, and without that staff such influence will be lacking. In fact, a study of the Senators who received the most frequent mentions in the news media, a certain sort of measure of their impact, found that their visibility in the press was linked to the size of their staff.[14] At the same time, a Senator who has a large staff tends to lose control of that staff. A Senator has many demands on his time, and he can necessarily be in only one place at any one time. As a result, staff has stepped in to fill those gaps in a Senator's time. Those gaps can be quite large. Since 1960 the Senate has been in large measure a farm team for the presidency. At various times during the 1976 presidential season, for example, Senators Frank Church, Birch Bayh, Henry Jackson, Lloyd Bentsen, Walter Mondale, and Robert Byrd were announced presidential candidates. Hubert Humphrey was contemplating a presidential campaign. Ed Muskie was campaigning for the vice presidential nomination, and Mondale and Senator Robert Dole were vice presidential candidates. Other

Senators were running for reelection that year. When the Senators are thus occupied, the day-to-day work of the Senate falls to the staff by default. When the Senate Governmental Affairs Committee considered a proposal in 1976 to set up a Senate Committee on Intelligence, hearings were held on rotating the committee membership throughout the Senate by limiting the length of time that any one Senator could serve on the committee. That way, some felt, the committee would avoid being captured by the very intelligence agencies that it was set up to oversee. But Frank Church, who was a prime sponsor of the proposal to create an Intelligence Committee demurred. Rotating the membership, he said, would only increase the power of the committee staff. Testifying before the Governmental Affairs Committee, Church said, "We should keep the Senators and rotate the staff."

The average voter, and for that matter even the sophisticated voter, believes when he casts his vote for a candidate to the United States Senate that he is voting for a man who will make his constituents' concerns his own. At one time that was true, but it is no longer. Senators are only peripherally involved at best in representing their constituents. Senators continue to exercise the symbolic functions of their office. They introduce bills. They cast votes on the floor and in committee. They deliver speeches and read testimony. They attend social and political functions that require their presence. But the real work of the United States Senate is carried on by the staff. Lloyd Bentsen, an able and conscientious legislator who was president of a conglomerate insurance company before his election, once said, "In a state the size of Texas it's impossible to know everything that's going on there. All you can do is hire a good staff and trust that they'll tell you what you should know." It is the staff that drafts the bills and draws up amendments, writes the speeches and committee testimony, plots legislative strategy and occasionally recasts a malleable Senator in its own image.

In the mid-1960s the consumer protection movement was still in its infancy, and Senator Warren Magnuson of Washington, chairman of the Commerce Committee, had only a passing interest in consumer-oriented legislation. Magnuson, however, did have a strong interest in securing his Senate seat after a near defeat in 1962 and in consolidating his power in the Senate. Fortunately for Magnuson, he was gifted with a bright, young, and aggressive Commerce Committee staff who saw in the emerging consumer movement a way of accomplishing both of these ends. Led by Michael Pertschuk who was later to be named chairman of the Federal Trade Commissions by President Carter, the staff set out deliberately to stake out consumer protection legislation for Magnuson and themselves. Under their tutelage Magnuson was to come to dominate a policy area of growing importance and public interest. Through their guidance he was to become the Senate's expert on consumer protection and a nationally recognized leader in the consumer movement. And as one consequence among many of all this activity, according to their plan, he would be regularly returned to Washington by the grateful voters back home.

Early on, the staff usurped the truth-in-packaging issue, which had been floating around the Senate in one legislative guise or another since 1961. It was Senator Phil Hart of Michigan who originally introduced a truth-in-packaging proposal. (Hart allegedly opened a box of cereal at breakfast one morning and, finding that it was half empty, said, "We've got to do something about this.") In 1966 Hart's truth-in-packaging legislation was suddenly reincarnated as Magnuson's Fair Packaging and Labeling Act. As chairman of the committee which claimed jurisdiction in this area, Magnuson was in the position to do something with the legislation. As Hart later told it:

> In fact, Maggie entered the picture at the right moment and in the right way to get the thing passed. A lot of opposition had been created. . . . So Magnuson's stepping in when he did probably saved the bill. After two or three executive sessions he called everybody together, including some boys from downtown, and hammered out a "substitute" bill. That it was supposedly a substitute and not merely an amended Hart bill made it a lot easier to get through. We lost some things, but by and large it was a good bill and much the same as mine. You know how Maggie can pull that sort of thing off, with his broad sweeping statements which everybody somehow accepts: "This is a *new* bill!"[15]

The "new bill," basically formulated by Hart but now bearing Magnuson's name, was passed into law later that year.

The legislation which finally cleared the Congress was a watered-down version of the bill which had been reported out of the Commerce Committee. The staff, however, were little concerned about such details. They had gotten what they wanted out of the legislation. From their perspective the important thing was that a piece of consumer protection legislation backed by Magnuson had become law. More meaningful legislation could come later. Furthermore, they were busy with other bills. That same year they were working on the Federal Cigarette Labeling and Advertising Act and the Traffic Safety Act, both of which were important consumer-protection bills. Still to come was the whole panoply of consumer legislation which would be written into law in the late 1960s and 1970s. By that time the Commerce Committee staff would have secured Magnuson's reputation as the natural and rightful champion of any and all bills in the consumer protection area.

The relationship between Magnuson and his staff was complex, as such relationships always are. Magnuson was not an unwitting dupe of an activist staff who manipulated their chairman for their own ends. Such an inference would be as inaccurate as it would be unfair, but it is true that Magnuson willingly went where his staff led him. Magnuson was flailing—and knew he was—in the mid-1960s and was receptive to the direction of his staff. Without Pertschuk and several other key staffers who were interested in consumer issues and who wanted to activate the committee, Magnuson would not have achieved his present preeminence in the consumer protection area. The staff's influence was aptly summarized by a student of the Commerce Committee at that time. "Onto the old Magnuson, interested in fishing, shipping and Boeing Aircraft and running a rather sleepy committee," he wrote, "was grafted a new one: the champion of the consumer, the national legislative leader, and the patron of an energetic and innovative staff."[16]

That particular staff coming to work at that time did something else which redounded to their and Magnuson's credit. They turned the previously moribund Commerce Committee into a major power in the United States Senate. The staff wanted to make the Commerce Committee and themselves into a force to be reckoned with. They could do that only if they pushed Magnuson as far as he was willing to go. There were invisible limits which had to be observed. If they exceeded them, all would be lost. So they pushed and pulled gently, but always in the direction of more activism for Magnuson, more power for the committee and, of course, its staff. And they succeeded. The committee, now renamed the Commerce, Science, and Transportation Committee, has one of the largest staffs and was among the most powerful in the Senate in the 1970s. It and its staff are considered a force to be reckoned with. Other committees and their staffs tread lightly in areas that infringe on the legislation and issues which the Commerce Committee claims, and when they become involved in these areas, they are sure, in the vernacular of the Hill, to touch base with this committee.

The problems that Pertschuk and the activist staff he brought to the Commerce Committee faced in revamping Magnuson's image were minimal compared to the difficulties that confronted the staff of Congressman Andrew Maguire of New Jersey in a similar situation a decade or so later. Magnuson, at least, had an image, however dull and pedestrian it might have been, to remodel. Maguire had none.

Maguire was swept into office in the post-Watergate elections of 1974. He is an unlikely Congressman for the seventh district in northern New Jersey. He is a Democrat in a district that went two to one for Nixon in 1972 and voted predominantly for Ford in 1976. He is an urban affairs specialist in a district that takes in some of the most beautiful and affluent suburbs in the country. Maguire, however, had two things going for him—the nationwide revulsion against the Watergate capers and an aging incumbent who was no match for his aggressive campaigning. Like most of the freshmen who took office that year, Maguire had no patience with the old "go along to get along" ways of the House. Maguire was used to getting ahead, not along. After studying economics on a Woodrow Wilson fellowship and earning a Ph.D. in politics at Harvard, Maguire worked at the United Nations and from there had gone on to the Ford Foundation. At thirty-five, Maguire was ready to make his mark in Congress.

Maguire saw things differently than most of the older members of the House and a lot of the newer ones as well. Having served on staffs at the UN and the Ford Foundation, he knew the importance of good staff work. At freshman orientation in December a senior Congressman told the incoming class, "The greatest contribution any of us can make to the welfare of America is to return here in two years. That's what you should concentrate on. Don't waste money hiring staff. Anything you need you can get through the DSG [the Democratic Study Group] or the committee. The sole purpose of your staff is to answer the mail." The older members of the House nodded sagely, but while Maguire listened politely, he didn't take the Congressman's advice. And as it happened, Maguire's staff ended up doing everything but answering the mail.

Maguire, in fact, chose to do exactly the opposite of what the Congressman advised. At the outset he hired Bob Kerr, a young political scientist from the University of Pittsburgh, as his administrative assistant. Kerr, having worked previously for Senator Hubert Humphrey, had decidedly Senate notions about the proper role for staff. The combination of Maguire's personality and Kerr's experience shaped subsequent happenings.

Maguire was both smart and brash, and he had come to Congress at a propitious time. That winter a sense of excitement was abroad in Washington and especially in the House. The changes wrought by the internal reforms of the 1970s were having their effect. Some of the stodginess of an earlier era in the House had been swept away. Moreover, the House still felt a kind of residual collective pride in the highly praised performance of its Judiciary Committee as it handled the articles of impeachment that summer against Richard Nixon. As a result, some of the debilitating feeling of inferiority to the Senate from which the House habitually suffers had worn away temporarily. And in general the nation was no longer morbidly glued to the national soap opera of Richard Nixon's demise. The long nightmare was ended. The nation was ready to get on with the business at hand.

The freshmen Congressmen arriving in Washington that winter believed they represented the first of a new generation of post-Watergate politicians. They were serious and idealistic. Starry-eyed, some of the veterans thought. Many had campaigned heavily for political reforms and owed their election to promises to change the system. The election had been heavily chronicled by the national media, and the media were watching over the shoulders of the incumbents to see if these notions of reform would be accepted. The House leaders were more willing to listen, more open to the freshmen's ideas than they had ever been. There was a sense of changing seasons when they came in December that had nothing to do with the plummeting temperatures which heralded the arrival of the Washington winter.

Andy Maguire correctly sensed that in this atmosphere he could play the power and status game in a new way. Instead of moving up through the committee hierarchy, hopscotching from a low-ranking committee to a high-ranking committee and wait-

ing for subcommittee chairmanships to open up, which would
ordinarily take years, he would force the establishment to let him
in immediately. The way to do that, he rightly reasoned, was to
become a national figure in some important area. As a nationally recognized figure he would be able to command the attention
of the leadership. Maguire and his staff set about creating a national image for him. The energy crisis provided an opportunity,
and the national press unwittingly became the means.

The freshmen were something of a novelty to the media,
which paid substantial attention to their initial comings and goings. Maguire, however, realized he needed to differentiate
himself from the rest of the newcomers if his strategy was to
work. The press is notoriously fickle, and Maguire knew that if
he were going to keep its interest, he eventually had to do
something that would be newsworthy. Press interest in the freshmen would last only so long.

The Ford administration's energy program created the ideal
setting. One of the centerpieces was a gasoline tax which would
raise the price of gas at the pump. Neither Al Ullman, chairman
of the Ways and Means Committee, nor John Dingell, chairman
of the Energy and Power Subcommittee, came out against it.
Maguire seized the opportunity to become the spokesman for the
consumers. Together with five other newly elected Congressmen,
Maguire put together an alternate program and held a press
conference to announce the freshman energy coalition. The
press conference attracted a number of key reporters and Maguire was on his way.

Maguire's press secretary was young and inexperienced, and
his naiveté proved to be a decided asset. An experienced press
secretary, more knowledgeable about the workings of the press,
would have known that the national media would not have the
slightest interest in the pronouncements of the 435th member of
Congress. But Gary Sardo, who had no experience as a press secretary, was blissfully unaware of that fact. He was also, in the
words of a fellow staff member, "obstinate as hell, totally charm-
ing and able to talk endlessly." He turned out to be as bold and
brash as his boss.

Soon the staffs at such papers as the *New York Times* and on
such programs as "Today" and "Not for Women Only" were receiving phone calls from Sardo. At the start they were non-
plussed. Why, they wondered in amazement, would anybody

imagine they would be interested in a freshman Congressman from, of all places, New Jersey? They became increasingly befuddled as the phone calls kept up. Sardo was completely undaunted by refusals. Eventually skepticism gave way to grudging admiration of Sardo's tenacity. He simply did not give up or go away. It took ten phone calls to the "Op Ed" page of the *New York Times* to place the article that Maguire had written, but in the end the editor accepted it. It took three months of badgering before Sardo placed Maguire on the "Today" show, but he got on.

"We were a group of zealots and generally regarded that way," said an aide, recalling that time. " 'Brash,' 'abrasive,' and 'aggressive' were favored adjectives in the press."

Meanwhile, Maguire's staff were focusing all of their attention on energy. Everything else was shoved to a corner of their desks. The district office staff back in Bergen County screamed at the Washington staff daily as the routine work of a Congressman's office piled up behind more statements on energy policy. Even the mail went unanswered for months at a time. One day as Maguire strolled into the office from the floor, he chided Kerr. Another Congressman had just told him that his office answered mail within two days. "Why can't we have a two-day turnaround?" he said. Kerr asked if he wanted the staff to answer mail or work on energy. Maguire shrugged his shoulders and wandered away. It was the first and last time anyone in the office heard Maguire complain about the mail.

Maguire had managed to assemble a large staff for a first-term Congressman by finding people who were willing to work long hours for hideously low salaries, but even so they could accomplish only so much in the course of a twelve-hour work day. Maguire knew he could not have everything, and he deliberately chose for them to spend their time to establish him as a spokesman on energy. He might not be picked as Congressman of the Year by his constituents, but he could make headlines in the *Washington Post*.

Moreover, the strategy was working. Outside of Congress Maguire was being recognized as an energy expert. Maguire took the toughest possible stands on energy. If Ford or Ullman or Dingell took one position, Maguire took the exact opposite. The reporters who covered the Hill for the Washington *Star* and *Post* came to realize that Maguire could be counted on for an articulate and highly quotable reaction to the energy proposals that were floating around the administration and Congress. They also realized that Maguire always knew the ins and outs of issues. Sardo managed to break through the initial resistance of the media through sheer force of personality. Their attitude was, as a Maguire aide described it, "Let's hear what this nutty guy has to say." Once they started listening, Maguire became that favorite thing—a good source. The "Today" show, which had initially laughed at Sardo's attempts to place Maguire, invited him back three times in a year. And Maguire's frequent appearances there were something more senior Congressman could easily envy. The press was beginning to trust the young Congressman from New Jersey. An aide said, "In the Senate you are automatically assumed to have credibility until you blow it. In the House you must establish it. So we did." The press began to see Andrew Maguire as the person to talk to on energy issues. Press coverage inevitably engenders press coverage. The more press a Congressman can get, the more he tends to be sought out by the press.

The press helped to build up Maguire's reputation inside the House. It was not just the sheer volume of press clippings he was accumulating, although that obviously added to his visibility. More important, it was the kinds of press he was getting. Newspapers such as the *New York Times* and the *Washington Post*, whose opinions carried weight with members of Congress, were taking Maguire seriously. And the Op Ed piece in the *New York Times* was a brilliant stratagem on the part of Maguire's staff. Other Congressmen, who were not privy to the effort which had preceded its acceptance, were impressed. As a young man in a hurry, Maguire had no time to waste. Since he was unwilling to put in the time on the inside that would ordinarily be required, he sought to build his expertise, a necessary prerequisite of power in the House, off the Hill.

Not all Congressmen were pleased by the attention which Maguire was getting and by his use of staff. Some were hostile outright. Others were merely affronted by his unwillingness to play the game in the old way. Once when Maguire brought an aide to sit beside him in a committee hearing, a Congressman asked, "Has that man been elected by the people?" But Maguire was able to deflect a lot of criticism by always doing his homework, always being prepared. He might speak out more than freshmen Congressmen were supposed to do even in 1975, but at least when he did, he had something of consequence to say.

The initial payoff was Maguire's reassignment to the Interstate and Foreign Commerce Committee. Maguire had sought that committee in the beginning but had been appointed to the Banking Committee instead. When Congressman John Jarman of Oklahoma switched parties, a vacancy was created among the Democrats. Maguire reapplied, as did Larry McDonald of Georgia, a self-proclaimed member of the John Birch Society. Ordinarily McDonald would have been able to claim the seat because of his seniority. But the leadership was anxious to keep McDonald, who had a regrettable tendency, from their viewpoint, to go his own way, off the committee. Maguire, having demonstrated with the help of his friends in the press a potential for leadership in energy policy, was the logical choice. He might not always support the party position but unlike McDonald he was considered a responsible dissenter. Through hard-headed bargaining, Maguire was able to get himself assigned to the Energy Subcommittee of the Interstate and Foreign Commerce Committee also.

Within a year of his election Maguire's staff had been able to accomplish for him what other Congressmen spend a decade or more doing. They built an image for him. They made other Congressmen take him seriously. And they had gotten him on the right committees. Maguire had emerged as a comer. Without an aggressive, dynamic staff that was incapable of taking no for an answer, Maguire would have been languishing in obscurity on the Banking Committee, still waiting, as political scientist Richard Fenno would say, to become a Congressman.

Maguire is a rare case, the proverbial exception that proves the rule that staff as an adjunct of power is a Senate, not a House, phenomenon. Maguire was successful, in addition to all the foregoing reasons, because the staffs of similarly placed Congressmen were not spending all their time promoting their bosses. Maguire simply had no competition.

The Senate is different. Senate staffs are routinely assumed to be as ambitious, as aggressive, and as brash on behalf of their Senators as Maguire's staff was for him. Not all Senators who have been swept along by this trend are entirely happy with it. Senator James Allen, who opposed government growth at all levels, once remarked, "I feel the staff is doing the philosophizing and Senators are too inclined to rubberstamp." Allen, who did his part to fight this trend, once introduced amendments which would have banned staff members from the floor while the Senate was in session and would have forbidden the reading of prepared texts, that is, statements prepared by staffs, on the floor. The amendments were enough to damage Allen's reputation as a conservative, for both were profoundly radical notions in the Senate of the 1970s. Needless to say, the amendments were never voted on. If they had passed, a loud silence would have abruptly descended upon the Senate chamber.

Even Senators who scramble for more aides themselves are not entirely comfortable with the idea of burgeoning staffs. There is the gnawing feeling that the Senate may have created a Frankenstein monster and the Senators may have ended up the servants, not the masters, of their staffs. This constant badgering by staff leads some Senators to seek refuge in the "Senators Only" room just off the chamber where they disappear for hours to the consternation of their aides. It also prompted Senator Ernest Hollings of South Carolina to say during a hearing on legislative branch appropriations, "There are many Senators who feel that all they are doing is running around and responding to staff. . . . Everybody is working for staff, staff, staff; driving you nutty. . . . It has gotten to the point where the Senators never actually sit down and exchange ideas and learn from the experience of others and listen. . . . Now it is how many nutty whiz kids you have on the staff to get you magazine articles and get you head-lines and get all those other things done."[17]

In their quest for power Senators have permitted their days to become, in the words of the Commission on the Operation of the Senate, "a scheduler's nightmare." Committee hearings are necessary to demonstrate power, so more are held. Legislation is needed to prove expertise, so more bills are introduced. Articles and speeches prove status, so more are written and given. Staff accompanies power, so more are hired and then in a variant of Parkinson's law the work expands further to occupy the people who are available to do it.

Nowhere is the pervasive influence of staff more visible than in committees and during roll call votes on the Senate floor. Senators typically do not bother to attend committee hearings unless they are supposed to be chairing or the hearing is unusually important. When they do show up, they arrive on the run, casting frantic glances around the room for the aide who has been monitoring the hearing in their absence. While the Senator's attention has been diverted elsewhere, the staff has studied the pros and cons of the legislation, drafted a statement to be read into the hearing record, and compiled questions to be asked of the witnesses. Often, the Senator has seen neither the statement nor the questions in advance. One aide to a young Senator was confounded when her Senator unexpectedly turned up at a hearing where then Secretary of State Henry Kissinger was testifying on a resolution which would create a Select Committee on Intelligence. Since the Senator had said the night before that he could not attend the hearing, she was as unprepared as he. "Quick," he whispered, "give me some questions." The aide, whose last contact with foreign affairs had been a course on Indian and Pakistani politics her senior year in college, suddenly found herself scribbling questions for the Secretary of State. "I shook," she said later. "I didn't even know what I was writing. All I could imagine was this loud outburst of laughter as the Senator asked some dumb question which I had written." Two minutes later the Senator was asking her questions. Coming from the Senator, the questions sounded more authoritative, and no one laughed. Thus hearing records on which the passage of legislation depends are compiled.

More Senators try to show up at committee meetings when legislation is being acted on, but they are not always better informed. The same aide found herself a year later working for newly elected James Sasser of Tennessee. The Governmental Affairs Committee was marking up the bill that would create the Department of Energy, and the Subcommittee on Civil Service and General Services, which Sasser now chaired, had prepared a minor amendment. The amendment was of little importance to the Department of Energy, but it was enormously important to the General Services Administration, over which Sasser now held jurisdiction. Somewhere along the way language had slipped into the bill which would authorize the Department of Energy to construct office buildings. This power had previously resided exclusively in the General Services Administration, and the people there were determined to keep it that way. The amendment was drafted and Sasser thoroughly briefed on the content and need for the amendment. The markup was called to order, and Senator Abe Ribicoff, the committee chairman, began skimming through the lengthy bill. Page after page was called out, and if no amendments were brought up, the page was approved by

unanimous consent. The subcommittee amendment belonged
on page 64. Ribicoff turned to page 64, read the page number,
and after a brief pause said, "Approved." The aide was stunned.
Then she noticed Sasser was looking at her in horrified bewilderment. Suddenly she found herself on her feet, saying, "Mr.
Chairman, we have an amendment." Ribicoff and Senator
Charles Percy, the ranking minority member, were gentle with
Sasser in his inexperience. They permitted the amendment to be
introduced. Halfway through Sasser's explanation of the amendment, he paused and rapidly riffled through the papers in front
of him. Somehow he had lost a page of his statement. He turned
to the aide and said in a horrified whisper that carried throughout the room, "What comes next?" As the committee waited and
a packed committee room watched, the aide told Sasser what he
was supposed to say and he repeated her words.

Sasser was really no less prepared than other Senators. His
lack of familiarity with what was allegedly his amendment was
simply more obvious because of his inexperience. Unlike other
Senators he had not yet learned to absorb a staff briefing in
minutes in order to fake preparedness or to cope humorously in
its absence.

At the end of 1977 the Senate Judiciary Committee was in the
midst of another of its interminable markup sessions on legislation that would revamp the 200-year-old criminal code. The
complex bill ran 360 pages. Senator Joseph Biden of Delaware,
then approaching the end of his first term in the Senate, had an
amendment which, unlike Sasser's amendment to the Department of Energy bill, would affect the policy that was ultimately
embodied in the reform. The discussion that day, in the words of
a *Washington Post* reporter who covered the incident, centered
on "the most awesome power the law can give one man over another—the license of a judge to take life, deprive liberty and con-
fiscate material wealth." In this instance it had to do with time
off for good behavior. Or so he thought.

"In other words, for every day of good behavior in prison—
excuse me, I am being corrected here," Biden said, as members
of his own staff thrust a copy of his own amendment at him.

Then, seemingly confused and stumbling somewhat over his
words, Biden attempted to digest and explain what his staff had
prepared. Finally he startled his colleagues and the audience
with a frank admission.

"Obviously," he said, "I don't know what the hell I'm talking about. I thought I had a two-for-one provision there. The staff, in its wisdom, rewrote it, so I guess I did not want that after all."[18]

Senators are normally conspicuous by their absence on the floor. The sessions are so scantily attended that authors of the literature prepared by the Senate and given free to all tourists who happen to wander through their Senator's office felt compelled to explain that if a constituent did not see his Senator on the floor, it was undoubtedly because he was occupied with important business elsewhere. Staff, however, are constantly monitoring the floor for the Senators. When the Senate is in session and a moderately important bill is on the floor, staff are everywhere. A special gallery is set aside for staff so aides of Senators who are not on the committee which reported the bill and are not sponsoring amendments can watch the proceedings. On the floor beside the one or two Senators who are present because they are introducing amendments sit one or more staff members juggling file folders and lengthy briefing books, handing their Senators the appropriate fact sheet to support the amendment. The floor managers of the bill also have their aides present, who with a casual nod often determine which amendments are accepted and which must go to a vote.

In the back of the room on long sagging leather couches sit the committee staff who have carefully shepherded the bill through committee and who have obtained unanimous consent from the Senate to be present throughout the debate. The Majority and Minority Leaders, who stand in the front of the chamber, have their own staffs nearby to keep them apprised of the significance of each amendment. In the Senators' lobby adjacent to the floor several other Senators huddle with aides. In the public reception room to the right of the Senate chamber more aides lounge — aides who have not gotten or not sought the special passes that will admit them to the floor for five minutes and are waiting to buttonhole their Senator as he emerges. The atmosphere is somnolent. It seems to harken back to another time, except for the fact that in an earlier time the Senate floor was the center of activity for Senators.

All of this starts to change when a roll call vote is announced. Senators begin to filter in as the roll is read, but most wait until the five bells which signal that five minutes remain before a re-

corded vote buzz throughout the Senate offices. Those six
buzzers bring Senators and staff running. The subway which
runs between the Russell and Dirksen Office Buildings is now
held for Senators. Capitol Hill police halt the subway and shep-
herd Senators into the cars. Tourists back against the wall as
Senators rush into the special "Senators Only" elevators that whiz
them to the second floor of the Capitol and disgorge them only a
few feet from the door to the chamber. Aides run down from the
staff gallery to the public reception room and try to flag down
their Senator as the employees who guard the doors to the chamber try to keep them back and out of the way. Aides jockey for
position around the small anteroom off the floor to call their offices. The arriving Senators who have been summoned from
other business have not the slightest inkling about the amendment on which they are called to vote unless it is that rare
amendment which has been announced and scheduled in advance. As they arrive, they beckon their aides from the reception
room or scan the chamber for their staff member, who is usually
bobbing up and down so he can be spotted easily. This aide
rushes to his Senator. He is apt to whisper hurriedly something
like "This is a motion by Helms to table the Kennedy amendment to require mandatory energy conservation standards." If
the Senator is a member of the committee that reported the bill,
he will add, "The committee is against" — or "for" — "the motion." Whether his Senator is on the committee or not, he will
say, "You want to vote no" — or "yes." The Senator casts his vote,
except in rare instances, in accord with his aide's advice.

For a few minutes all is turmoil. The clerk who is calling the
roll can barely hear the votes of individual Senators above the
babble. Then, as the vote is announced, Senators begin to drift
away. The aides drift back to the staff galleries, their perches on
the couches in the rear of the chamber, and the public reception
rooms.

On an important vote the pandemonium may last a bit
longer. When the Senate was voting in 1978 on the Carter administration's arms deal which would provide military weapons
to a number of Arab countries as well as Israel, the crucial vote
came on a motion to table the resolution approving the arms
deal, rather than a straight up-or-down vote on the resolution itself. The staffs of several Senators who had not learned precisely
what they were voting on panicked as they heard their Senators

cast their votes the wrong way. As the seconds ticked away, aides sprinted to the floor to find their Senators while there was still time to change their votes, and frantic calls were made to the staff in the cloakroom "to find Senator So-and-So and tell him what is going on."

Soon, however, the Senate is back to normal. The aides have returned to their vantage points and the Senators have vanished.

A comic aspect hovers around the more public aspects of staff as the fiction of the Senate as the world's greatest deliberative body, carefully studying the issues and making good public policy, collides with the reality of a Senate dominated in most crucial aspects by staff through their sheer omnipresence. But the humor hides the ironic fact that the scramble for staff has had an unintended consequence. The growth in staff has enabled Senators to step up their legislative activity and thus add to their stature within the body, but it has brought about a diminution of real power. Senators are increasingly less able to influence the outcome of events.

Before legislation is ever introduced, aides outline the policy alternatives, and as an aide pointed out, the staff tends to "frame the options and if you frame the options, you can often frame the outcome." The staff puts inchoate ideas into legislative language and drafts the introductory statement that accompanies a bill, detailing the purpose and need for the legislation. Once a bill is referred to a committee, the committee staffs take over. The committee staffs organize all hearings on legislation, select the witnesses, and then write the questions to be asked of them. Drafts of committee bills are written at staff meetings where aides work out the language that will be ratified or amended in committee markups. When a bill is reported out, the staff writes the report that is filed along with it. The reports are the major source of information for other Senators and more importantly their staffs. They become the basis for interpretation of legislative intent by courts and administrative agencies.

Along the way the staff performs the delicate negotiations which can keep a bill alive or doom it to a premature death. The staff of Senator Pete Domenici, a first-term Republican from New Mexico, managed in 1977 through just such negotiations to keep his inland waterways bill afloat. Domenici's bill was going to force barge operators to pay for the use of government-built waterways. Domenici could expect the most hospitable hearing from members of the Public Works Committee, on which he served. But several obstacles stood in the way. The Finance Committee would logically claim jurisdiction over any bill that would tax the barge owners, and its chairman, Russell Long, was an implacable foe of waterway fees in any form. In drafting the bill, the staff decided the fees would not be called taxes. Instead they would be called charges, in the hopes that such legislative sleight of hand would cast the bill into the jurisdiction of the Commerce Committee, which had authority over inland waterways. The Commerce Committee might be slightly better disposed to the bill. However, the staff discovered that the chairman of the appropriate subcommittee was none other than Russell Long. Domenici's aides searched for a way that the bill could legitimately be referred under the rules to the Public Works Committee.

Meanwhile, the Senate was taking up committee reorganization. In the process of the debate committee jurisdictions were being discussed, and on the afternoon of February 3 Domenici innocently asked Senator Adlai Stevenson of Illinois, who was managing the committee reform bill, about the inland waterways fee bill.

"Would it not make sense to have user charge legislation in the Public Works Committee?" he said.

Stevenson, who was fighting to salvage as much of the reorganization proposal as possible and wanted Domenici's support, readily acceded. "I agree," he said. "It appears to me that is logical."

Domenici's triumph was short-lived. When S. 790, the inland waterways bill, was introduced, the savvy Murray Zweben, parliamentarian, assigned jurisdiction jointly to the Public Works and Commerce Committees. "I saw that colloquy with Stevenson," Zweben said later. "I knew what they were up to. You don't think these guys can fool me with some canned legislative history, do you?"[19]

A week later the Ford administration sent its inland waterways bill to the Hill. Warren Magnuson had already agreed to introduce it, and when he did, an assistant parliamentarian unaware of the dual referral of S. 790 assigned the Ford administration bill to the Commerce Committee alone.

At that point Domenici was back to start until the staff once again stepped in. Staff member Hal Brayman had worked occasionally with some of the staff on the Commerce Committee and had contacts there. He made a few telephone calls, which turned up some surprising news. Although Magnuson himself and a number of the committee members were likely to oppose S. 790, the staff thought it was not a bad idea.

The aides negotiated an agreement. Magnuson would return to the floor and request that the Ford administration bill be jointly assigned. Public Works could then proceed to hold hearings and report out S. 790. Commerce would not raise a point of order challenging the right of Public Works to report the bill to the floor before Commerce could consider it.

That is precisely what happened. Magnuson went back to the floor. The Ford administration bill was reassigned. And eventually the Domenici bill was reported unchallenged.

Aides who specialize tend to survive year after year. They provide an institutional memory, a repository of facts and experience as well as a network of personal contacts. Long-term staff members are often no match for their alleged bosses who simply lack the expertise and knowledge to challenge their recommendations.

One of the best examples was Laurence Woodworth, who at the time of his death in 1977 was Assistant Secretary of the Treasury for tax policy and President Carter's top adviser on tax matters. Before that, he spent thirty-two years on the staff of the Joint Committee on Internal Revenue Taxation. During his last fourteen years he served as staff director. Woodworth understood the intricacies of the tax code as well as anyone in the country and better than most. As the staff director of the little-known committee which drafts all tax legislation for both houses, he was responsible for all the revisions of the Internal Revenue Code for over a decade. During the 94th Congress, when the House Ways and Means Committee was grappling with energy tax legislation under a new chairman, Woodworth guided the committee day after day. The committee's bewilderment was such that an oil lobbyist remarked during the extended markup sessions, "I'm moving to a safe country. Like Libya." It was Woodworth who time and again brought the committee back from the fringes of total disarray. The new chairman, Al Ullman of Washington, found himself turning to Woodworth repeatedly. "Restate it again very simply," Ullman said one day. "I'm totally confused here. Will you please clarify it?" Moreover,

Woodworth was on occasion the only one who could explain to reporters covering the sessions what the committees had done. At his death Ullman said, "In his quiet way he was as much an influence in shaping tax policy in this country as any committee chairman or Treasury secretary or President in recent memories."[20]

Another such aide was Harley Dirks, the long-time staff director of the Appropriations subcommittee which controls the budget of the Departments of Labor and Health, Education, and Welfare. For twelve years Dirks played a major role in shaping the second-largest appropriations bill in the federal government. The budget for the two departments in 1976, the year that Dirks resigned, totaled $56.6 billion and affected the lives of millions of Americans.

Dirks and his boss, Warren Magnuson, the chairman of the subcommittee, were an outstanding example, to a greater degree even than Woodworth and the chairmen of the tax-writing committees, of the way that the power of aides and that of their Senators are interdependent. Everyone in Washington—lobbyists, bureaucrats, and Hill people—knew that the man to see on anything that had to do with labor, health, education, or welfare appropriations was Harley Dirks. The officials who ran the programs sought his help in restoring funds that had been cut by the Office of Management and Budget. Dozens of lobbyists who work for the poor, the sick, and the elderly curried his favor. Hill aides and members who wanted money for a pet project found their way to his crowded office on the first floor of the Dirksen Office Building. So many programs and so much money are involved that no Senator, and certainly not one like Magnuson, who is also chairman of a major committee, could possibly hope to master the entire budget on his own. The chairman of a subcommittee like that would inevitably rely on the staff, but Magnuson's dependence on Dirks grew over the years until it was difficult to tell where one ended and the other began.

Dirks and Magnuson first met in 1964 when Dirks was running the Lyndon Johnson presidential campaign in Washington state. Magnuson was impressed by Dirks, who was then a farmer, banker, and owner of shoe, clothing, and liquor stores in tiny (population 4,559) Othello, Washington. Magnuson asked if he would be interested in helping to shape up his Washington office. Dirks was. He first came for only three months, which soon stretched into five months and then into years.

The two got along well, and Dirks worked hard. Most mornings he was up at 5 a.m., studying reports and briefing materials stuffed into the two or three battered briefcases which he lugged home every night. He never got home early, and after dinner there were papers and memos to read out of the same briefcases that were opened again early in the morning in the recreation room of his home in the suburbs. Dirks did what Magnuson was unable to do. He mastered the programs. He fed Magnuson good advice. And through Dirks's help Magnuson was able to stay on top of his subcommittee's work and by doing so to increase his power in the Senate.

The responsibility of the subcommittee grew as Johnson's "Great Society" added ever more programs to the Department of Health, Education, and Welfare in particular. As the budget increased throughout the 1960s and into the 1970s, Magnuson came to depend on Dirks even more. Before long, Dirks's recommendations to cut or not to cut a program, to add or not to add funds, to reinstate or not to reinstate money were accepted more often than not. And as his recommendations tended to be accepted, Dirks's power grew. People around town learned that Dirks was, in the vernacular, a heavyweight. If Magnuson couldn't be reached, perhaps Dirks could be. Eventually, Dirks's phone rang first.

Self-aggrandizement is an occupational disease among staff on Capitol Hill as common as the flu in winter. Cajolery, flattery, and blandishment accompany all politicking and ease the way of all kinds of lobbyists in much the same way that scotch and soda does. And sooner or later, most staff succumb. There are few foreign affairs advisers to Senators, for instance, who do not in their heart of hearts believe that they are as important as the Secretary of State. Officially, they will always disclaim their importance, but their unguarded statements often reveal more than they intended. So it was with Dirks. Once in a conversation with a reporter about staff power he said, "A lot of staff guys kid themselves about how much power they have. I've got a lot of guys who know who Harley Dirks is but if Magnuson dropped dead tomorrow, there'd be a lot fewer of them." Dirks was right. Ultimately, an aide's power stops where the desk of the man who employs him begins. It is a political cliché that Washington is a harsh town, and there are thousands of aides who never understand why their telephone stops ringing the morning after a Congressional or presidential election. After a while, aides forget that their power is derivative. Earlier in the conversation, Dirks unwittingly revealed more about the way he actually viewed himself. Talking about the demands of his job on his family, he said, "It was difficult when [the children] were small but they've survived 12 years of their father *being in the Senate*."[21]

In the end Dirks was hoist with his own petard. His power proved to be his downfall. He resigned in disgrace at the end of 1976 after columnist Jack Anderson revealed that the hearings on which the $56 billion appropriations bill of that year was based were never held. The 4,500 pages of transcript, which contained written testimony submitted by witnesses and written remarks by members of the subcommittee, were sprinkled with remarks that made it appear that the hearing was actually held. At one point, for example, the transcript had Magnuson gaveling a subcommittee session to order and welcoming witnesses. Four months earlier Dirks, in a letter to subcommittee members, said changes in the way the testimony was handled had allowed printers to prepare a full transcript of the budget hearings and make it available to Senators in near record time.

When the phantom hearings came to light, Magnuson called what had happened "an inexcusable mistake made by a staff member."[22] But some Hill veterans felt that Dirks was merely a scapegoat. "Didn't Magnuson ever ask when the budget hearings were scheduled or why they hadn't been?" an aide said. "Didn't they ever talk over the budget?" Wherever the responsibility rested, it was natural for Dirks to assume the blame. The staff inevitably becomes the fall guy for the boss.

The extreme dependence of the Senate on its staff was clearly evident during the Governmental Affairs Committee's hearings in 1977 on the tangled financial dealings of Bert Lance, whom Jimmy Carter appointed director of the Office of Management and Budget. Before the committee and the Senate confirmed Lance's appointment, the Governmental Affairs staff had conducted a routine background investigation. The staff recommended confirmation, and on that basis the committee approved the appointment. Six months later the press began unraveling Lance's wheeling and dealing as president of a small bank in Georgia. The Governmental Affairs Committee re-opened its hearings on Lance. A crucial aspect of the hearings was exactly what Lance had told the staff during its precon-firmation investigation and exactly how thorough the staff had been in conducting it. Before a nationwide television audience the committee members were forced to quiz their own staff about the activities which had been carried out in their name but about which they knew nothing. Those days of sworn testimony by three aides were an unusual rent in the curtain of illusion which both staff and Senators conspire to draw tightly across the inner workings of the Senate.

Behind that curtain such aides as Woodworth and Dirks con-stitute a vast network of influence and power. Some aides have gone on to elective office themselves. Senator Dick Clark of Iowa once worked for Senator John Culver, also of Iowa, when Culver was in the House. Until his 1978 defeat Clark was the senior Senator from his state, and his former boss was the junior Sena-tor. Most aides, however, are happy to remain behind the scenes, where many feel they have more power than their bosses. Con-gressman Norman D. Dicks of Washington spent eight years as an aide to Senator Warren Magnuson before his election to the House. He said, "People asked me how I felt being elected to Congress and I told them I never thought I'd give up that much power voluntarily."[23] Dicks was only partially jesting.

A private world of staff exists which reflects the private world of Congress. Staff, like Congressmen, have perquisites or "perks," that go along with their position. (See Chapter 5 for a discussion of perks for Congressmen.) Staff have private elevators reserved for them and marked "Staff Only." Staff have their own cafeterias, which are barred to the public during lunch hours. A newsletter titled *STAFF* is published periodically by the Joint Committee on Congressional Operations. Like other professional and trade journals, it runs articles of interest to its readership, such as "Software, Hardware and the Hill: A Guide to Computer Use," "New [Congressional Research Service] Director Plans Im-proved Service," and "How Congress Plans for the Future." Parking places are set aside for staff, further reducing the num-ber of public parking slots in space-conscious Washington. And lobbyists and other interest groups routinely fete Congressional staff at lunches, dinners, and receptions. Most staff see no con-flict of interest in accepting such invitations. They tend to agree

with the Douglas rule, formulated by former Senator Paul O.
Douglas, that "anything you can eat, drink, or fornicate in an
afternoon" is okay.

These are the general perks. But as it is with Congressmen,
all perks are not distributed equally among staff. Senior staff are
entitled to their numbered parking spaces, carefully guarded
every morning by Capitol Hill policemen. This is an important
perk on Capitol Hill, where the parking permits outnumber the
spaces by a better than two-to-one margin. The more senior
staff, like their Congressional bosses, are invited on junkets
which are fully paid for by trade associations or foreign governments. These take them to Florida or Hawaii in the winter or
around the world during Congressional recesses. They often fly
first class, sometimes receive liberal expense accounts, and are
always ensconced in plush hotels.

Within this private world of perks and privilege staff pursue
power and influence not just for their nominal bosses but also for
themselves. The bitter rivalries and infighting among the Watergate Committee staff are part of the folklore of the Hill. Many
felt that they had finally arrived at the right place at the right
time and were determined to use the hearings for all they were
worth to advance their own careers. Some members of the staff
frequently had themselves paged in the Senate staff cafeteria so
other staff aides would be impressed with their importance. Publicly, the majority staff members were after the White House
staff but behind the scenes they were often after each other. En-
mity lingers on years later among the former aides to Senator
Sam Ervin, the committee chairman.

The year 1977 was unusual in another way. While the Bert
Lance hearings spotlighted the reliance on staff, the investigation into South Korean influence buying on Capitol Hill exposed
the ambitions of staff in a particularly raw way. The fact that
this happened in the House, where staff are traditionally much
more subservient to their bosses, made it just that much more bi-
zarre. But significantly, the aide involved, Philip Lacovara, was
a member of the Watergate Special Prosecutor's staff and was
well versed in the politics of the Watergate committee. He knew
that such investigations could make staff reputations. He also
knew he could go only as far as the committee was willing. In the
summer of 1977 the Korean investigation was on and off the

front pages of the newspapers. The press, sensing a major scandal, was intrigued by the investigation. In fact the press had taken to calling it "Koreagate." There seemed to be the possibility that if the investigation went forward and wrongdoings were exposed, the person who was in charge would be able to make his fame and fortune. The problem, as Lacovara saw it, was that the investigation was not going forward. He and the chairman of the House Ethics Committee, John J. Flynt, Jr., of Georgia, differed in a number of substantial ways. In June of that year Lacovara sent two memos to other members of the committee, without Flynt's knowledge, complaining that Flynt's failure to hold timely committee meetings was delaying the investigations. The memos found their way into the press, and Lacovara was splashed across the front pages of Washington newspapers in a way that he had not intended. The conflict between the committee chairmen and the special counsel became the major source of gossip among the Washington press corps. And the other committee members, as Lacovara should have predicted, did not rally behind him. As far as Flynt was concerned, Lacovara had overstepped his boundaries as a staff member. At a press conference Flynt said, "I did not seek this apparent confrontation. As far as I'm concerned it was unilateral." Flynt told reporters that he had hired Lacovara because he felt that he was the "best qualified" person to lead the South Korean investigation as a result of his work on the Watergate Committee. Although Flynt was saddened by Lacovara's actions, he was not about to go along with it. He said, "I think he's got to realize that he works for the committee and that he is not the committee."[24] Lacovara left shortly afterward.

In the wheeling-dealing atmosphere of Capitol Hill the ambitions of staff induce a kind of general paranoia within their private world. Staff, even more than their bosses, want to be first to introduce legislation. When Senator Birch Bayh of Indiana introduced "gasahol" legislation that would explore the possibility of making gasoline out of alcohol at the beginning of the 95th Congress, his energy aide received howls of protest from the staffs of Senators who were also interested in alternative fuels. Although the aide had been working on the bill between Congresses and the general idea was circulating around the Hill, other staffs who had not been so quick in drafting legislation felt that their Senators should have had a chance to cosponsor Bayh's bill. After his bill was introduced, anything they did would appear imitative.

Staffs are constantly afraid that their ideas and bills will be stolen. Their concern is not groundless. The staff of Senator Tom Eagleton of Missouri once was startled to pick up the *Congressional Record* and find out that the day before, another Senator had introduced a bill to amend the Older Americans Act. Eagleton was chairman of the Subcommittee on Aging, had always introduced such legislation, and fully intended to do so that year. But before he could, an aide to Senator Lloyd Bentsen through personal ties to the staff of Congressman John Brademas of Indiana, who was the House sponsor, obtained the bill shortly after passage and prevailed upon his Senator to introduce it.

Aides are relentless and determined protectors of their legislation. A staffer who discovers that his bill has been co-opted is outraged and his anger is likely to exceed that of his boss. After all, he was the one who did the work. Aides to freshman Senator John W. Warner learned a quick and brutal lesson in staff protocol when he announced a proposal that would solve the financial problems of the Washington, D.C., subway system. The funding of the metro system, which includes the Virginia and Maryland suburbs, was a long-standing problem in the area.

Warner's office issued a press release that invited elected officials in Northern Virginia to a meeting "to discuss federal legislation Sen. Warner plans to introduce to provide capital, operation and bond-retirement funds for Metrorail." A reporter who called for further information was told that Warner and Senator Charles Mathias were working together and that Mathias was a potential co-sponsor.

There was one error in that statement. Mathias had already introduced his own bill to resolve the tricky issues. When Mathias's office was called for confirmation, a long disbelieving silence followed. An aide finally said, "Give us a moment to call Warner's office for clarification. And then you should get back to Warner's people."

The second call to Warner's office drew a different response. A terrified aide said the reporter must have misunderstood. Mathias was the senior senator from the area who had been working on the problems of metro for years. Any co-sponsoring would be done by Warner, not by Mathias.

Warner personally called the reporter into his office the next day. He said, "We are working from [Mathias's] legislation. That is the starting point. He is the senior person actively working on it. He has the corporate knowledge and I'm delighted to co-sponsor with him. There's not likely to be a separate Warner proposal. I don't know how that happened." As Warner spoke, four aides took notes.

Mathias's aides reported that Warner stopped by to apologize to them and to invite them to meet with his staff to avert future misunderstandings. Mathias, meanwhile, was in West Germany speaking to the Atlantic conference in Hamburg, serenely unaware of the power plays that were going on back in Washington in his name.

Personal ties among staff are all-important in the Senate. When the Government Operations Committee agreed to consider Senator Ed Muskie's sunset bill on its own and not in conjunction with Senator Charles Percy's regulatory reform bill, the staff director of Muskie's Intergovernmental Relations Subcommittee, Al Fromm, was instrumental. As noted in Chapter 3, some Democratic members of the committee were not too keen on the alliance between the chairman, Abe Ribicoff, and Charles Percy, the ranking minority member, feeling that the Republicans had too much say in running the committee. The majority staff on the subcommittees were even less pleased about it because it reduced their influence. They habitually chafed at the high-handed treatment they thought they received from the full committee staff, especially staff director Dick Wegman. Ribicoff tended to defer to other Senators and to leave the committee in the charge of Wegman, who was less deferential to the rest of the staff than Ribicoff was to the committee members. Many subcommittee staff members had running battles with Wegman, who, they said, refused to assign legislation to their subcommittees or to schedule markups on their bills. Fromm, playing on their feelings, managed to convince aides smarting from their generally losing fights that this was the perfect opportunity to give Wegman his comeuppance. They rallied behind Fromm and in turn convinced their Senaors to back Muskie.

More formal ties supplement these informal relationships which spring up based on personal rapport, ideology, and home state ties. Press secretaries and administrative assistants have organized groups which meet regularly. The most influential and powerful of these associations is called the Chairmen's Representatives. They number less than two dozen of the top-ranking Senate staff, the staff directors of the standing committees, and aides to the leadership. Every Friday at 8 a.m. they huddle over breakfast in the staff dining room of the Capitol, discussing and rehashing the events of the past week. The meetings have no agenda. The purpose is not to reach formal decisions. Instead, it is a way for them to stay in touch, to keep abreast of the flow of legislation through the Senate, to patch up differences. If all Congressmen are not equal, neither is staff, and this group consists of those who are more equal. They are the eyes, ears, and right hands of the most powerful men in the United States Senate. Few things happen there without their knowledge and personal participation.

Just as their bosses reach crucial compromises over Perrier and lime on the official Washington party circuit, they too find socializing an indispensable part of their jobs. Washington is a town where "workaholic" is considered high praise and parties are just an extension of business hours. The Chairmen's Representatives launched their 1978 social season the day after the Panama Canal treaties were signed, at the Monocle restaurant. Located just around the corner from the Senate office buildings, the Monocle is a favorite lunch and after-hours drinking spot for staff, who find the brown banquettes a convenient place to draft legislation and launch presidential campaigns. The Chairmen's Representatives are among the most frequent patrons. As a gesture of appreciation Connie G. Valanos, the owner, scheduled a celebration. The party was dutifully covered by the *Washington Post*, and Frank Moore, head of the White House Congressional liaison office, showed up to nibble cold cuts, stuffed eggs, and pizza. Moore took the occasion to tender formal apologies to the Chairmen's Representatives for his slapdash operation when he first arrived in Washington. He came, he said, "green as a gourd but this group was very patient until we got our act together." Moore stressed he now realized he must work through the group if the administration's programs were to be passed. "The President was talking to the Speaker and the Majority Leader at the leadership breakfast this morning about some priorities for the rest of the year," he said. "And Senator

Byrd said he needed a report for the Chairmen's Representatives before we start. That shows how important you are."[25]

Thus staff, which started out as a symbol of status and an adjunct of power, has become a formidable power in its own right. It has emerged as an independent force in Congressional politics. Aides play the same games as their bosses and reap many of the same awards. And *they* need never face the electorate.

5

A Word about Perks

IN THE PRIVATE WORLD of Congress the perquisites of office, or "perks," distinguish those who have power and status from those who do not. All perks are not distributed equally, and the most important are reserved for the powerful few. Seven-term Congressman George E. Brown of California noted, "While the basic emoluments of office or fringe benefits are essentially the same for all members of Congress, these constitute only 75 to 80 percent of the total number of perks." The remaining 20 to 25 percent which are allocated unevenly possess enormous symbolic significance in the power and status game. Despite this, the public and the press have usually fixed on the general perks, which are relatively unimportant within Congress itself.

Although these common perks are not important in determining status, they are still subtly alluring. They contribute to the general ambiance of Capitol Hill. They help to remind Congressmen, who rank near the bottom of occupations in terms of public trust, that they are in fact people of consequence and deserving of respect. They help to soothe the frustrations of constant demands and too little time. They buffer and cosset and they are almost impossible to relinquish. Of all the losses that defeat entails, perks may be the hardest to give up. The House in its wisdom has tried to ease the way somewhat by extending a few perks to former Congressmen. They are given privileges of the floor, and once a year a reunion is held. A day is set aside for former Congressmen, who come from around the country, to make speeches on the floor again and to address the House. For a brief moment they are permitted to savor the power that was prematurely taken from them.

Former Congressmen have lost, however, much more than the right to speak on the floor. Congressman Bob Mathias of California, reflecting on the perks he would lose after his defeat

172

in 1974, said wistfully, "I'm going to miss having that special parking place at the airport and a free telephone in my office. I was able to call up my friends in California anytime I wanted."[1] Others miss the foreign junkets and the first-class hotels, Chivas Regal, and limousines that go along with them. They miss the deference of escorts from the embassies abroad and from the Defense Department, and the convenience of all the arrangements made in advance by others.

Gone, too, are less exciting perks. There is the members-only restaurant with its famous bean soup and the private bank, off the beaten track in an obscure corner of the Capitol, with its "Private—Members Only" sign. The bank, whose existence is a little known mystery to outsiders, arranges easy loans for members. There is the staff allowance ranging up to $225,000, free office space in Washington and back home, expense allowances ranging up to some $50,000 a year for travel, telephones and newsletters, a free trip to the district every other week, liberal retirement benefits that offer over $35,000 a year after thirty-two years service, a $47,000 life insurance policy for $434 a year, and government subsidized health insurance and free medical care. There are swimming pools, gymnasiums, steam rooms, plants and flowers from the Botanic Gardens, $2 haircuts at the barber shop, most of the books ever printed at the Library of Congress, and numerous small items such as calendars, maps, office furniture, and copies of the *Congressional Record*.

Senators who are defeated are similarly bereft. Senator Barry Goldwater of Arizona, who takes great pride in his position in the Air Force reserve, once lashed back at critics of defense spending by attacking the amount of money that Congress expends on itself. He called these perks of office the "little known and often blatant privileges enjoyed by legislators in this glass house on the Hill." He said, "In all this groveling about military allowances, I have not read one critical word in the Congressional Record about our own side benefits." Goldwater went on to catalog senatorial perks at great length. As he said, "They range all the way from free shoeshines and haircuts to ascending amounts for travel, greatly increased staff allowances and political contributions available for special purposes." Specifically, he said they included "basement stores which sell at reduced prices," "free haircuts and free towels and even ad gratis combs and hair brushes," "fine gymnasiums and excellent swimming pools," "pictures for

display in our offices . . . framed free of charge," "free potted
plants from the Botanic Gardens," and a "1,000-volume set of
lawbooks" packed "in the handsome, custom-made storage
trunks presented free for each year of service." If Senators require medical care, he said, "At the Capitol legislators have fine
medical offices, courtesy of the taxpayers. We get free medical
examinations on a priority basis—no waiting. Free prescriptions
are included. And if we are ill, two of the finest hospitals in the
world are available—Walter Reed and Bethesda Naval. The
charge is $60 a day, including any surgery we need. The govern-
ment also pays 40 percent of our group health insurance." Furthermore, Goldwater said, "Our parking garages are magnificent. Throw in parking spaces of our staff and we have a
situation where an ordinary taxpaying citizen can't find a spot to
park anywhere on the Hill or at the airports." The perks do not
end with retirement. Afterwards, Goldwater said, Senators are
hired by "big fee lobby and law firms downtown." He added,
"The lawyers among them are not hired primarily because of
their great legal skills. They are sought out because they know
the ropes of the Hill; they have special privileges on the House
and Senate floors and they have friendships that pay off for their
employers."[2]

Goldwater was nearly encyclopedic, but he missed a few general perks which make Senators' lives that much better. There
are elevators in the Senate office buildings reserved for Senators
only. All elevators can be summoned at once by three rings.
That signal requires the operators to arrive immediately at that
floor regardless of the number of other passengers or their
destinations. And he neglected a parochial perk. As the result of
a resolution passed by former Senator Norris Cotton of New
Hampshire, the desk of Daniel Webster is reserved for the senior
Senator from the state of New Hampshire.

Goldwater also failed to mention that a host of technicians
and specialists wait to attend to his and his colleagues' every
need. Among the many specialists on the Senate staff are a chief
cabinetmaker ($27,566 a year); and assistant chief cabinetmaker
($23,807 a year); three cabinetmakers ($17,000 to $18,437 per
year); a finisher ($18,437 a year); an upholsterer ($18,437 a
year); six automatic typewriter repairmen (each making $17,542
a year); and numerous other specialists, from messengers (making $10,000 to over $19,000 a year each) to computer specialists.

The House, like the Senate, is served by specialists in virtually every area a member would want to make his life on Capitol Hill comfortable. The office of the clerk and the doorkeeper match all of the specialists that are employed on the Senate side, and have a few unique ones of their own, including a venetian-blind cleaner ($14,000 a year), a library technician ($15,000 a year), a carpet technician ($20,000 a year), a carpet serviceman ($16,400 a year), a carpet cleaner ($14,000 a year), and carpet layers ($18,000 a year).

There are so many specialists on Capitol Hill that some members have even complained that overattention to their comforts causes confusion. The office manager for newly elected Senator John Heinz III, who was elected to the Senate after five years in the House, complained, "It took us three days to have someone hang a picture." She continued, "The House was never like this. Everyone is a specialist here. You want to put a nail in the wall, it's one person. You want to attach a wire to the nail, it's another person. You have to call one person to get one kind of envelope, another person to get another kind of envelope. The supply room in the House was great. Here, when we first came, the supply room was out of everything. We couldn't even get Scotch tape."[3]

Some members rate more perks than others. Perks are attached to the rank a member has in the power and status hierarchy. George Brown commented, "It is the marginal benefits of office that assume greater importance than they are actually worth, for they become a means of distinguishing members one from the other. Perks become important as you continue to advance in status and power. Perks and increments in perks over the years are another tangible way of illustrating upward mobility, as opportunity increases. Perks are to be distinguished from legislative clout, which also increases with seniority."

At the outset, Senators possess more power and status than Congressmen. Senators who previously served in the House are surprised at the deference accorded them, and the inherent power that resides in their offices. "All of a sudden I'm making a difference," said Senator John Heinz. "You have more say, more of an input, you're more intimately involved with the executive branch, your vote, you feel, counts for much more." Newly elected Senator Donald W. Riegle of Michigan said, "People do seem to pay more deference." Hawaiian Democrat Spark Matsunaga, another member of the Senate freshman class of 1976, said, "I have been on nationwide television, '60 Minutes,' how do you like that?" He added, "When I went to the House floor recently, they applauded."[4]

The distinctions between the House and the Senate reflect the informal ranking of members that always occurs on Capitol Hill. Perks are a vital part of this ranking within as well as between the House and the Senate. In the House, perks have become increasingly important as a sign of status, for the perks of senior members are symbols of power that are inviolate. As young Congressmen succeed in encroaching upon what used to be the unchallengeable private power preserves of the senior members, the perks of power remain intact. Even under the extraordinary circumstances where committee chairmen are deposed (for example, at the beginning of the 94th Congress in 1975, when three senior members lost their chairmanships) the perks that accrue to seniority, such as choice office space, remain unchanged. Once obtained, chairmanships are generally assured; however, this does not by itself guarantee the power of a chairman outside of his committee. But while the power of chairmen may fluctuate, the perks that distinguish them from their colleagues stay the same.

One House chairman, discussing the importance of his perks as chairman, said, "Power can peak and then go down. This has happened to quite a number of people. But perks do not go down." One of those perks is control over staff. Another is foreign travel. The chairman said, "Seniority and the chairmanship that goes with it carry a large increase in options for foreign travel. As a chairman you can choose where and when you want to go on foreign trips. When I first got here I wondered how this was done, and now I know. If I want to go anywhere, I simply instruct my staff to find a plausible reason and then we go."

Chairmen control substantial budgets and large staffs. At the end of the 1970s the Senate was authorizing $29 million and the House was spending $40 million annually on committee operations. Even subcommittee chairmen are in charge of hefty funds. In 1978 the House Committee on Interstate and Foreign Commerce budget was $828,500 for the full committee. At the same time Paul Rogers's Subcommittee on Health and the Environment had a budget of approximately $400,000, John Dingell's Subcommittee on Energy and Power had a budget of $764,000, and John Moss's Subcommittee on Oversight and Investigations had a budget of close to $1 million. The three chairmen controlled respectively thirteen, twenty-nine, and twenty-one staff members. The budget submitted by Paul Rogers for the 95th Congress, second session, is given in Table 1.

In the Senate, budgets are equally immense, even for relatively minor committees. In 1978 the special Committee on Aging had a budget close to $700,000 and twenty staff members. The Select Committee on Indian Affairs had a budget of $528,000 and twenty-six aides. And the Select Committee on

Table 1. 95th Congress, Second Session (1978), Budget of the Subcommittee on Health and the Environment

Personnel

(1) *Existing Filled Positions at Present Salary Levels*

Chief Counsel	$47,500
Director, Research & Planning	47,500
Staff Associates (4)	129,879
Assistant Counsel	23,551
Administrative Assistant	17,128
Staff Assistants (5)	66,508
	$332,066

(2) *Proposed New Position*

Minority Staff Associate	$25,000

(3) *Merit and Cost of Living Increases*

5 percent of all salaries excluding those of individuals paid at statutory maximum	$13,103
Total	$370,169

Other Expenses

Travel	$15,000
Stationery & Supplies	250
Telephone & Telegraph	7,000
Periodicals	1,750
Miscellaneous	13,000
Total	$37,000
TOTAL BUDGET ESTIMATE	$407,169

Nutrition and Human Needs, which was consolidated with the Agriculture Committee, had a budget close to $500,000 and seventeen staff members.

The House Administration Committee and the Senate Committee on Rules and Administration clear committee budgets. The degree to which these bodies exercise control over committee budgets is largely determined by the personalities of their chairmen. When Wayne Hays ran the House Administration Committee (see Chapter 3), he exercised a far tighter rein over House expenses than his successor, New Jersey Democrat Frank Thompson, does. But the Hays tradition occasionally reappears. For example, in the legislative branch appropriations bill for 1979, the House, with an eye on California's Proposition 13 (passed in 1978 mandating cuts in property taxes and government spending) and the spreading taxpayers' revolt, voted a 5 percent cut in its own budget. Angered by the vote against his committee's bill, Thompson began vetoeing requests for committee and office operating expenses that in the past were routinely approved. Congressman John Krebs of California found himself a victim of Thompson's new policy when he requested the relocation of one of his office telephones. "Dear John," Thompson wrote him, "in the spirit of that amendment [to the legislative appropriations bill], I must regretfully defer your request. This will result in a saving to the House in the amount of $35. Kind regards." Krebs replied acknowledging "with gratitude your letter . . . in which you were kind enough to deny the relocation of a telephone instrument in my palatial office." The telephone was eventually moved, and Krebs thereafter requested funds to frame his "Dear John" letter. Thompson said, "I was just trying to teach those guys a lesson, nothing serious."

Congressman John Brademas seized the chance to become chairman of the Accounts Subcommittee of the House Administration Committee in the 96th Congress. In order to do so he resigned the chairmanship of the Subcommittee on Education. Brademas had made a name for himself in the education field. But while the Education Subcommittee gave him visibility outside Congress, the Accounts Subcommittee offered him power within. Although committee budgets must be formally approved by the full Administration Committee, the Accounts Subcommittee performs the close scrutiny that chairmen fear. Brademas quickly authorized an increase in the budget of his parent Committee from $599,200 to $845,000. Simultaneously, he boasted that his committee had reduced the budget requests of every single other committee in the House. The reductions were minor but sufficient to alert House members that as chairman he would not rubberstamp their requests for funds.

The Senate Rules Committee, when it was chaired by Howard Cannon, exercised a certain amount of rhetorical control over committee budgets by close questioning of the chairmen and occasional budget cuts, but the legislative appropriations process remains largely pro forma. In the annual Senate budget is an item entitled "Inquiries and Investigations." Under it $28,542,700 was authorized for the 95th Congress, second session. The Rules Committee holds hearings, usually in February, based on the prior year's Inquiries and Investigations amount. Those hearings consider the budget resolutions submitted by each of the committees and determine whether or not any increases in expenses will be granted. After the Rules Committee has completed its work, the total amount of allocations becomes the next year's Inquiries and Investigations budget recommendation. The resolution goes to the Subcommittee on the Legislative Branch, which formally appropriates the funds authorized by the Rules Committee. The Legislative Branch Subcommittee does not control individual committee budgets. Officially it must vote up or down on the total Inquiries and Investigations budget compiled by the Rules Committee. "For all practical purposes, it is the Rules Committee that makes a decision [on individual committee budget allocations]," said Senate financial clerk Robert Malstrom. Senator Richard Schweiker of Pennsylvania, a member of the Appropriations Subcommittee on the Legislative Branch, said, "As long as I have been on the committee, for five years, I have never seen it [change anything]. We just rubberstamp what [the Rules Committee] gives to us."[5]

While most of the budgets of the large standing committees are shared with their subcommittees, this is not always the case. Senator Edmund Muskie, chairman of the Budget Committee, controls close to $3 million, since the Budget Committee has no subcommittees. Control over the committee's budget is a perk of Muskie that helps to distinguish him from the chairmen of smaller committees and from Senators without committees. This has not gone unnoticed. During the Rules Committee meeting in May 1977 on the next year's budget, Ed Muskie's aggrandizement alarmed his colleagues. Muskie was requesting an average salary of $30,000 for five professional staff members.

And space too, both in terms of square footage and location, is an important status symbol on Capitol Hill. Committee chairmen and ranking minority members constantly seek to enlarge these perks. The Senate Rules Committee and the House Administration Committee both face inevitable conflict among committee chairmen when they allocate space because only a limited number of rooms are available. The space crunch due to the constant demands of members and the needs of staff encourages the House and Senate leadership, in conjunction with the Architect of the Captiol, to expand Congressional office buildings into the surrounding community, despite the objections of residents. Limited budgets add to the difficulties of negotiating committee demands for more perks.

Conflicts over the perks of staff and space also occur within committees between chairmen and ranking minority members. Although the minority is supposed to receive its fair share of staff and space, the balance between chairmen and ranking minority members varies. The differences between the majority and minority continually appear and reappear as the Senate Rules Committee holds hearings on these issues.

In addition to space and staff, a grandiose hearing room is a perk of prestigious committees. A hearing room's size, location, and decor are important symbols of a committee's status. The large and ornate hearing room of the House Ways and Means Committee in the Longworth Building, with its crystal chandeliers, conveys an immediate sense of the committee's importance. The status of the House Appropriations Committee, one of the most important committees on Capitol Hill, is symbolized by its location in Suite H-218 on the House side of the Capitol. Similarly, the Senate Appropriations Committee occupies several stately rooms near the Senate chamber, in addition to a large suite of rooms in the Dirksen Office Building. Altogether the Appropriations Committee is assigned seven hearing rooms while the other committees have only one.

The limitations on space on Capitol Hill, due to the proliferation of committees and their staffs, is a severe handicap for members who are not yet chairmen, and few who lack twenty years seniority are. Edward Kennedy found after a decade on the Hill that although his subcommittees were extraordinarily active, his chairmanships alone did not guarantee sufficient space. Kennedy's imperialism in building up a large and active staff created an acute space crunch. Committee staff were often forced to work out of the personal offices of committee members, including Kennedy's. This in turn was the subject of a *Washington Post* series by Stephen Isaacs, who accused Kennedy and members of his subcommittees of co-opting committee staff for this very reason. In 1975, when Howard Cannon attacked Kennedy for his foray into the preserve of the Aviation Subcommittee (see Chapter 2), he raised the space issue. In the Rules Committee hearings on the budgets of Kennedy's subcommittees, Cannon asked about the *Washington Post* articles and about the location of staff. Kennedy replied, "I believe there are seven in the office, and over in the building — ten in the subcommittee, and up until about two weeks ago there were nine in the subcommittee and one at home. Because there was no space. As I say, I would move them all this afternoon if there is any opportunity for space. And I would say to my good friend from Michigan [Senator Robert Griffin, a vigilant defender of Republican rights to staff] if he wants to take a walk with me just down the corridor, I will show him rooms that are the size of either of ours assigned to us, in which there is one person. And [they] get the space. But there are seven at the present time [in an equivalent amount of space on my subcommittee]. There are ten in that office, seven in my other office."[6] Cannon asked, "You say there are ten in the subcommittee offices?" Kennedy replied, "Ten in the subcommittee." Cannon said, "[The] subcommittee has six rooms, so —" Kennedy interrupted, "No, no, no, no; we have two, one minority, one majority. Six rooms was an error." Cannon said, "My staff information shows six rooms." Kennedy said, "I wish we did." Finally Cannon admitted, "I am sorry, I am sorry, [there are only] two rooms, 3214 and 3216."

Cannon's questions about space and staff brought up another question: why a Senator from a relatively small state should have control over one of the largest staffs in the Senate, a staff so large that many must be housed outside the committee rooms. Senator Griffin said, "I think it also goes to the basic question, why does one Senator, by use of committee budgets have more staff for his representative state or representative political interest, if that happens to be the case, in a particular situation than other Senators when we all have or are supposed to have an office allowance for our staff to take care of our state. It gets down to that, of course, basic thing." Kennedy replied, "I mean, I think also whether we like it or not, Mr. Chairman, we have the divisions of power in the Congress, we have those that are going to be chairmen and those that are going to be ranking minority members on it. And, quite clearly, the position of chairman comes with additional responsibilities in terms of the whole leadership role in the development of a legislative body."

Inevitably, Kennedy continued, some people are going to have more power. And with that power go the trappings of power, including staff. "I am not unduly surprised," said Kennedy, "at the fact some people [have more power than others], either we are going to accept a seniority system [or not], [and] as a result of seniority [some of us] come to positions of responsibility, and therefore have to discharge those responsibilities. I mean, I think that is the way our particular system functions and works." Kennedy went on, "I do resent quite deeply as just an individual member of the Senate, in not being afforded the kind of staff opportunity to meet responsibilities as a member of the Senate." There must be perks to accompany power in the Senate, Kennedy was saying, including staff and space to house them. His staff should have the same amount of space that other staffs enjoyed.

Committee chairmen and ranking minority members also seek to increase their power and status by hiring the best possible staff, which usually translates into the highest paid staff. Aides themselves hope that working for the most powerful committee chairmen will increase their own perks, which can be measured concretely in terms of their working conditions and salaries. A Congressman who cannot provide perks to his staff that are at least equivalent to the perks that may be obtained from their Congressional peers will find himself at an acute disadvantage in attracting staff. As Abraham Ribicoff and Charles Percy presented the budget of the Governmental Affairs Committee in 1977, the Rules Committee quizzed the two Senators on the unusually high salaries of the committee staff, particularly on the Permanent Subcommittee on Investigations. Cannon told the chairman and ranking minority member of the Governmental Affairs Committee, "I may say that you have also some of the highest paid staff people in the entire Senate on the average."[7] Ribicoff replied, "Well, that may be so. I think they are good. I mean I am proud of the staff we have; they are able, they are capable, and they work hard. And one of the consequences is less friction in our committee than any other committee, I believe, in the whole Congress. Senator Percy and myself and our staffs work very, very carefully together. The staff works Saturdays and Sundays. As I say, last week we reported out three major pieces of legislation which required practically working around the clock and Saturdays and Sundays — and the staff did it." Ribicoff added, "I would rather have a well paid good man than two salaries paid at the half price to two other people." Cannon injected, "You are not implying that the other Senators don't have good staff on their committees, are you?" Said Ribicoff, "No, no, no reflection at all on that." Cannon continued, "[Your staff] is extraordinarily high [paid] at the top level." Percy explained, "We do require an unusually high number of professional people, such as lawyers. Moreover, there is no way we can pay less than comparable [salaries in the private sector] and get the quality people we need." Said Cannon, "Well, your top level salaries are higher than the Committee on Agriculture, the Committee on Armed Services, the Committee on Banking, the Committee on Budget, the Committee on Commerce, the Committee on Finance, the Committee on Foreign Relations, the Committee on Energy — and you have six people higher [in salaries], seven people higher, than all but two of the subcommittees on Judiciary, just to give you some kind of comparison." Percy said, "We need extraordinarily competent people, and in terms of cost-effectiveness the payoff is very large." To illustrate the need for well-paid aides, Percy cited the example of a committee investigation of the independent accounting and auditing profession. "You can't have an investigation of that consequence, with the whole industry pitted against us, and then trying to work toward a common solution, without very high-quality professional people," he said. "I just wouldn't dare to go into hearings like that with second-grade people." Cannon replied, "Well, I don't think some of these other committees would appreciate your referring to their staffs as second-rate people simply because they are not being paid as high as your people are, particularly when you talk about Foreign Relations, and Finance, and Commerce, and Budget and Banking, and Armed Services and Agriculture, you know."

While members of the Rules Committee tried to apply equal standards in budgeting for staff and committee space, they also

revealed inadvertently that these things had become more perks
of power than perks of office. As the Rules Committee high-
lighted Kennedy's "excessive" number of staff, it now challenged
the "excessive" salaries of the Governmental Affairs Committee
staff. It questioned its space which also appeared larger than
other committees. "The one place we are really short is space,"
Percy said. "The minority is short of space—we want to house
our people in the committee area, but we are very short of
space—but so is the majority short of space. And that is the only
request that down the line we would hope that it would be taken
into account that people simply can't work efficiently crowded
into the kind of areas that they are crowded into now." Griffin
said, "Compared to other committees, the Governmental Affairs
Committee does very well in terms of assignment of rooms. This
[chart] indicates that Governmental Affairs has 61 rooms assigned to it. I don't see any other committee on the chart that has
more than that, although I suspect that Judiciary does, but the
figure isn't here." After discovering that the Judiciary Committee had 62 rooms, Griffin went on to say, "The next highest
[committee] I see on here is the Appropriations Committee,
which has 42 rooms. I don't know whether you know where the
61 rooms are that are assigned to you, but—" Ribicoff interrupted, "Well, I think Marilyn [the chief clerk of the commit-
tee] does. The Permanent Investigations Subcommittee has 20,
but many of them are just cubby-holes that they have divided
up." Percy chimed in, "And they are over in the Annex; very
small rooms over there—where in Appropriations, some of those
rooms are like ballrooms." Percy told the Rules Committee, "We
will swap, hands down, any time with the Appropriations Committee."

While committee space is often affected by the power and
status of the chairmen, based in part upon their seniority, personal office space is allocated solely on the basis of strict seniority
formulas. In the House those who have served a certain number
of consecutive terms rank directly above those who have served
the same number of nonconsecutive terms. Except for personal
office space in the Capitol, which is controlled by the Speaker,
Congressmen select office suites in the three House office building in order of seniority. Lotteries are held among members who
have served the same number of years to determine the order in
which they will choose their personal offices. Most senior members are uniquely placed, so lotteries are unnecessary. However,

even among members who are in their fourteenth and fifteenth terms there are sufficient numbers of Congressmen so that a lottery may be the only means of resolving disputes. Approximately ten years are required to move into the Rayburn Building, and fifteen or more years are necessary before Congressmen can claim desirable space there. Paul Rogers waited twenty-two years for a corner office overlooking the Capitol dome in the Rayburn Building. The Rayburn Building is considered the prestige address by many House members. One Capitol Hill staffer remarked, "The pushy status-seekers are still scrambling to get into Rayburn, but those with real taste would just as soon stay in Longworth."[8]

Immediately after the election, Congressmen who have been returned to office send out their scouts to appraise the office suites of their defeated colleagues. Congressmen seek suites with high-status locations—for example, a corner suite in the Rayburn Building overlooking the Capitol—and some relief from the universal overcrowding. The public generally sees only the relatively spacious reception area of a Congressman's office. Outside of public view the desks of eight or ten aides are jammed into a single room. When the new Congress convenes, the office lottery is held. In 1975, for example, the lottery lasted more than eleven hours and attracted more than 200 participants. Most Congressmen sent their aides, but some House members, including Henry Reuss, Brock Adams, and John Erlenborn, went in person.[9] After the lottery, members use the numbers they have drawn as chips to claim the most desirable office they can find. Delicate maneuvering is required to prevent a member being bumped from a choice office by more senior colleagues. As Eric Nathanson and Norman Ornstein described the process, "A delicate calculus is involved here, for a member who places his bid too early or is too talkative about the virtues of the little-known-but-delightful suite he has discovered can wake up to find that he has been 'bumped' by someone with more seniority. To protect themselves against this kind of unpleasant surprise, Congressmen try to work out deals with colleagues who have drawn higher numbers. As one observer put it, 'It's like the National Football League draft—they make trades and give up priority over a good office for future considerations.'"[10]

The complicated nature of disputes over space was illustrated at the beginning of the 93rd Congress in 1973. Morris Udall came out ahead of Don Fraser in the lottery (both were equal in seniority). Both sought to move to larger and better situated quarters—a corner suite vacated by a retiring Republican. Udall's victory was short-lived, however, as he was bumped by the more senior John Ashbrook of Ohio, who, after discovering the empty suite Udall wanted, decided to move in himself. As a second choice Fraser tried to move into Edith Green's former suite, but found that one of her rooms was being converted into a hearing room. He appealed unsuccessfully to Speaker Carl Albert to retain Green's suite intact. Both Udall and Fraser, defeated in their quests for better space, kept their old offices. Meanwhile, Congressman William Steiger, who had sought Udall's office thinking the Arizona Congressman was about to move, decided that Green's quarters would be better than his present office. To Steiger's chagrin Indiana Congressman Andrew Jacobs, whose eccentricities included a Great Dane called C-5A who occasionally accompanied him onto the House floor, made an end run and, with the help of the House building superintendent, was assigned Green's suite. But Steiger had more seniority than Jacobs. Although each had served four terms, Steiger's were consecutive and Jacobs's nonconsecutive. Steiger appealed to the House Building Commission and won.[11]

The most prestigious personal offices of members are those located in the Capitol. In both the House and the Senate, Capitol offices are talked of in hushed terms, and exactly who occupies which office is a closely guarded secret. Even powerful members of the House and Senate who are supposed to know about the allocation of rooms in the Capitol are mystified. When a vitriolic debate occurred in 1976 over the construction of a new Senate office building, Senator John Culver claimed that the building was unnecessary because space in the Capitol could be allocated more efficiently. South Carolina Senator Ernest Hollings, the chairman of the Legislative Appropriations Subcommittee and a proponent of the new building, retorted, "I do not know how he [Senator Culver] knows what is going on behind the doors [of the Capitol] as he says. Sure, there is wasted space. Can you put the OTA [Office of Technology Assessment] or a Senate office in the Capitol building? What is behind the doors? We never have knocked on the doors and asked what is going on behind them. It is pure nonsense."[12] In the Senate these offices are assigned strictly on the basis of seniority, and fifty-five Senators have Capitol "hideaways." In the House fewer offices are

available to members because of the large number of rooms assigned to such support staff as the Sergeant-at-Arms, the doorkeeper, and the clerk. The Architect of the Capitol also occupies
a large number of rooms in prime space to the continuing consternation of the House leadership, which exercises control over
the allocation of rooms in the Capitol. The final report of the
House Commission on Information and Facilities, chaired by
Congressman Jack Brooks, proposed in 1977 to abolish many of
these space perquisites, including those of the Architect's office,
to make more room for House members. The commission proposed that the Architect give up some of his Capitol space "for
possible reassignment for the use of members and committees."
The Brooks report further recommended shuffling other Capitol
room assignments. The House documents room, which is located
just off the House floor, would move to the Longworth Building,
opening up this space for the clerk of the House, who would in
turn vacate a two-level office on the third floor of the Capitol.
This would provide Captiol work space for twenty additional
members who could then "do certain types of official business
while remaining close to the floor." The Capitol Architect, who
has steadfastly refused to vacate his offices, argued that his office
"is required by law to be in the Capitol Building in order to provide the required centralized supervision, control and direction
of the activities of the Office of the Architect." This prompted
an indignant outburst by Congresswoman Elizabeth Holtzman of
New York, who had been thwarted previously by the Architect
when she tried to obtain floor plans of the Capitol. She said, "I
think it is extraordinary that the Architect would assert that his
functions take precedence over the needs of members for additional space near the House floor." As an aide to Speaker Tip
O'Neill commented, "That's a bunch of recommendations"
which incorporated good ideas but which would be almost impossible to carry out.[13]

The space near the House and the Senate chambers is most
cherished, for it is of the greatest status on Capitol Hill. The
space squeeze, which was the subject of the Brooks Commission,
continues. Even senior House members are often disappointed in
their quest for rooms in the Capitol, because seniority alone does
not guarantee that the Speaker will assign a member a Capitol
office. "Offices in the Capitol are not assigned on the basis of
strict seniority," said Congressman George Brown. "Seniority

only establishes bargaining power, the right to talk to the Speaker about the assignment of rooms in the Capitol. There is a certain irrational element in the assignment of Capitol space and when space becomes available several people will of course make a claim to it. However, the Speaker decides on whatever tangible grounds he wants. The process is not subject to clear standards, and a purposeful effort is made to maintain flexibility in the system of assigning space and personnel so that these can be kept as much as possible in the largess of the Speaker." Brown pointed to the "convenience for chairmen of committees not to have to be running back and forth all the time to the Capitol" that stems from a room near the chamber. But he added, "Less than two dozen members have been given rooms in the Capitol."

In the Senate offices in the Russell (old Senate) and Dirksen (new Senate) Office Buildings, as well as in the Capitol, are assigned on the basis of a strict formula that is not within the discretion of the leadership. The number of rooms assigned to Senators is based upon state population. Eight-room suites are assigned to Senators from states with populations over 15 million; six-room suites go to Senators whose states have 7 to 9 million people, and five-room suites are given to Senators representing states with fewer than 7 million people. The Senate rules provide that the selection of office space start one week after the November elections and that assignment lists be compiled on the basis of seniority. Each Senator is given a number. The Senator who has the longest service receives number one. However, while House members with the same length of service are ranked by the lottery, incoming Senators, according to the rules of the Senate, "are arranged pursuant to the following formula: 1) those who have formerly served in the Senate; 2) those who have served as Vice President; 3) those who have served in the House of Representatives; 4) former Cabinet officials; 5) former governors of states; 6) preference based on the size of state populations; 7) in the possible instance where all other factors are equal, according to the alphabetical order of their surnames." The Senate rules on space assignment are so detailed that they provide for attic lockers "available from the superintendent of buildings on the same basis as room assignments and assigned, when possible, in the same building as the Senator's office." Senators are furnished with floor plans of Senate office buildings so they can assess their space needs. Space assignments are coordinated by an aide to the Rules and Administration Committee, who asks each Senator in order whether he wishes to move as suites become available. There is considerable movement among office suites after each election as Senators seek more desirable locations, often near their committee rooms or overlooking the Capitol, and more space. Some are forced to move three or four times before they settle into their final offices months after Congress has convened.

To help solve its space problems, the Senate in 1973 voted to construct an elaborate and luxurious new office building, which was named the Philip A. Hart Office Building in 1976. The Hart Building, which one Senator estimated will cost $185 a square foot, will be occupied by fifty Senators. Among other amenities, the building is to include 100 private bathrooms (two for each Senator's office), an indoor tennis court, a 3,000-square-foot multimedia room, wood paneling in the Senators' offices, and a rooftop restaurant.

While it is considered elaborate by many, including some Senators, and it even provoked a satiric comment in *The New Yorker's* "Talk of the Town" column, Senator Richard Schweiker expressed the attitude of most Senators and staffers. As the new building was debated, Schweiker said, "We put up with crowded conditions in the Senate that no other executive agency of the federal government puts up with. We also put up with crowded conditions that many businesses would not put up with. The General Services Administration says that for a matter of a healthy environment . . . we should have at least 150 square feet per employee. We have 65 square feet per employee." To the applause of Senate staffers Schweiker said, "You do not have to talk to many Senate staffers to find that out. Anybody who moves downtown is just aghast at the grandiose space they have there and the spaciousness of their offices compared to what we deal with here. There is no magic here. It is clearcut, 65 square feet to 150 square feet."[14]

South Carolina Senator Ernest F. Hollings, the enterprising chairman of the Subcommittee on Legislative Appropriations, was a staunch supporter of the new Hart Building. He had always fought for more space for the Senate. The fiery South Carolinian found himself embroiled in acrimonious debate in 1976 over his plan to buy for the Senate a large office building located on North Capitol Street, about a mile from the existing Senate

buildings. The debate over the Hollings proposal immediately
became entangled in a power and status battle between Hollings
and Senator John Culver of Iowa, who, as one of the principal
authors of the resolution creating the Culver Commission on the
Operation of the Senate which studied space allocation, considered the problem of space to be in *his* preserve. Hollings was
elected to the Senate in 1966, and soon became a respected
member of its inner corps. Although he was originally considered a conventional Southern conservative, Hollings led successful Senate fights in support of legislation to reduce the oil-
depletion allowance for big producers and to bring an end to
hunger in America. Some of his colleagues, especially liberal
Gaylord Nelson of Wisconsin, backed him for the position of
Majority Leader in 1976. Hollings's political antennae accurately deduced that he would have no chance in a race that might in-
volve Hubert Humphrey and Robert Byrd, and he withdrew before the Senate voted.

Out of public view, Hollings had been an active chairman of
the subcommittee that controlled internal expenses. He delved
deeply into Senate operations, quizzing closely the Architect of
the Capitol, the Secretary of the Senate, and other support agencies whose appropriations came from his committee. He not only
was a leading proponent of the new Hart Building but also supported an even greater expansion of space. When he placed before his colleagues his proposal to buy the North Capitol Street
building, he argued that it would provide "a bonus of 948 additional parking spaces which would help terminate the silly situation we now have of 2,758 permits issued for the 595 unreserved
spaces in the general parking lot, with the result that the surrounding neighborhood is inundated with the cars of Senate
staff."[15] And that ever expanding Senate staff was an additional
reason another building was needed. In a "Dear Colleague" letter Culver charged that Hollings was "unsystematic." The South
Carolinian replied that he and his subcommittee "have been
engaged in a series of hearings relative to the development of
Capitol Hill. We have been about as systematic as we possibly
could be. We had all kinds of studies." In a statement that could
only endear him to colleagues and staff alike, he added, "We
have to respond because life in the Congress is just not that
deliberate. We have to act and move as a result of the necessities.
The necessities would mandate now, if we had a systematic way,

that we all go off to jail with the OSHA [Occupational Safety and Health Administration] inspector. He would come in and he would find that we have half of the per square footage necessary for safe, healthful, operable office staff that would be found in what everybody loves today in this election year, that which is known as private, free enterprise." To Culver, he said, "I am sure the distinguished Senator from Iowa understands this, because he has been asking, like other Senators, for extra space in order to do his work."

As the debate proceeded over the building, it became a contest between Hollings and Culver on who would become the spokesman for space. Culver called attention to "his" Commission, whose report was due at the end of the year. He established his expertise from his experience as a member of the Bolling Committee that looked into space allocation in "the other body." He referred to Hollings's proposed acquisition as "a boilerplate speculative building" and "a greenhouse," because of the extent of glass in the building. Hollings replied, "I did go to La Scala last night, and I thought it was pretty good entertainment until I heard my colleague from Iowa," and added, "He has a great glamorous bunch of malarkey if I ever heard it in my life." Hollings characteristically defended his proposal with passion on the floor. The Senate was unconvinced, however, and finally voted 53–28 against the Hollings amendment to purchase the North Capitol building.

Space is a constant topic of conversation on Capitol Hill. However, the various commissions and committees which study space almost always ignore the dimension of the power and status game that is involved. In the House, for example, the Brooks Commission report recommended various rearrangements of space that would affect such powerful entities as the Architect of the Capitol. Even the House documents room, which the Brooks Commission blithely proposed to move, is powerful in its own right. Moreover, the commission recommended relocating such informal House groups as the Democratic Study Group, the Congressional Black Caucus, the Democratic Policy and Steering Committee, Democratic caucus offices, and campaign committees of the two parties that have space in the three House office buildings. Brooks suggested these groups relocate in the far less desirable and prestigious House Annex 1 or the old Congressional Hotel, often called House Annex 2. Such moves are difficult if not impossible, however, because of the internal power that these organizations have developed. In effect, the arrangement of space represents a delicate balance of power and status in each body. Although Congressmen and Senators always desire more space and better office locations, they are loath to isolate space allocations from internal politics by appointing an impartial administrator who presumably would neither understand nor follow the complex rules of the power and status game.

The Commission on the Operation of the Senate in its 1976 report echoed many of the suggestions for the Senate that the Brooks Commission was in the process of developing for the House. Significantly it was composed mostly of persons who had no Senate experience. Well-meaning they may have been but the commissioners generally failed to appreciate the political implications of their recommendations. An aide to the Senate Rules Committee said, "It simply did not know what it was doing because it did not understand the way we work around here."

Even the commissioners could not overlook the fact that the problem of space was at or near the top of Capitol Hill priorities. "Many of the most serious and recurring administrative problems of the Senate have involved such elementary needs as office and parking space," said the commission.[16] But the commissioners did overlook the political ramifications of office space and parking. If they had not, they would have refrained from suggesting that the Senate appoint an administrator to handle such matters. Many of the "antiquated" procedures the commission criticized in the Senate reflect current political realities. They are antiquated only if an attempt is made to apply managerial techniques to a Senate steeped in tradition and reverence for its own way of doing things. The commission, for instance, found, "It is often difficult for committees and subcommittees to find rooms to hold meetings at desired times. Simultaneously, other rooms stand vacant because of the possibility that meetings might be called." Inefficient as this may be, it respects the political turf of committees which have fought for their own space and have no intention of sharing it.

It is the politics of Capitol Hill, too, that results in a number of other administrative practices the commission labeled "inefficient." For example, the commission found, "The officer of the Senate in charge of parking had no list of those assigned parking spaces." Anyone who has attempted to park on Capitol Hill knows that those in charge of parking for the Senate want to maintain a certain amount of flexibility to increase their own power as they assign spaces. Any fixed parking list would reduce their discretion. The travails of parking on Capitol Hill received semiofficial recognition when humorist Art Buchwald devoted an entire column to the matter. In a column which was appreciated by people on Capitol Hill, Buchwald said that the freshman class of 1974, which rode into office on the crest of post-Watergate morality, had lost its zeal for reform due to the scarcity of parking places on the Hill. He quoted a fictitious freshman Congressman who said that if the freshmen pressed for reform, they would anger Congressman Wayne Hays, then at the zenith of his power as chairman of the House Administration Committee. As a result, they would *never* have a parking place and would never be able to make votes in time. And, consequently, they would never get reelected. Buchwald concluded that reform floundered because of a lack of parking spaces on the Hill. The lack of adequate parking space is a constant frustration and aggravation. A parking space remains an important perquisite of top staff and members. In the House each office is allocated a certain amount of space for parking, and while all members have their assigned parking spaces, parking can be a perk of power even among members. A senior Congressman pointed out that some members get to park in restricted space by the Capitol steps. "I honestly don't know how this is arranged, but certain senior members, who spend time at the Democratic Club near the Capitol, simply park their cars there and no questions are asked. They can get away with things others cannot," he said.

Attempts to do away with the parking perks of members and staff have failed ignominiously. In the Senate, Charles Percy once offered an amendment to an energy bill that would have required government employees, including Congressmen, to pay a parking fee for the use of federally maintained lots. The amendment was defeated 56–25. Senator Gary Hart of Colorado also has proposed fees for parking. This matter is taken so seriously on Capitol Hill that Nordy Hoffmann, the Senate sergeant at arms, prepared a lengthy parking questionnaire which asked Senate employees about their particular parking problems and whether they would support pay parking. Hoffmann revealed the results of the questionnaire in testimony before the Legislative Appropriations Subcommittee in 1978. Committee chairman James Sasser asked Hoffmann if he would care to comment on Senator Hart's proposal to charge up to $50 a month for parking. To laughter Hoffmann responded, "I just thought you might ask that question." He continued, "I had prepared for me a Senate parking questionnaire which we just completed. Question No. 8 reads: Paid parking may again be proposed for the Senate. Please indicate your attitude toward this issue. Answer: 210 were for it; against it, 1,670. 88 percent are opposed to that. The total response to the question was 1,880." As laughter continued to ripple throughout the room, Senator Richard Schweiker asked, "Who were the 210?" Hoffman responded, "They belong to the Independent Party. If you think I am not partisan, you are crazy." Hoffmann opposed paid parking, he said, because with only 3,500 spaces for 4,350 people, it was helpful to stagger parking hours. A pay system would make this more difficult since each employee would be entitled to a set number of hours. "I just think we are not ready for it yet," said Hoffmann. "Unless you people want to build an underground garage someplace. I haven't found the Senate is too much interested in that. I tried to buy a building a year ago and got knocked down, so I am leasing space in it now."[17]

Failing to deal with the politically sensitive parking issue, the Culver Commission turned to other examples of "inefficiency." The commission was surprised to find that "carpentry shops are maintained by both the Architect of the Capitol and the Senate sergeant at arms for different, though sometimes overlapping, purposes." The Architect of the Capitol and the sergeant at arms are entirely different political entities on Capitol Hill, and they do not want to share their employees under any circumstances. Tradition, too, is responsible for the fact that the commission found numerous instances "where official job descriptions no longer reflect actual duties but continue to appear in Senate reports. At the time of our study, for example, barbers were described as laborers. The nominal assistant chief telephone operator, was, in reality, the chief maid. In numerous instances committee employees are listed for budgeting and accounting purposes as temporary when, in fact, they are permanent employees. In one case, a committee staff director was unable to distinguish between temporary and permanent employees without consulting the files, and, in fact, misguessed as to which was which." These results often occur because the secretary of the Senate and the sergeant at arms, who are in charge of personnel policies carry out their responsibilities in their own fashion.

More staff and better space are two of many perks that are distributed among members on the basis of their power and status on Capitol Hill. As committee chairmen are gathering extra staff, office space, and travel funds, they find that in the power-oriented world of Washington their elevated positions on the Hill bring them into closer contact with the top ranks of the executive branch. George Brown mentioned as an important perk of his chairmanship and seniority the "greatly improved communications with the executive branch the longer you stay here. Secretaries, assistant secretaries, deputy and undersecretaries are almost always available to come over to your office to chat." He added, "I felt highly flattered when Jim Schlesinger called me at home and told me he was going to make the appointment of an assistant secretary for the environment, whose responsibilities fall within the jurisdiction of my subcommittee." Even with Republicans in power in the White House, top bureaucrats defer to senior members of Congress because the bureaucrats' agencies and ultimately their power depend upon Congress.

Committee chairmanships also bring with them highly prized invitations to the White House, for bill signings in the Oval Office and to state dinners. Carter's failure to understand the use of these accepted perks contributed to his constant troubles with Capitol Hill. When Carter took office, he intended to draw up new rules to replace the old-style politics that he had so vehemently assailed throughout his campaign. Everyone was to be dealt with equally, and the grandeur of the White House was not to be used for political manipulation. The powerful chairmen and leaders of Congress were not to be given special privileges. For as long as anyone could remember, the Speaker of the House, for example, received extra seats for his friends and cronies to the inaugural parade and the balls that followed. Speaker Tip O'Neill was chagrined to find that he could not get the seats that he wanted for the inaugural festivities from President-elect Carter.

Congressman George Brown pointed to a number of other benefits which accrue to those in the top echelon of the power hierarchy in the House. Only the more senior members, he said,

can hope to exercise control over the more than 500 patronage
jobs in the House. These include pages, elevator operators,
various employees in the clerk's office, the office of the doorkeeper, and the office of the postmaster, and the Capitol Hill
police force under the sergeant at arms. House patronage is controlled by the Speaker through his power to appoint the chairman of the Democratic Personnel Committee, which handles all
patronage appointments. Persons appointed under the patronage system have in their official personnel file the statement that
they have been "appointed on the patronage of Congressman
X," even after the Congressman has left office. Generally a Congressman's retirement or defeat means a turnover in his patronage appointments, although some, such as the Capitol Hill
police force, are not so casually treated. Congressmen claim that
it is at least ten years before the patronage committee pays any
attention to them, and then, in the words of George Brown, they
tell a Congressman that "we will try to help you if we can."
Brown said, "The most senior Congressmen control approximately six patronage slots, although patronage allocations are
purposely kept as fuzzy as possible." The perk of patronage is
generally unknown to freshmen, who are apt to say, as one in
fact did, "What patronage? I didn't know there was such a
thing." Patronage is also a perk of power and status in the Senate
and is controlled similarly by the leadership of both parties and
the senior members.

Another key perk in both the House and the Senate, although more important in the House, is the appointment to
boards, commissions, and joint committees. In the House this is
at the sole discretion of the Speaker. In the Senate this power
resides in the President pro Tempore, which essentially means in
the hands of the Majority Leader and senior Senators. Since the
Joint Committee on Atomic Energy was abolished in 1977, the
only remaining joint committee of any consequence has been the
Joint Economic Committee. The chairmanship of this committee
rotates between the House and the Senate every two years as a
new Congress takes office. In the 95th Congress Richard Bolling
of Missouri was the chairman of the JEC. The membership included such powerful Democratic Congressmen as Henry S.
Reuss of Wisconsin, chairman of the Banking Committee; ten-
term William S. Moorhead of Pennsylvania, chairman of the Economic Stabilization Subcommittee of the Banking Committee,

and Gillis Long of Louisiana, a rising star in the House power structure.

Seniority also brings appointments to joint boards such as the Technology Assessment Board. This board is the result of the same legislation sponsored by Edward Kennedy in the early 1970s that created the Office of Technology Assessment. The board oversees the activities of that office. "It's a symbol of status," said George Brown, who was appointed to the board by O'Neill. "It also is a political value to the holder of it." Brown is rapidly moving up in seniority on the House Science and Technology Committee, ranking fourth in the 96th Congress, and is chairman of the Subcommittee on the Environment and the Atmosphere. He finds that membership on the Technology Assessment Board fosters his House reputation in the scientific field.

International conferences and international travel constitute a perk that is taken seriously in both the House and the Senate. Congressmen fought to become members of a special Congressional honor guard to escort the Magna Carta on loan from the Queen of England to the U.S. Capitol where it was displayed during the Bicentennial.

The Magna Carta trip was approved after heated debate in both bodies of Congress. The selection of delegates was an important leadership perk. In the House, the Speaker was given the authority to appoint twelve members on the recommendation of the Majority and Minority Leaders. In the Senate the Majority and Minority Leaders were to select twelve of their colleagues as delegates. Richard Bolling was the floor manager of the resolution authorizing the trip in the House and Senate Majority Leader Mike Mansfield guided the legislation there.

On the day the resolution was introduced in the House, Maryland Republican Robert Bauman, a second-term Congressman who was gaining a reputation as a humorless gadfly, called the proposed trip an unwarranted junket. Minority Leader John Rhodes, who was eagerly looking forward to going to London, told his Maryland colleague, "I am sure the gentleman from Maryland would not want a delegation from this body to go in any way other than in a manner in accordance with the dignity of this body. There is a considerable amount of dignity in this body, I maintain, and it would be my hope, certainly, that we could go ahead with this piece of legislation."[18] The resolution was first introduced in the House as Senate Concurrent Resolution 98, but since the leadership had not paved the way for its acceptance, it was rejected by a vote of 167–219. However, Bolling reintroduced the resolution as H. Res. 1086 a week later, and after a lengthy and acrimonious debate, costing by one member's estimate almost twice as much as the Magna Carta trip itself, the House voted for the resolution 294–98. Bauman again led the attack, which included a remark slighting the ancestry of Wayne Hays who strongly supported the trip.

Hays had irritated Bauman, who was partly of German extraction, by acidly saying that the real purpose of the American Revolution was to give the opportunity for "a bunch of Englishmen on this side of the Atlantic to kick the hell out of a bunch of German mercenaries." Bauman replied, "I would like to inform the gentleman from Ohio, whose name does not suggest any particular ancestry, that the gentleman from Maryland is indeed of German extraction but his grandfather was a British civil servant." Hays rose. "Mr. Speaker and members of the House," he said, "in view of the abysmal lack of knowledge displayed on other matters by the gentleman from Maryland, I am not surprised that he would not know the origin of my name. I do not think it really worth taking much time to explain it to him, except to say that it predates the Magna Carta by about two centuries. And if he would take some time to go to Aberdeen, in Scotland, and make a speech there that nobody ever heard of Hays, we would be spared having him in this body any more, especially if he made it in some pub on Saturday night." Wayne Hays was not the only colleague Bauman irritated. California Congressman James Corman, a senior member of the House who held an important Ways and Means Subcommittee chairmanship, suggested that the Speaker appoint Bauman to the Magna Carta delegation. "He is young," Corman told his colleagues, "he looks vigorous, and I think this would be a better House if he would travel some."[19]

The Senate too had its difficulties with the Magna Carta trip. After routine approval on March 4, 1976, the Senate, which had now received the House resolution, voted on April 5 to reduce the size of the Congressional delegation from twenty-four to eight members. It was an evening session, and the Senators present were ready to go home. Alabama Senator James Allen suggested that those going on the trip should pay their own expenses. There would be fewer junkets, he said, if members had to pay for their own foreign travel. This prompted Colorado Senator Gary

Hart to ask if even members of the Senate Armed Services Committee should have to pay for their own travel. As Hart and Allen exchanged verbal blows, John Pastore of Rhode Island interrupted. "Mr. President," he said, "this may be funny." "It is not," replied Mansfield. "I never thought it started out to be funny," said Pastore, but he continued, "all of this comedy, all of this nonsense, I think is a disgrace. It is a disgrace. Do you want the Magna Carta? Then do it the way the people over there asked you to do it, and if you do not want to do it, just tell them that you refuse the invitation. That is what you ought to do in a manly, courageous fashion." He concluded, "All these gobbledygooks about junkets, and this and that, you ought to be ashamed of yourself." Mansfield agreed. He chastised his colleagues, "I do not know whether we are acting like barons or not, but I do know that we are making a ridiculous spectacle of ourselves." He continued, "Do we have no appreciation of an offer extended in good faith by those . . . whom we defeated to acquire our independence? Do we not have any sense of decency and dignity and decorum? Talk about junkets. I have never made a trip overseas that I did not, on my return, file a report. Junkets. Almost every trip I have had has cost me money, not the government. Here we have one plane going over, supposedly to take 25 members of the Congress of the United States, it costs just as much for 12 as it does for 25. I hope we will get away from this immaturity. This body of mature people are supposedly capable of acting. I hope we will get down to the realities of the situation." In conclusion, he said, "Have your fun. Cut down the funds. Make a mockery of these trips that we make overseas. Call us junketeers, if you will. But you are only making fools of yourselves, and, in doing that, you are making a fool out of this institution."[20]

The Senate rescinded its previous action and went on to approve a twenty-four-member delegation. Fifty-one persons went on the London trip. The delegation included nineteen members of Congress, fifteen of their wives, the son of Congressman Peter W. Rodino, Jr. of New Jersey, ten Hill staffers, the chairman of the American Revolution Bicentennial Administration, and five escorts from the State and Defense Departments. The Defense Department supplied the plane and liquor and food for a sumptuous in-flight meal. For the twelve-hour round trip, the plane stocked eight quarts of vodka, four quarts of Beefeaters gin, four quarts of Jack Daniels whiskey, two fifths of Wild Turkey, two

quarts of Canadian Club, six fifths of Chivas Regal, and a quart
of Bacardi rum.

Foreign junkets are not limited to senior Congressmen and
committee chairman, but they have more frequent opportunities
to travel abroad. They control their own committees' budgets,
and their positions can lead to thank-you's for favors done in invitations for foreign trips. In 1976, a typical year, 204 members
of Congress took at least 309 trips abroad at government expense. The total cost to the government was $2.4 million. Usual-
ly members of the Senate Foreign Relations Committee and the
House Foreign Affairs Committee travel frequently and far. Senator Jacob Javits and Congressman Steven J. Solarz, members of
the New York delegation on these committees are among the
most peripatetic Congressmen. Congress is one of sixty members
of the Interparliamentary Union (IPU) and periodically elects
delegates to visit the parliaments of other countries. Illinois
Republican Congressman Edward J. Derwinski, who was a senior member of the House Foreign Affairs Committee, visited
Greece, Cyprus, Switzerland, Great Britain, and Mexico as an
IPU delegate in 1976. Steven Solarz, whose trips are often publi-
cized because of his unusual restlessness for a junior member of
Congress, said that the perks of power continue even overseas. As
a member of the Africa Subcommittee, he traveled extensively in
Africa in 1976. Stopping at Timbuktu with the chairman and
the ranking member of the committee, he found that chairman
Charles Diggs was provided with a room, a fan, and a mosquito
net. The ranking Republican member of the committee, Charles
Whalen, was supplied a room and a mosquito net, but no fan.
Solarz was given only a room. The "murderous mosquitoes and
sweltering heat" drove Solarz out of his room and into the Sahara
Desert, where he slept. "That was no pleasure trip," he said. By
contrast, when five-term Congressman James Scheuer of New
York visited Great Britain as an IPU delegate at the beginning of
1976, the American Embassy in London provided rented limousines and chauffeurs, including a Rolls Royce on New Year's
Day. When it was revealed that the limousines cost the taxpayers
$1,094.58, Scheuer decided to use taxis in the future. In the 95th
Congress he became chairman of the Domestic and International Scientific Planning, Analysis, and Cooperation Subcommittee, which was created for him. At the end of second session
of the 95th Congress, he scheduled a trip to China, and invited

members of the parent Science and Technology Committee to go along. Scheuer's subcommittee, with its unlikely name, seemed to require international travel.

Travel possibilities increase if a member sits on the Senate Foreign Relations Committee, the House Foreign Affairs Committee, or either Armed Services Committee. Membership on these committees is highly sought after in its own right, and the committees are generally composed of the more powerful and influential members. In one three-month period, for example, the House Armed Services Committee spent over $133,000 on two trips that required Defense Department planes and personnel. Members of the committee have frequently circled the globe at government expense. While most junior members of Congress travel seldom or not at all, the senior members, especially the leadership, may take three or four expensive trips during Congressional recesses. (To escape the idle connotations of "recess," the House renamed these periods "district work week" in 1977.) During one such week, Congressman Jack Brooks of Texas, chairman of the Government Operations Committee and its Subcommittee on Legislation and the National Security, took the members of his subcommittee to Paris and London to examine the operation of the American embassies there.

The special perks of committee chairmen are magnified in the offices of the leadership in both the House and the Senate. The leadership is furnished extensive and prestigious space both in the Capitol and in the House and Senate office buildings. Some of these offices offer breathtaking vistas along the Mall all the way to the Washington Monument. Others glitter with gold leaf painstakingly applied to walls and ceilings. Crystal chandeliers sway above thick carpets. Red velvet curtains drape the windows, and oversized, tufted leather couches provide quiet comfort. Floor-to-ceiling mirrors in gold frames reflect the comings and goings of visitors and aides, while massive oil paintings of past leaders encased in ornately carved frames look on.

Due to their positions, leaders control substantial funds for staff. In 1979, House leaders received the following appropriations: Speaker, $545,300; Majority Leader, $384,100; Minority Leader, $479,100; Majority Whip, $416,800; Minority Whip, $321,800. Tip O'Neill managed to bring both the Steering Committee and the Rules Committee under his control which netted approximately $500,000 more for extra staff. Republican leaders also gain additional staff and space by controlling party groups. Congressman John Anderson of Illinois, chairman of the House Republican Conference, controls twenty-nine extra employees. Congressman John Rhodes, the Minority Leader, has six more aides at an average salary of over $40,000 a year.

Both the Majority and Minority Leaders of the Senate received $410,984 in fiscal 1979 for the operation of their offices. In addition, each of these leaders has a staff assistant paid $51,500. The Majority and Minority Whips in the Senate are budgeted at $238,428. Moreover, Majority Leader Robert Byrd controls an additional $131,386 as chairman of the Democratic Conference. The same figure is budgeted for the Senate Republican Conference.

Leaders are set apart by other important perks. Chauffeured limousines are provided for the Speaker, the President pro Tempore, and the Majority and Minority Leaders of the House and the Senate. When Lyndon Johnson was Majority Leader, he demanded a telephone in his limousine when he found out that Minority Leader Everett Dirksen had one installed in his limousine. On his way to the Hill, Johnson delighted in calling Dirksen. "Ev," he said, "you're not the only one with a telephone now."

A final perk is the weekly leadership meetings at the White House. Since Carter began the practice of billing the Speaker's office for the coffee and doughnuts at the breakfasts with House leaders, these meetings may be less cherished, but they remain an important symbol of status on the Hill.

In the House, which in some ways has more esprit de corps than the Senate, the prerogatives of leadership linger on even after retirement. A former Speaker, like former Congressmen in general, retains some of the perks which he enjoyed in office. He is entitled to a budget for staff which he may use at his discretion. In 1979, for instance, Carl Albert was allocated $649,200 for his staff in Oklahoma.

An important part of the cachet that attaches to position and power in Congress is based on perks. Their unequal distribution makes them a valuable indicator of status. The intricate maze of perks helps to answer the vital question of the Hill—who has power and who does not.

6

Power and Reform
in Congress

WHILE REFORM AND reorganization on Capitol Hill are almost exclusively an internal matter involving struggles for power and status among members, the rhetoric describes the need for a more effective Congress in making policy and for a more powerful Congress in dealing with the President. The rhetoric of reform masks the underlying forces at work.

The major effort to reform the House in the 1970s can be viewed as nothing more nor less than a power play by Congressman Richard Bolling of Missouri. Elected in 1948, Bolling was a protege of Speaker Sam Rayburn, who tutored him in the arcane ways of the House. He aimed at the leadership from the very beginning. He won a seat on the Rules Committee, which then tightly controlled the flow of legislation to the floor. But after Rayburn's death, Bolling's career faltered. He was passed over for Majority Whip by John McCormack, who succeeded Rayburn. He ran for the Majority Leadership in 1962 against Carl Albert but the votes were not there and he withdrew his candidacy. Bolling became disenchanted with the House in the 1960s. He turned to writing and published two books that criticized severely House organization and procedure and Speaker John McCormack's leadership: *House Out of Order* and *Power in the House*.[1]

Bolling remained on the Rules Committee during the 1960s, and emerged a close adviser to Speaker Carl Albert. Although the committee was dormant during the latter 1960s, Bolling, the third-ranking member, clearly saw a future for himself there. (He became chairman in the 96th Congress in 1979.) Early on he decided to exploit his newly recognized expertise in House orga-

203

nization and procedure. He became an active chairman of a Rules subcommittee that recommended the establishment of the Committee on Standards of Official Conduct, which eventually produced a code of ethics for the House. He was also a member of a Rules subcommittee that drafted the Legislative Reorganization Act of 1970. His mastery of the ways of the House was unmatched.

Through reorganization Albert and Bolling hoped to expand and solidify their power in the House. The resolution to create the Select Committee on Committees, commonly called the Bolling Committee, was voted out of the Rules Committee on January 30, 1973, and brought to the floor under a closed rule which prevented any amendments. The committee was embroiled immediately in controversy, since key members of the House, particularly Wayne Hays, the chairman of the House Administration Committee, rightly felt it was a threat to their power. Hays believed all matters which dealt with House administration properly fell within his jurisdiction. The resolution creating the select committee carefully established its budgetary independence. Bolling would never have agreed to any other arrangement.[2] The select committee, which the House approved 282–91, was appointed by Speaker Carl Albert. Although Albert formally selected the committee, he and Bolling worked together.

Bolling had promised his colleagues that the committee members would represent the overall views of the House. The committee was composed of conservatives and liberals and members from all geographic regions. This balance, however, could not insure its success because reform was not an ideological issue, but a matter of internal power. The Bolling Committee included neither powerful committee and subcommittee chairmen nor representatives of the various factions of the Democratic caucus leadership. Eventually these groups banded together to defeat the work of the select committee.

The Rules Committee dominated the select committee. Bolling was chairman, and the ranking minority member of the Rules Committee, David Martin of Nebraska, was vice chairman. Naturally enough, as the committee proceeded with its deliberations Bolling and Martin attempted to defend and enlarge the power of the Rules Committee.

The select committee mandate was broad. House Resolution 132 required "a thorough and complete study . . . [of the] committee structure of the House, the number and optimum size of committees, their jurisdiction, the number of subcommittees, committee rules and procedures, media coverage of meetings, staffing, space, equipment, and other committee facilities." The committee was directed to report out a resolution that contained its organizational and procedural recommendations.

At the outset of the hearings, Speaker Carl Albert made an unprecedented appearance. For over 100 years Speakers have refused to testify before committees of the House to maintain the appearance of impartiality. This was an unusual situation, however, since the Speaker had helped to establish the committee in order to strengthen his control over the burgeoning subcommittee fiefdoms. Albert wanted to be on the record in support of reorganizations that would strengthen the position of the leadership and, rhetorically, make the House more efficient. He left no doubt that the task of the committee was solely a matter of internal concern, and that the committee's work would serve the interests of the leadership. As far as Albert was concerned, the principal issue of reform was the ability of the Speaker to control the House. He said, "I do not wish to impose the powers of my office or my personal views upon this committee. Every member of the House views the committee system from his own unique perspective. The Speaker, however, feels the impact of the committee system in a particularly personal way as he attempts to fulfill his responsibilities to the House and to the nation."[3]

While the committee system has its own rationale and often works very effectively, Albert said, it is the Speaker who ultimately is responsible for legislation. The Speaker is judged by his ability to exercise leadership in the legislative process, but, Albert argued, House organization and procedures prevented the kind of leadership his colleagues demanded. He implied that the real power of the House rested not in the hands of the Speaker but in the committees. Albert knew that he was considered a weak leader, and his statement before the select committee constituted a partial excuse for his ineffectiveness.

As the Bolling Committee began its hearings, it sought to build a public record in support of reform. However, the testimony before the committee, particularly from chairmen who had a vested interest in the status quo, was decidedly hostile to the commitee's objectives. The ranking minority members of committees were willing allies of their chairmen, since they too benefited from the system. For the Democratic establishment of the House—the committee chairmen, the caucus leaders, and aspiring leaders such as Phil Burton, and even for junior members whose seats on desirable committees were at stake—the select committee posed a serious threat.

Chairman after chairman of the major House committees appeared to testify publicly against any reform efforts that would reduce his jurisdiction. Privately, the chairmen pressured Bolling and his staff to keep the existing arrangements. The strategy of the committee chairmen was characteristic of reform politics on Capitol Hill. Each chairman cited the need for reorganization but pleaded for the exemption of his committee.

The chairman of the Committee on the Post Office and Civil Service, Congressman Thaddeus J. Dulski, a sixteen-year veteran of the House, confronted a particularly difficult uphill battle. Dulski could not justify his committee's existence by pointing to an executive department under his jurisdiction. In fact, the Post Office Department had been abolished and replaced by the independent Postal Service Corporation in 1970. Martin, the Republican vice chairman, pointed out to Dulski, "Since we now have a postal system and it is pretty much removed from the jurisdiction of the Congress . . . it would appear that your committee does not have nearly the work load that it previously had." Dulski was unabashed. In the best traditions of Lewis Carroll political logic, Dulski argued that as a result of the abolition of the Post Office Department the committee was needed now more than ever. "Well, Mr. Martin," Dulski responded, "let me put it in this perspective. Since postal reorganization we have had more complaints on service than we had before. In fact, the only legislation we no longer consider are rates and postal employee benefits. Yet, I should add that last Congress we were involved specifically in post employee benefits and this year we have a major rate bill under consideration." Moreover, Dulski added, "We are conducting extensive hearings right now because of our oversight responsibilities. There has been a great deal of difficulty to get the postal organization into operation, and that's the reason we have these hearings . . . to see if we need legislation to correct the situation."[4] He even pleaded for more staff to meet the increased responsibilities of his committee.

Some chairmen defended their committees by employing the old political strategy of "Don't touch me, don't touch him, touch the fellow behind that tree." Richard Ichord, chairman of the

Internal Security Committee targeted for elimination, suggested that if the committee was bent on reorganization it should delve into such areas as transportation where jurisdiction was scattered. Ichord testified, "Jurisdiction over transportation matters is now shared by at least five committees of the House."[5] The creation of the Department of Transportation, consolidating transportation responsibilities in the executive branch, justified a similar consolidation over transportation on Capitol Hill.

Ichord knew that he was touching a sensitive chord in even mentioning the scattered transportation jurisdictions. The Merchant Marine and Fisheries Committee, under its scrappy and combative chairwoman, Lenore K. Sullivan of Missouri, would be a major target of such a consolidation. Merchant Marine and Fisheries had long been under attack by Congressmen whose own interests were not at stake, because, they said, it was a captive of the industries under its purview. Their access to the committee had been greatly strengthened over the years by regular contributions to the reelection campaigns of its members.

Again, at stake was not the policies or practices of the committee, but internal power. Its jurisdiction overlapped a number of committees including Interstate and Foreign Commerce and Public Works. Many members felt that it was a good target of reform because its abolition would in no way affect their turf.

Sullivan, naturally, scorned such reform notions.[6] She had served in the House for twenty years, winning election after the death of her Congressman husband in 1952, and she had just become a committee chairman. She had not taken over the chairmanship to preside over the dismemberment of her committee. She was outraged by the behind-the-scenes maneuvering that was aimed at her committee. In definite terms she told the Bolling Committee, "I am confident that you will agree after hearing my statement that the Merchant Marine and Fisheries Committee rests on a logical, coherent jurisdictional base and has established an impressive legislative record." The abolition of her committee would toll the death knell, she said, of an already beleaguered maritime industry.

Sullivan justified her committee's continued existence on the basis of the number of bills it reported out. In her statement for the record Sullivan wrote, "The record of legislative production of the House Merchant Marine and Fisheries Committee is as big or greater than any other committee in the House and I would point out that this legislative record is compiled by a committee staff of only approximately 21 individuals."

Sullivan eventually turned to the staff of Merchant Marine and Fisheries to mobilize the committee's outside constituency in its defense. Even more than Sullivan, the staff felt that their power as well as their jobs were threatened by attacks upon their committee. The staff and industry lobbyists produced a letter-writing campaign. Some 175 letters and telegrams were received by the Bolling Committee on behalf of Merchant Marine and Fisheries.[7] The Federal Maritime Commission, a regulatory agency, unanimously passed a resolution supporting the Merchant Marine and Fisheries Committee.

As committee chairmen continued to defend their power before the Bolling Committee, members realized that real reform — that is, meaningful redistribution of power — was impossible. Congressman James C. Wright of Texas, then the chairmen of the Committee on Public Works and later the Majority Leader, articulated the views of many senior members when he said, "I suppose there is inherent in each of us a certain tendency toward empire building, and every committee of the House undoubtedly feels that it is best qualified to handle the subject matter that it now handles and probably most competent to take on additional subject matter."[8]

The select committee prepared a controversial working draft of a report in early December 1973. It proposed, for example, to abolish the Merchant Marine and Fisheries, and the Internal Security and Post Office Committees. The Small Business Committee was to be merged with Banking and Currency. It recommended enough jurisdictional transfers among committees to alienate a number of influential chairmen, who allied themselves against the Bolling report. Many members whose committees would be abolished or substantially reduced through jurisdictional transfers were also opposed. The select committee's recommendations were enough to alienate the Democrats who had the most at stake and virtually every other member of the House as well.

Bolling had set out to do a job for the leadership and to boost his reputation as an expert in House organization and procedure, and he succeeded. Although the committee's report angered many members, Carl Albert was pleased. (A section of the report specifically detailing the assistance to the leadership was struck to avoid further antagonizing members.) Both the Speaker and the Rules Committee would benefit from the proposed reorganization of the entangled jurisdictions of competing House committees. However, as a practical political matter, it was suicidal to transfer control over elections and campaign financing from the House Administration Committee to the Committee on Standards of Official Conduct. Eliminating the Merchant Marine and Fisheries Committee was, as Bolling admitted during the committee hearings, another politically dangerous move. And even the seemingly relatively minor shifts in jurisdictions of the Ways and Means Committee—for example, its control over trade to the Foreign Affairs Committee—angered powerful members, who worked vigorously behind the scenes to defeat the Bolling plan and who voted almost unanimously against it on the floor..

As the 94th Congress convened in January of 1974, the House began to digest the initial Bolling report. Predictably, the response depended on whether a member stood to lose or gain. Newly elected freshmen who had little at stake were willing at first to support the select committee publicly. However, as they began to sense the powerful opposition building as the plan wended its way to the floor, the majority withdrew their support. The freshmen, realizing that Bolling had managed to bestir every power center in the House, saw that their support would antagonize the committee chairmen whose approval was essential to their careers.

Even before the opposition began to mount, the select committee reconvened to try to salvage its plan. First of all, it reinstated the Merchant Marine Committee in face of the vociferous opposition fomented by members and staff. Second, it took a new look at the jurisdictional realignments.

Among the most controversial proposals were the reduced jurisdictions of the Interior Committee over forest and wilderness areas and of the Merchant Marine and Fisheries committee over wildlife, fisheries, and marine affairs. These jurisdictions were to be transferred to the Agriculture Committee. The select committee argued that this would broaden the narrow commodity orientation of the Agriculture Committee. Congressman John Dingell, a member of Merchant Marine and Fisheries, was beside himself when he learned of the intended transfer. Other members of Merchant Marine and Fisheries and the Interior

Committee were equally mad, and they were supported by the Sierra Club and other environmental groups. Agriculture chairman W. R. Poage, of course, was delighted. The select committee, however, retreated and, in response to internal Congressional pressures, struck these provisions from the report.

The select committee altered its initial draft in other ways. It originally recommended an Energy and Environment Committee that would have been superimposed on the Interior Committee. This was scuttled because the proposed new committee would have been far more attractive and powerful than the Interior Committee. The jurisdictional transfers which were needed to set up the new committee alarmed chairmen of existing committees. Congressman Chet Holifield of California, chairman of the Government Operations Committee that would receive jurisdiction over Indian affairs, objected that this would be inappropriate for his committee. The select committee could not very well change jurisdictions with objections both from the committee that would lose and the committee that would gain. In the end, the revised draft established a separate Energy Committee that would take jurisdiction from more than a score of House committees. This only served to make the revised report even less acceptable than the original.

Even relatively minor changes stirred strong protests from some of the most powerful members of the House: Wilbur Mills, Congressman Herman Schneebeli of Pennsylvania, the ranking Republican on Ways and Means, and Armed Services chairman F. Edward Hebert of Louisiana. Bolling had tiptoed carefully around the fringes of Ways and Means and Armed Services jurisdictions, but even a little encroachment was too much. Hebert strongly objected to sharing jurisdiction over foreign intelligence with the Foreign Affairs Committee. The Armed Services Committee even circulated rumors that some members of the Foreign Affairs Committee were security risks who could not be trusted with military intelligence. Bolling ordered his staff to consult Hebert's staff and to redraft the proposal, so that primary jurisdiction over military intelligence would remain with the Armed Services Committee.

The select committee drafted H. Res. 988, which incorporated the political compromises that had been worked out, in March 1974. All ten members cosponsored the new resolution. By now Bolling realized that his Democratic colleagues, especially the caucus leaders, who saw themselves as his rivals for power in the House, would offer strong and perhaps fatal opposition to his plan. The timing could not have been worse. The unfolding revelations about Watergate increased the likelihood that the House would become embroiled in impeachment proceedings. The drama of reform, which was very real to members and staff alike, was overshadowed by the drama of Watergate. When the Bolling Committee was circulating its first draft in December 1973, the Ervin Committee had already completed its Watergate hearings, and the Judiciary Committee, under chairman Peter Rodino of New Jersey, was preparing for its investigations of President Richard Nixon. When the Bolling Committee completed its markup and brought the resolution before the caucus in May 1974, Rodino was scheduling a series of closed hearings before his committee that eventually would lead to a committee vote on three articles of impeachment. House Democratic leaders, particularly Tip O'Neill, Phil Burton, and caucus chairman Olin Teague, wanted to avoid at all costs Democratic infighting that would split their ranks and blunt the impeachment inquiry.

The Bolling Committee itself intensified partisan feelings in the House, as did the impeachment proceedings. The membership and the recommendations of the committee were bipartisan, since the Republicans contributed to a great extent to the committee proposals. But the power structure of the House was Democratic, not Republican. Reform would affect the powerful majority, not the already dispossessed minority members. Republican recommendations such as increased funds for minority staffing could only anger the Democrats. The chairmen knew that in many cases the proposals to reduce the jurisdiction of their committees came from the Republicans and not the Democrats on the committee.

Besides this, the Bolling Committee aroused internal conflict within the Democratic Party and among its committee chairmen. Most importantly, the Democratic caucus and its leaders feared Bolling was a rising power in the House. Bolling recognized that without the support of the caucus neither his plan nor his career would advance. Therefore, instead of asking the Rules Committee to report H. Res. 988 to the floor, he first sought the approval of the Democratic caucus. It was in the Democratic caucus that the real battle over the Bolling plan was fought and lost. Bolling had few supporters in the caucus. Almost all those who counted—the chairmen, the committee staff, the leadership, and the relevant industry groups—were already against him. So Bolling, lacking the support of insiders, was forced to resort to seeking outside support. In doing so, he was already admitting defeat. He courted publicity, speaking before the National Press Club in Washington and mailing copies of a favorable *New York Times* editorial to more than 300 journalists around the country. Bolling also found ready allies in John Gardner of Common Cause and Ralph Nader, who stood to gain in their own way from reform.

Bolling enlisted the support of Gillis Long, a young colleague who was building his House career through the Rules Committee. Long agreed to meet with selected committee members. To the strategy sessions Bolling invited Congressman Lloyd Meeds of Washington, a respected liberal House member; Paul Sarbanes, who was instrumental in drafting the original report; and John Culver, who had backed reform from the beginning. Carl Albert joined the group as they blocked out a strategy for winning caucus approval. The group also appealed to the Democratic Study Group, that offshoot of the Democratic caucus composed of liberal Democrats. The Democratic Study Group increased its power in 1971 when Congressman Phil Burton of California became its leader. Burton was—and is—both an activist and a liberal. An early opponent of the war in Vietnam and a vocal proponent of abolishing the Internal Security Committee, Burton at one time stood on the farther fringes of the Democratic Party. But unlike many liberals, Burton relished exercising power as well as protesting its abuses. He was willing to compromise to acquire that power, and politicians of the old school could admire his instinct for classic political deal making. Burton latched on to the Democratic Study Group early in his career. For him the DSG became a means of acquiring power. In December 1974, through adroit use of the DSG, he became chairman of the caucus itself. Burton had clear ambitions to become Majority Leader and Speaker of the House, and he saw as his archrivals in his quest for power Speaker Carl Albert, Majority Leader Tip O'Neill, and Richard Bolling. Burton set out to defeat the Bolling proposal with the considerable resources and political skills at his command.

Burton had ready and powerful allies. The foremost was Wayne Hays. A Bolling-Hays alliance was forged that later led Burton to defend Hays's chairmanship of the House Administration Committee after the revelation that Hays kept his mistress on the committee payroll. Young Congressmen realized that they had to choose between Burton and Bolling, and a wrong decision could ruin their careers. Burton sensed that the best way to defeat the Bolling report was to rally his supporters behind something. That way they would not simply be voting against the Bolling report. He offered a motion to refer the Bolling plan to the Hansen Committee that had been set up long ago to study House organization and procedure. Unlike the Bolling Committee, the Hansen Committee, named after its chairwoman Julia Hansen of Washington, clearly represented the House Democratic establishment. It included Wayne Hays, several members of the Ways and Means Committee, and representatives of the Education and Labor Committee. Burton knew that a vote for referral would effectively kill the plan. But members would be spared the embarrassment of voting against reform, with all that implied for a more efficient and effective Congress. Burton, Hays, and their allies won by a vote of 111–95.

Reform was now co-opted by Bolling's rivals. Antagonism developed immediately between the staffs and members of the Hansen and Bolling Committees. After an initial staff meeting Bolling forbade his staff to consult with the Hansen staff without his prior approval.

As the Hansen Committee met, Burton and Hays fought to revamp the Bolling report. Julia Hansen was sympathetic to them. The Hansen Committee adopted a provision which allowed the Speaker to recognize members who wanted to present their own rules on legislation, thus bypassing the Rules Committee. Bolling and his colleagues on the Rules Committee who had backed reform would have their power directly reduced by this procedure. The Hansen proposal further weakened the Rules Committee by removing its authority to arbitrate jurisdictional conflicts among committees, a power Bolling and David Martin had wanted to strengthen the Rules Committee. Burton's strategy was to disperse power in the House generally, thus weakening the present leadership, while strengthening the caucus, which was essential to his career. The Hansen Committee scuttled the centralizing thrust of the Bolling plan by requiring that standing committees with more than fifteen members have at least four subcommittees. The Hansen resolution also omitted the Bolling limitations, which kept members to one major committee assignment.

In mid-July Carl Albert became alarmed at the growing ani-

mosity between Burton and Bolling. Two of the most powerful
Democrats in the House were at loggerheads, and the other
Democrats were choosing sides. The Democrats seemed set on in-
ternecine warfare at the precise moment that they would be
faced with the very real prospect of the first impeachment vote in
over 100 years. Albert was now willing to compromise. He asked
Bolling and the Hansen Committee to negotiate their differences. But things had disintegrated too much for a last-
minute compromise. Bolling was intransigent.

The caucus held its critical meeting on reform on July 23.
After a heated and acrimonious debate, the caucus directed the
Rules Committee to report the Bolling resolution under an open
rule that would allow the House to substitute the Hansen resolu-
tion on a section-by-section basis. The next day the Supreme
Court announced its decision in *The United States* v. *Nixon*,
ordering the President to surrender his tapes to Judge John
Sirica, who was trying the Watergate case. That same day the
Judiciary Committee began its impeachment hearings. The re-
form resolutions were lost in the constitutional crisis.

Reform might have died quietly that year except for Richard
Nixon's resignation on August 9. With the crisis averted, the
House could once again focus its attention on the internal battle
for power between Bolling and Burton. Time, however, was
short. Congressmen were eager to adjourn. The midterm elections were only three months off, and the furor over Watergate
had kept most of them in Washington for a good part of the
summer. They were ready to go home and to start campaigning
for reelection.

Despite the caucus instructions, the Rules Committee did not
report the resolution smoothly. Chairman Ray Madden naturally loathed the Rules bypass procedure and mistakenly feared it
was part of the Bolling resolution. He said he did not want his
committee to be reduced to a mere "sewing circle."⁹ Numerous
witnesses clamored to be heard and a filibuster loomed.
Through a series of delicate and controversial maneuvers Bolling
succeeded in winning an open rule to bring reform to the floor.

Those who opposed reform, however, were unwilling to give
in. Opponents called for a special meeting of the caucus, which
they hoped would reverse its previous instructions to the Rules
Committee. Bolling managed to forestall another caucus meeting, and the floor debate opened with hostility and suspicion on
all sides.

The bitter debate took six days. Opponents still hoped that any reform, no matter how minor, might be defeated. Lenore Sullivan, chairwoman of the Merchant Marine and Fisheries Committee, and twenty-five of her colleagues voted against the rule that would permit the resolution to be brought to the floor. John Dingell tried to convince the House that the resolution was out of order.

Some of the young members felt that they were used and abused in the power struggles over reform. Freshman Pat Schroeder, an unconventional Congresswoman who became the first woman on the Armed Services Committee, said, "I am shaken and appalled that some opponents of committee reform have resorted to thinly veiled threats to more junior House members in an attempt to scuttle the bill before us. Not so subtle hints to junior members that a vote for reform will put them on the priority list of members who will have to lose seats on preferred committees in the reshuffling necessitated by the Bolling reforms have not been uncommon."[10]

Once the House turned its attention to the substance of the resolutions, it further weakened the so-called reforms of the Bolling and Hansen committees. Congressman Richard Ichord argued persuasively on behalf of his Internal Security Committee, and it was retained by a comfortable vote of 246–164. The Committee on Small Business was similarly restored, and the Rules Committee retained its existing power over the rules under which legislation was brought to the floor. Congressmen, whose impatience mounted daily, pushed for a final vote, and the Hansen substitute was adopted by a vote of 203–165. The changes on the floor were scarcely surprising. As Majority Leader Tip O'Neill stated earlier, "The name of the game is power and the boys sure don't want to give it up."[11]

While a majority of Republicans, particularly the freshmen, favored the Bolling report, a majority of Democrats, including freshmen, were against it. Only two of the standing committee chairmen voted against the Hansen substitute — George Mahon, chairman of the Appropriations Committee, and Thomas Morgan, chairman of Foreign Affairs. Neither of these chairmen was threatened by the Bolling resolution. The Foreign Affairs Committee actually gained jurisdiction. Those who voted for the Hansen resolution voted in their own self-interest. It was the lesser of two evils. The Bolling resolution threatened too many powerful members too much for it to be passed. Even so, the fight which preceded its defeat was so bitter that Wayne Hays and the House Administration Committee refused to authorize funds to reprint the hearings and meetings of the select committee. It was not until March 1975 that the House Administration Committee reluctantly authorized the printings.

The internal power struggles stopped for four years after most of the reorganization proposals were defeated or forgotten. In the 96th Congress Richard Bolling, the new chairman of the Rules Committee, revived the reform issue. Phillip Burton was now chairman of the Caucus Committee on Organization. At Bolling's insistence, the House voted to establish a new Select Committee on Committees in March 1979, which would once again study the committee structure, jurisdictions, rules and procedures, and staffing and facilities.

The committee was established by a close vote, 208–200, divided mostly along party lines, with Democrats in favor and Republicans opposed. In a repeat of 1974, those Democrats who felt threatened by reform voted against the resolution. Among the seventy-four Democrats opposing the new panel were five committee chairmen: Don Fuqua of Science and Technology, Harley W. Staggers of Interstate and Foreign Commerce, Frank Thompson, Jr., of Administration, Al Ullman of Ways and Means, and Jamie Whitten of Appropriations. Henry Waxman, who had finally captured the Health Subcommittee, also voted against.

Al Ullman in particular opposed a new study of the committee system because he knew that the broad powers of his Ways and Means Committee would reemerge as a likely target of reformers. He helped to persuade twenty-one of his thirty-five committee members to vote no. Many committee chairmen, both liberals and conservatives, shared Ullman's fears. In response, Speaker Tip O'Neill appointed Congressman Jerry Patterson of California, a moderate, to head the new committee. Patterson promised to soften demands for major alterations of House organization and procedures.

While the junior Congressmen were the troops and the senior Congressmen were the generals in the early 1970s, the freshmen began to demand a certain redistribution of power on their own as they entered their third and fourth terms. Flouting the seniority rule and the leadership, they backed their own candidates for subcommittee chairmanships when they thought they had a good chance of winning. (See Chapter 3 for a discussion of the in-fighting that occurred over subcommittee chairmanships in the 96th Congress.) The freshmen of the past were no longer willing merely to follow where the leadership conflicts among the senior members led them. They were encouraged by the knowledge that almost half of the members of the 96th Congress had been elected since 1974. At the start of the 96th Congress, Congressman Christopher J. Dodd presented a motion in the Democratic Caucus that would prevent full committee chairmen from chairing any subcommittees. The reaction of the committee chairmen was predictable. They felt Dodd was going too far. One of the leaders of reform in the past, Interior Committee chairman Morris Udall, said, "You can't put power in the subcommittee, then prevent the full committee chairman from sharing in the action." The chairmen uniformly rejected the Dodd plan, which would have reduced them to mere figureheads. Without subcommittee chairmanships they would lose substantial control over the legislative process. The Democratic caucus agreed that this would be too extreme, and rejected the Dodd motion, 85–21. Meanwhile, the Republicans voted to diffuse power in their own ranks by limiting each member to only one ranking minority position on the committees.

In the House, reform originated with the Speaker and a senior member of the Rules Committee, but in the Senate it was the Democratic freshman class of 1970 that raised the issue of reform in the guise of reorganization. Kenneth Gray, who was to become the staff director of the Senate Committee on Committees, said, "We never called what we were doing 'reform' because reform means the redistribution and sharing of power, particularly between senior and junior members. We were always careful to call our effort 'reorganization' because that does not imply tampering with the intricate power relationships in the body."

The freshmen who took office in 1970 were bolder and less quiescent than their predecessors. They were willing to challenge traditions and procedures that denied them their fair share of power. They balked at the notion of lengthy apprenticeships. They had no desire to languish on the sidelines; they wanted to be in the midst of the fray. This activism was something they had in common with the young Senators, such as Edward Kennedy, who were already challenging the Senate powers that be. The older, more traditional Senators of the establishment still controlled most of the chairmanships and exercised a disproportionate amount of influence. However, they could no longer take this power for granted, as they once had.

Senator Adlai Stevenson III of Illinois was a member of the 1970 class. Stevenson was—and is—a puzzle to many, a political figure who does not fit neatly into any of the stereotypes. He bears one of the most distinguished names in Democratic Party politics. Like his father he is quiet and sometimes aloof, wrapped up in ethical and philosophical issues that no one else cares much about. He seems to enjoy his chairmanship of the Ethics Committee, while most Senators would shy away from such a position. He is also enough of a practical and pragmatic politician to have won the support of Mayor Richard Daley of Chicago during his election campaign and to have hired the prosecutor of the "Chicago Seven" as his campaign manager. Stevenson's involvement in reorganization smacks of both sides of his cerebral personality. Reorganization is not an issue to excite most politicians unless it can be used to increase their own power, which, of course, is precisely what Stevenson intended. Stevenson, however, also seemed to believe that reorganization was the right thing for the Senate to undertake.

In 1971 Stevenson and his Republican colleague Senator Charles Mathias of Maryland held a series of ad hoc hearings on improvements in Senate organization and procedures. But it wasn't until 1976 that Stevenson, now finishing his first term, began to tackle reorganization in earnest. Sixteen Senators had been elected in the intervening years. Twenty percent of the Senate now belonged to the freshman caucus chaired by Senator Lloyd Bentsen of Texas, who was also interested in reorganization. This group was a potentially potent force for change. Stevenson wrote a letter, signed by fifty of his colleagues, to the Rules Committee calling for a select committee to study the committee system. A resolution setting up a Committee on Committees was reported out of the Rules Committee with surprising ease.

Senator Howard Cannon, chairman of the Rules Committee, sensed that a reorganization movement might be rippling through the normally placid Senate. The year before, newly elected Senator John Culver of Iowa, a key figure in House reform, had succeeded in winning Senate approval of the Commission on the Operation of the Senate. This commission undertook a "comprehensive and impartial study of the organization and operation of the Senate." The Culver Commission, as it came to be known, however, lacked the imprint of the Rules Committee. Majority Leader Mike Mansfield, according to an aide, "simply sprung the commission on the Senate." If there was to be reorganization, Cannon wanted to make sure that he and the Rules Committee would have some say about it. The Committee on Committees was his way.

There were fundamental differences between the Culver Commission and the Stevenson Committee. As noted in Chapter 5, the Culver Commission was composed largely of outsiders. The Stevenson Committee was made up of insiders. Its members were Senators and its staff had Hill experience. And this shaped its approach. While the Culver Commission studied the problem in relative isolation, the Stevenson committee was co-opting the Rules Committee. Ken Gray, the staff director, said, "I made it a point to make every effort to work hand in hand with the Rules Committee staff, to parallel interests that were developing there so there would be no threat to the Rules Committee."

Gray and Stevenson set precise limits to the study. Two things were immediately ruled untouchable—the Rules Committee and staff. The Committee on Committees needed their carefully cultivated allies on the Rules Committee. Without the help of the Rules Committee, their recommendations would die a quiet death. But not even the Rules Committee could save their recommendations if they succeeded in alienating enough powerful members. And the quickest way of doing that, Gray and Stevenson knew, was to start tinkering with the sensitive subject of staff. The existing allocations of staff were delicate and fragile, and the balance could be upset at any time. It was best to leave staff alone altogether.

Moreover, if their jobs were not threatened, the Senate staff could be powerful supporters. Gray started dropping by the regular Friday morning breakfasts of the Chairmen's Representatives, the informal association of staff directors and chief counsels. He made a point of meeting with the staff directors individually and sometimes the chairmen as well. Wherever he went, his message was the same. The existing committees need not worry about the Committee on Committees. As Gray said later, "I pleaded with the [Stevenson] committee not to do too much. We were not in the business of threatening committees. Effective reorganization comes from not biting off too much."

Gray need not have worried. In the summer of 1976, an election year and one with a presidential election at that, most Senators and their staffs were preoccupied with the various campaigns. Although the Bolling Committee held fourteen days of lengthy and sometimes acrimonious hearings, the Stevenson Committee met only three times. The testimony was cursory and hastily prepared as Senators rushed to escape the humidity which wrapped the Capitol like a wet mohair blanket. Gray said, "We couldn't get anybody interested. We knew we would not be taken seriously until January at the beginning of the new Congress." Nevertheless, the staff went ahead and drafted a resolution that embodied the committee's recommendations. It was introduced on September 30, 1976, and introduced again in January 1977 after the new Congress convened.

Unlike the Bolling report, the resolution did not completely scramble the existing committee structure. The Stevenson Committee did not, as Gray originally promised, try to redistribute power within the Senate. Nevertheless, its recommendations were far-reaching. The overall number of committees was reduced from thirty-one to fifteen. The Select Intelligence Committee was the only special committee to be continued. The jurisdiction of virtually all committees was changed to some degree. Six relatively minor standing committees—Aeronautical and Space Sciences, Indian Affairs, Veterans Affairs, the District of Columbia, Post Office and Civil Service, Small Business—were to be abolished. Senators would be limited to two major committee assignments and two subcommittees on each. They could also serve on one minor committee and one subcommittee under it. Senators could chair only one major standing committee and one subcommittee of each standing committee.

In December 1976, Senator Robert Byrd, soon to be elected Majority Leader, Howard Cannon, and Adlai Stevenson met to discuss strategy. Each saw the Committee on Committees resolution from his own perspective. Byrd was a man with an innate sense of order, and as the natural successor to Mike Mansfield, he preferred a new streamlined Senate to the old unwieldy one. Byrd, it was often said, was a man who liked to see the trains run on time. Byrd's support could not but help him with the freshmen Senators. The 1976 elections produced a record number of new Senators, the most since 1958. In fact, in the preceeding six years there had been a 40 percent turnover in the Senate. Many of these new Senators thought Byrd was too conservative, too establishment, too protective of the existing order to be Majority Leader. By championing reorganization, a new Byrd could emerge. Byrd's election was expected, but over a month remained before the actual ballots would be cast. The 1976 elections had already produced a few surprises, and Byrd wasn't taking chances on another. Byrd and Stevenson persuaded Cannon to take up S. Res. 4 in the Rules Committee.

Gray knew that January was the most auspicious time for reorganization. In fact, it was the only time. It was now or never. Gray said, "We had to get things done before the new committees were appointed for once members are given their committee seats they won't budge." Stevenson was backing Byrd for Majority Leader, but that did not necessarily mean that Byrd would be willing to go all out for reorganization. His support was crucial, and he gave it wholeheartedly. He eased the way with Cannon and spent several hours discussing the reorganization resolution with the other committee chairmen. Most importantly, he got the Senate to agree that committee appointments would not be made until S. Res. 4 had been taken up.

As the Committee on Rules considered S. Res. 4 in January, the Senate realized that it must take reorganization seriously. As Senators returned to Washington for the opening of Congress, they were deluged with complaints from pressure groups such as the American Legion and the National Small Business Association about the proposed elimination of "their" committees on Capitol Hill. Behind the scenes the staffs of threatened committees either were already garnering outside support or were mapping concerted campaigns to persuade their colleagues to reverse the proposals for reform. During the first week of hearings Rules Committee member Mark Hatfield said, "Committee reform is . . . like reducing federal taxes. Everybody is for it so long as the end result does not affect their pet projects or programs."[12] The "pet projects" of Senators and staffs were their committees.

As Senator after Senator appeared to testify before the Rules Committee, a familiar theme emerged. Most Senators were in favor of reorganization, as long as their committees were unaffected. On the fifth day of hearings, after Hubert Humphrey argued against abolishing the Joint Economic Committee, which he had served as cochairman, Howard Cannon said exasperatedly:

> This committee finds itself in a position that we have now heard from thirty-six Senators and two members of the House plus some special interest groups and public members; and everyone has started off by saying that they think reorganization is a great thing and they want to commend the committee for the great job they did, but they do not agree with what the select committee did in different particulars. . . .
>
> So you see, we have a difficult job. The question then comes down to: Are we going to try to reform, or are we not? If we are not, what are we going to do?[13]

Cannon asked Humphrey which committees should be abolished. Humphrey in effect replied "none"! Each committee, he said, has its own raison d'être and its own legitimate jurisdiction. Abolishing the Veterans Affairs Committee would deny adequate representation to veterans. Folding the Select Committee on Nutrition into the Agriculture Committee would mean disappointment for millions of Americans. Humphrey added drolly, "I gather my colleague, Senator McGovern [the committee chairman], may very well have commented upon this." Humphrey concluded, "Representative government does not lend itself always to a neat and cleancut operation. I mean, it is just not that way."

Stevenson pleaded with the Rules Committee to avoid reinstating individual committees under pressures. "Piece by piece, brick by brick, as the pieces are pulled out, the whole edifice will collapse," he said. As the hearings continued, renewed public and private pressures on the Rules Committee made amendments inevitable. Senior Democrats and many Republicans, especially ranking members of powerful committees, united against the resolution. John Sparkman of Alabama and Clifford P. Case of New Jersey, the chairman and ranking member respectively of the Senate Foreign Relations Committee, testified together against a proposed reduction in the committee's jurisdiction. Senator Jacob Javits of New York, second-ranking Republican on Foreign Relations, also strongly opposed the transfer of some of the committee's jurisdiction. Since the Chairman of the Veterans Affairs Committee had been defeated it was up to Clifford P. Hansen of Wyoming, ranking Republican on the committee and also a member of the Stevenson Committee, to support the continuation of Veterans Affairs. Barry Goldwater, the ranking Republican on the Aeronautical and Space Sciences Committee, counterattacked with a lengthy written statement proposing an expanded jurisdiction.

George McGovern enlisted the support of Robert Dole of Kansas, the ranking Republican on the Agriculture Committee, in his fight to retain his select committee's independence. Senator Edward W. Brooke of Massachusetts, second-ranking Republican on the Select Committee on Standards and Conduct, defended that committee against termination.

The Republicans were motivated by power and status. If they were not ranking minority members, they had enough seniority to anticipate they would be before long. Javits, for example, became ranking member of Foreign Relations in the 96th Congress in 1979.

Those who fought the hardest, however, were those who had the most at stake, the chairmen of committees who felt their jurisdiction and discretion were threatened. Russell Long, for instance, was not at all happy with the select committee's recommendations. Although five Finance Committee members were on the reorganization committee, Long felt that the traditional prerogatives of his committee were threatened. Among his allies was Senator Robert Packwood of Oregon, who once said that his special responsibility on the Committee on Committees was to protect the Finance Committee. Long opened his testimony with praise for the Rules Committee which had become the real power in the reorganization struggle. "As much as I admire those who served on the [Stevenson] committee that made the recommendations that led to the hearings," said Long, "I have a tremendous regard for those of you who served here on the Rules Committee. I have not the slightest doubt that you can improve on their suggestions. I hope very much that you will." Long was particularly distressed by the proposal that standing committees review tax expenditures related to their jurisdiction. "Any committee now, if it wants to," said Long, "can hold hearings and make whatever recommendations it wants to make with regard to tax expenditure provisions in the Internal Revenue code. There is nothing to keep them from doing it, but there is nothing in the rules of the Senate that suggests they should do it. The resolution pending in your committee suggests that they should do that. I am concerned lest when we are considering a major tax bill, we would have not only one set of hearings by the Finance Committee but another set of hearings by practically every other committee up here which feels it should be involved in tax expenditures." Long concluded, "If you pursue this thing to the ultimate, I would think that the involvement of a Senate committee in tax provisions would be limited only by the imagination and ambition of its own chairman."

In a new skirmish in his ongoing battle with the Budget Committee, Long argued that the Budget Committee should be upgraded to major committee status. This would mean members would be able to serve on only one other major committee. Long knew this would weaken the Budget Committee. Most members would resign rather than surrender their seniority on long established major committees for the Budget Committee whose eventual power was still in doubt. Muskie argued that Budget Committee members should be exempted from any limitations at least through the 95th Congress. Long countered, "The Budget Committee is such a significant committee that it should not be considered as a third committee. We may find, if its power and influence continues to expand, and if its jurisdiction by practice continues to expand, the Budget Committee may well be the most sought after committee up here. It is one of the most sought after already. If that is the case, I see no reason why the Budget Committee should be somebody's third or extra committee." In short, the Budget Committee members should not be given the special privilege of being able to serve on two additional standing committees.

Muskie replied, "If the Senate is to achieve a committee structure in which all of its committees have reasonably comparable legislative workloads, then some of the burden on those committees which now have the heaviest responsibilities must be shifted to committees which now carry a lighter load." Muskie added, "We all know that under our current system a handful of committees are responsible for the bulk of the Senate's legislative burden." He continued with deceptive casualness, "Take the Committee on Finance as an example. That committee is already under such a crushing legislative load from the first day of each Congress until the last that I sometimes wonder how my good friend from Louisiana manages to survive that ordeal. Yet there is talk in this committee of adding additional burdens to the Finance Committee's already overwhelming workload." General revenue sharing, for instance, should be transferred from the Finance Committee to the Governmental Affairs Committee. Muskie neglected to mention that he was the chairman of the Intergovernmental Relations Subcommittee of Governmental Affairs that would capture the general revenue sharing jurisdiction. Muskie's attacks and behind-the-scenes attempts to acquire some of his Finance Committee jurisdiction failed to upset Long's aplomb. "The Finance Committee," he stressed, *"will* continue [despite proposals to the contrary] to have jurisdiction over the vast bulk of federal expenditures for income maintenance through social security, welfare, and unemployment benefits."

Senators, whether insiders like Russell Long or mavericks like William Proxmire, are always interested in maintaining and expanding their power. Proxmire, chairman of the Committee on Banking, Housing, and Urban Affairs, testified that while he favored in principle many of the select committee's proposals to realign committee jurisdictions, he believed his committee's should be increased. Proxmire was determined to keep all of the Banking Committee's existing jurisdiction although he admitted that rationally some of it might be located elsewhere. The Banking Committee had jurisdiction over certain aspects of energy policy and urban mass transit which it was not about to relinquish voluntarily. Proxmire said, "We are unilaterally opposed to giving up jurisdiction over the urban mass transit program." Warren Magnuson, chairman of the Commerce Committee, urged the consolidation of transportation into his committee. "My colleagues on the Rules Committee know," said Magnuson, "that the Commerce Committee does not covet its neighbor's jurisdiction. Highways and mass transit bring more headaches than glory, but if the logic of the reorganization plan is the redistribution of jurisdiction so as to centralize authority, then the Commerce Committee must become a true transportation committee with the power and the authority to examine and develop a rational national transportation policy." The Rules Committee decided they didn't want to fight that battle and left mass transit in Banking.

In his quest for additional jurisdiction, Proxmire attacked the Foreign Relations Committee. He argued that its control over the World Bank and the International Monetary Fund should be restored to his committee. In 1959 Senator J. William Fulbright moved from the chairmanship of the Banking Committee to Foreign Relations and took this jurisdiction with him. Proxmire now wanted this "historic jurisdiction" back. Proxmire did not succeed.

Barry Goldwater warned the committee that reorganization "must be performed with surgical care, because if the past is any guide to the future, a pattern will be set that will last for one or two decades." John Stennis agreed. "I fail to see what seems to me to be the rush of things," he said. "Why does this have to be done so rapidly and pushed through? It is the most sensitive and most serious part of all the operations of the Senate. It is the committee system and I almost worship it."

Howard Cannon had work ahead. His initial ambivalence had waned and Cannon was rapidly becoming a fervent supporter of reorganization. He made the issue his own. He was a powerful chairman who kept a tight grip on his committee. This was his approach to reorganization.

The most unsettling of the issues before him was that of the committees that Stevenson wanted to abolish. Three of those, Aeronautical and Space Sciences, Veterans Affairs, and Post Office and Civil Service, had lost their chairmen in the 1976 elections. They could be merged with relative ease into existing committees. The Joint Economic Committee could rationally be restored since it had House as well as Senate sponsorship. Its preservation would not seriously undermine reorganization. The select committees—Small Business, Nutrition, Aging, and Indian Affairs—posed problems. Although Cannon and Stevenson agreed these should go, the committee chairmen and staffs opposed the slightest change.

The Rules Committee was now in the middle of the reorganization fight. Cannon tried to appease some members by grandfather clauses, which would exempt them from the new rules on committee assignments. Grandfathering was common in the Senate. At the time S. Res. 4 was being debated, most Senators were limited to two major standing committee assignments. However, due to past grandfathering, Henry Jackson, for instance, served on three major committees. He was chairman of Interior and Insular Affairs, ranking member of the Armed Services Committee, and a member of Government Operations, where he chaired the Permanent Subcommittee on Investigations. Through this subcommittee Jackson controlled a large staff and the largest subcommittee budget in the Senate. Jackson would be protected again through the appropriate grandfather clauses. The Rules Committee resurrected the Veterans Affairs Committee and the Small Business Committee. S. Res. 4 as amended was reported to the floor on February 1, 1977.

Although the resolution was weakened considerably by this time and posed no threat to significant power centers, the debate was heated and acrimonious. Senator George McGovern, infuriated by the abolition of his Nutrition Committee, attacked S. Res. 4 because it favored "the most established power centers in the Senate. It is a fine piece of irony that a plan with such consequences could be called 'reform.' "[14] The fight over the select committees was renewed on the floor.

Senator Frank Church, whose Aging Committee had been eliminated, worked vigorously for reinstatement. In his campaign he was fortunate to have the assistance of a large and able staff. The staff solicited "seniorgrams" and letters from senior citizen groups, state agencies on aging, and gerontology experts on behalf of their research and oversight efforts. During the markup sessions Mark Hatfield pointed out in a rare burst of candor, "I think one could say without it being in any way demeaning to anyone, that a select committee is a staff-dominated committee."[15] He added, "I can understand why the staff is always reluctant to see change." And in this case he was right. The staff secured fifty Senate cosponsors for an amendment to reinstate the committee. Arguing for this amendment, Church said, "I do question the denial of 23 million senior citizens the same consideration which we are extending to veterans, Native Americans, and small business." The committee was "a home for the elderly in the Senate." The Senate restored the committee by the overwhelming vote of 90–4.

Church's victory encouraged other Senators to fight for their turf. George McGovern immediately introduced an amendment to retain his Select Committee on Nutrition and Human Needs. McGovern rightly feared he would lose control over his staff if the committee were to be merged into the Agriculture Committee. "The Agriculture Committee is one of several in the Senate," said McGovern, "which traditionally have not had separate subcommittee staffs appointed by subcommittee chairmen; instead a professional staff under the supervision of the committee chair-

man serves all subcommittees and all members of the committee." McGovern saw a threat to his future power if his new
subcommittee were to be forced to conform to the traditional
practices of the Agriculture Committee. McGovern won a brief
victory—a one-year extension for his committee. Afterwards it
became a subcommittee of the Agriculture Committee.

Not all of the debate over S. Res. 4 concerned committee reorganization and changes in committee jurisdictions. Dick
Clark, a first-term Senator from Iowa, wanted more power for
junior members. Clark was a former political science professor,
with practical political experience at the grass roots level. He
helped elect John Culver, now a Senator, to the House. As
Culver's administrative assistant he learned reform politics in the
House. In 1972 Iowa Democrats asked Culver to run for the Senate against Jack Miller, a conservative, who easily won election in
1960 and reelection in 1966. When Culver refused, Clark ran instead and defeated Miller by a wide margin, but his attempt to
build power on Capitol Hill was abruptly ended with his defeat
in 1978. Clark sought to make his mark on reform in the Senate.

Clark proposed to limit the number of chairmanships that
could be held. He hoped to open up subcommittee chairmanships on the major standing committees which could be filled by
the junior members. This, of course, was precisely the way the
House Democrats played the reform game back in the sixties. His
amendment would limit the major committee chairmen to only
one additional subcommittee chairmanship. The Stevenson proposal, by contrast, would have allowed standing committee
chairmen to chair one subcommittee for each committee on
which they served. Clark believed that committee chairmen had
too much power, and some of their power should be redistributed to their junior colleagues. When Clark brought up his
amendment in the Rules Committee's markup sessions, he explained, "It is my judgment that this amendment would do more
than almost anything possible to share the responsibility of the
work of the Senate." He continued, "This would be the kind of
change which would effectively give junior members an opportunity to chair subcommittees."[16]

Clark was eyeing twelve subcommittee chairmanships that
would open up if his amendment passed. Cannon knew that a list
of the subcommittees would immediately produce at least twelve
opponents to the amendment, and he asked Clark to note which

subcommittees would be affected. Clark simply responded that a subcommittee chairmanship on each major standing committee would become vacant. The amendment was defeated in the Rules Committee, 4–5. All the Democrats voted against.

Clark, not so easily defeated, took the amendment to the floor. Stevenson, who strongly opposed the amendment, said, "I just do not see any point in punishing a few members of this Senate because they are chairmen." The committee chairmen unsurprisingly agreed. Cannon for one claimed that his Rules Committee would have trouble operating under the limitation. Russell Long melodramatically said the Clark amendment implied "even the crumbs off the table are too much for the chairman to wind up with." Clark was undeterred, however. He insisted that the Stevenson proposal did not go far enough. Senator Lawton Chiles of Florida, who was just beginning his second term, said that the Senate "is a little bit like Orwell's Animal Farm. All us pigs are equal. But some are more equal than others."

Stevenson's motion to table the Clark amendment lost, 42–47. All the chairmen whose power might potentially be reduced, including Russell Long, Henry Jackson, Abraham Ribicoff, William Proxmire, Jennings Randolph, James O. Eastland, Warren Magnuson, and Howard Cannon, voted to table. Majority Leader Robert Byrd also voted to table. Aspiring members of the Senate establishment, such as Sam Nunn, sided with Stevenson. The Senate outsiders, such as James Abourezk, George McGovern, Howard Metzenbaum, and virtually all Republicans voted with Clark.

When the Clark amendment itself came to a vote, it passed, 79–10. Most of the Senators previously voting to table the amendment now realized that passage was inevitable and switched. Clark was encouraged to introduce another amendment that would also redistribute power between senior and junior members. Under this amendment each standing committee would be forced to establish at least three subcommittees which would acquire jurisdiction over all appropriate legislation to the subcommittees. The amendment contained an escape clause for standing committees, however, that permitted them by majority vote to keep legislation at the full committee level.

Clark would thereby increase the power of subcommittee chairmen. This, too, was a replay of House reform efforts. After subcommittee chairmanships were opened up, the power of the new chairmen was cemented through the Subcommittee Bill of Rights. "I have seen what has happened when the chairman [of a standing committee] trespasses on the prerogatives of a subcommittee chairman," said Russell Long. Implying that subcommittee chairmen already had too much power, Long continued, "I have seen subcommittee chairmen point their finger in a chairman's face and say, 'You so-and-so, I will never speak to you again,' and keep that commitment for years. I do not want that, and nobody else wants it."

All of the committee chairmen felt threatened by this new Clark amendment, and it was tabled, 63–20. Most of the Senate establishment voted in the majority. The Senate upstarts had gone as far as they could for a while. Further redistributions of power would have to wait.

On February 4, 1977 the Senate voted, 89–1, in favor of S. Res. 4. The resolution succeeded because it did not significantly disturb the power structure of the Senate. As Ken Gray said, it was reorganization, not reform. It did not significantly redistribute power except for the restrictions on the number of chairmanships and the number of major committee assignments that could be held. The other changes engineered by S. Res. 4 were on the periphery of power, not at the core. The District of Columbia Committee could no longer be justified, and it was dropped. With the passage of home rule, the committee had become a mere holding company for the staff of its chairman, Tom Eagleton. Two standing committees whose chairmen were defeated — Aeronautical and Space Sciences, and the Post Office and Civil Service Committees — were abolished. The Select Committee on Nutrition and Human Needs, chaired by outsider George McGovern, was eliminated. The Senate establishment in the end prevailed.

The Senate is a confederation of sovereign powers who are the senior committee chairmen. Nothing happens without their collective approval. And they can exempt themselves from resolutions that would reduce their power. When Ed Muskie, for example, saw that major committee status would not buttress the power of the Budget Committee, he persuaded the Senate to release its members from the restrictions on committee assignments.

Senate outsiders also fight for power. Senator James Abourezk continued his fight to preserve the Indian Affairs Committee for another year. He proposed a permanent extension, and Senator Mark Hatfield, the ranking minority member, sought a two-year extension. In 1978 the Rules Committee was once again considering committee reorganization. Barry Goldwater appeared to support an extension. When Goldwater was asked about the conflict with S. Res. 4, he said, "I was much better off before S. Res. 4—I think we can all say that." He added, "It didn't do a damn thing." Senator Wendell Ford pointed out that if S. Res. 4 had not passed, he would have become chairman of the Aeronautical and Space Sciences Committee, "a major committee with thirty or more employees and a large budget." If the Senate was to begin major exceptions to S. Res. 4 such as continuation of the Indian Affairs Committee, he said, "maybe I should reconsider my vote [in favor of S. Res. 4]." Howard Cannon started a filibuster against extension of Indian Affairs, but while he was summoned elsewhere, the committee voted to report a two-year extension. Cannon put a "hold" on it, which would prevent the resolution from coming up on the floor in his absence. Despite his hold, the resolution was mistakenly brought to the floor on August 2 and passed. The action was quickly vacated on August 3 to allow Cannon to express his opposition, but Cannon's delaying tactics failed to prevent the extension of the Indian Affairs Committee.

Attempts to circumvent the limits on the number of chairmanships and committee assignments imposed by S. Res. 4 surfaced in the 96th Congress. The "reformers" of the past, who had outwardly supported the moderate redistribution of power embodied in S. Res. 4, moved quickly to remove themselves from its restrictions. Senator Kennedy successfully obtained an exemption for John Culver that permitted his friend to retain his seat on three major committees, including Judiciary. The exemption for Culver was important to Kennedy because he wanted Culver to be chairman of Kennedy's former Administrative Practice and Procedure Subcommittee.

Veteran Senator Harrison A. Williams, Jr., of New Jersey also attempted to skirt the restrictions. He had long been chairman of the Human Resources Committee, which is a major committee under Senate rules. He was chairman of its Labor

Subcommittee and chairman of the Securities and Labor Subcommittee of the Banking Committee. He was also first in line to
become chairman of its Housing Subcommittee. Williams had
built his reputation in labor and securities legislation around
these subcommittees. Williams knew that the Housing Subcommittee could further enhance his reputation. There was only
one problem. Under S. Res. 4 he would not be allowed the Housing Subcommittee. He worked out a strategy to optimize his
power. He persuaded the Human Resources Committee to dis-
band the Labor Subcommittee and move its jurisdiction to the
full committee where he could retain control over labor legislation. He then convinced the Banking Committee to dissolve the
Securities Subcommittee and to transfer its jurisdiction to the
full committee where he could retain control over labor legislation. He then beseeched the Banking Committee to dissolve the
legislation while he also acquired chairmanship of the Housing
Subcommittee.

Williams failed to accomplish his goal. Behind the scenes
North Carolina Senator Robert Morgan maneuvered against the
proposal. He believed that if the Securities Subcommittee were
continued, Williams would be content to remain its chairman
and he, Morgan, could take over the Housing Subcommittee,
which he ardently wanted. Morgan's strategy backfired, however, when Williams, confronted finally with a choice between
the two subcommittees, moved to the chairmanship of the Housing Subcommittee.

The history of the Bolling and Stevenson Committees reflects
the fact that reform and reorganization on Capitol Hill arise out
of internal power struggles. Outsiders may have an interest in
Congressional reform, but if they play a role, it is as pawns in a
game for insiders.

7

Power, Status, and Public Policy

WE HAVE DESCRIBED the increasing isolation of Capitol Hill as members advance their political careers by seeking power and status within Congress. An electoral base must, of course, be secured first. But after a term or two most Congressmen have developed political organizations that can defeat even the strongest challengers. Those who serve in the electoral organization of a Congressman are not those who buttress his position on the Hill. A Congressional office is partially staffed by aides who answer letters and play ombudsman for constituents. But these functions are incidental to members as they strive to gain power in Congress. The electoral connection is mostly irrelevant to committee work, the passage of legislation, the infighting among staff, and the constant power plays that constitute "reform." The time that members and staffers devote to cultivating perks has nothing at all to do with the electorate.

This quest for power profoundly affects public policy. It buttresses the system of checks and balances. The President is no longer simply pitted against the Congress. Now the White House opposes approximately 300 "little legislatures" in the form of committees. These committees have assumed many of the same powers that Congress was given under the Constitution. The President must deal with their chairmen and their staffs if he is to succeed in administering the government and implementing his programs. And he must deal with them by appealing to their need for recognition among their *colleagues* not the electorate. Presidents from time to time may gain Congressional support by helping Congressmen in their districts. Popular Presidents may help campaign or back federal projects in their communities.

But Presidents are usually of negligible help and may even be harmful. Constituents do not like to feel that "their" Congressman is a pawn of the President or of Congress.

Regardless of what Presidents may seek to do to appeal to voters, they cannot consistently influence Capitol Hill without paying attention to the internal power incentives of members. The dispersion of power on the Hill enormously complicates the task of the White House. As legislation is sent to Capitol Hill, Congressional protocol must be observed, and chairmen given the necessary incentives to promote the President's legislation as their own. The President cannot govern by fiat. He must persuade Congressmen ·that their interests coincide with his. To do this he must have a good grasp of Capitol Hill politics and the knowledge that Congressmen are constantly struggling to augment their power within Congress. Supplying legislation to committee chairmen who are searching for fresh proposals and who are seeking recognition as "effective legislators" will generate important allies for the President. California Congressman James Corman, chairman of a House subcommittee with jurisdiction over welfare, pushed President Carter's welfare program (see Chapter 2) because passage would elevate his legislative reputation. Despite his eighteen years in the House no major legislation bore his name. While the President found that Corman was easily won over, other White House legislation met with a mixed response, depending upon how Congressional leaders and chairmen thought they could use it to buttress their internal power. Presidents find that appeals to the people do not persuade their elected representatives to back him. Rather, support must be garnered by respecting a member's power and seeking to enhance it.

The private world of Capitol Hill fortifies the constitutional separation of powers and the overall pluralism of the policy process. Power is diffused and directed inward in an environment that isolates itself from external forces. Members of Congress and staff manipulate external politics for internal purposes. Their legislative activities are aimed at their colleagues, who are their real constitutents. Outside cosntituencies are mobilized to gain internal support for legislation. Congress is not the captive of lobbyists. Rather the chairmen of committees exercise leadership within their policy spheres as they attempt to boost their reputations on Capitol Hill. Passing legislation requires a broad consensus within Congress, but this is not the same as a broad consensus outside of Congress. In the House and the Senate consensus is built through personal relationships and courtesy; a reputation for expertise, hard work, and effectiveness as a legislator, including skill in drafting legislation; and respect for turf and for seniority. Even such controversial legislation as the original airline deregulation bill can be passed in the end almost unanimously if legislators with power and status are adroit. The examples of Congressmen Paul Rogers in health policy and Edward Kennedy in health and regulatory policy illustrate legislative leadership and the successful development of national policy that builds power on Capitol Hill. Their constituency was Congress itself not voters back home.

Understanding the drive for internal power and status explodes the misconception that the activities of Capitol Hill are geared to reelection. It explodes other myths as well. The "resurgent Congress" after Watergate was not an attempt by members to increase their collective power at the expense of the White House. Congress does not exist in the collective sense. In the post-Watergate era individual members, such as Edward Muskie in the Senate and Richard Bolling in the House, moved quickly to capitalize on a general restlessness on Capitol Hill over the ability of Congress to counteract the excesses of the imperial presidency. The Budget Act of 1974 was as much a power play by Muskie as a reflection of the collective wisdom of Congress that control needed to be exerted over the president. Organizational reform in the House was a power play by Bolling, not an attempt to strengthen the ability of the House to legislate and exercise oversight. Congress must be considered always in terms of its members' pursuit of their Capitol Hill careers. A resurgent Congress is individual members using the theme of resurgence in their quest for personal power. The result is more power and status for members and staff on the Hill, not a more powerful Congress as a whole.

Outside groups are useful in building careers on the Hill. Administrative agencies in particular supply expertise to members that helps them provide the necessary rationale to support legislation. The existence of the agencies also increases the visibility on Captiol Hill of the policies they implement and the committees that oversee them. A committee without oversight of an agency or department in the bureaucracy will have difficulty justifying itself, not to the public, but in the House and Senate. This was the case of the Senate Committee on Nutrition and Human Needs. The status of committees and their chairmen is directly related to the importance and aura of the executive departments and agencies in their control. Their perks may also come from the bureaucracy. The Defense Department takes grandiose care of members of the Armed Services Committees and Appropriations defense subcommittees.

Because members of Congress need the bureacracy for internal power and status, vigilant oversight of the agencies is rare. Congressmen have much to lose and little to gain by alienating powerful departments through a close scrutiny of their activities and policies.

The quest for personal power on the Hill fortifies the pluralism of the vast administrative establishment and buttresses the bureaucracy against incursions on its power from the White House. The bureaucracy has become an integral part of Capitol Hill. Despite the campaign rhetoric agencies are the friends, not the adversaries, of Capitol Hill. They fortify the isolation of the Hill by joining with Congressional committees to forge an impenetrable link in the Washington power establishment.

The preoccupation of Congress with institutional power and status casts public policy into a mold that is not understood by those who continue to believe in the imperial presidency and the watchful electorate, which rewards or punishes Congressmen for their performance on the Hill. Congress is strenuously legislative but legislation is responsive to institutional norms. Congressmen are not legislating for the people, but for themselves. This explains the multitude of legislative proposals and the scarcity of legislation. It explains why bills generally pass by large majorities. These majorities reflect, not the will of the people, but the internal consensus.

This book describes the politics of Capitol Hill as it is played by the residents—the members and staffers. Politics is an occupation that involves insiders and outsiders in different ways. Outsiders—the electorate, pressure groups and their leaders— think that politics serves them. This idea is central to democratic theory, which requires that public policy be attuned to popular and group interests.

Politics has always existed in varying degrees apart from the people. All governments tend to take on a form and life of their own. Constitutions may set up the formal arrangements of government but informal forces are often more important in shaping the real character of politics.

The framers of the Constitution established the House to be the voice of the people in government. It alone was to be truly representative of popular interests. Legislation from this body of the people was to reflect popular and local interests. The Senate was never intended to represent the people directly. Senators were to be selected by the state legislators for six-year terms to permit rational deliberations on national issues in an environment free of emotion and electoral pressures.

The framers of the Constitution were well aware of the doctrine of original sin and based our system upon the premise that there is an intrinsically evil element in government. Government must be forced to control itself, for even popular checks upon political leaders will be insufficient to prevent the arbitrary exercise of political power. "What is government itself," wrote James Madison in the fifty-first paper of *The Federalist*, "but the greatest of all reflections upon human nature? If men were angels, no government would be necessary. If angels were to govern men, neither external nor internal controls on government would be necessary. In framing a government, which is to be administered by men over men, the great difficulty lies in this: you must first enable the government to control the governed; and in the next place, oblige it to control itself."

The framers ingeniously devised a system of separation of powers and of checks and balances that raised numerous obstacles to government action and thus controlled it. They saw the dimensions of power revolving primarily around the three major branches of government, but at the same time they installed a checks and balances system in Congress by pitting the Senate against the House. The framers knew that Congress would have a propensity to legislate and they wanted to insure that its legislation would reflect neither the hasty conclusions nor the intemperate passions of the majority. Instead it would emerge from compromises between a prudent Senate and a popularly elected House.

While many of the assumptions of the framers have passed the test of time, Capitol Hill politics do not fit into the constitutional model. The writers of the Constitution did not foresee the possibility of a House unto itself. James Madison wrote in the fifty-seventh paper of *The Federalist*:

> The House of Representatives is so constituted as to support in the members an habitual recollection of their dependence on the people. Before the sentiments impressed on their minds by the mode of their elevation, can be effaced by the exercise of power, they will be compelled to anticipate the moment when their power is to cease, when their exercise of it is to be reviewed, and when they must descend to the level from which they were raised; there forever to remain unless a faithful discharge of their trust shall have established their title to a renewal of it.

If Madison had seen the growth and institutionalization of the House of Representatives, he would have changed his sanguine view that the House would be forever dependent upon the people.

The dimensions of the power game have changed since the Constitution was adopted. The constitutional rhetoric survives in our folklore. The realities of the power game on Capitol Hill have important new consequences for the political system that are not all bad.

The extraordinary fragmentation of power on Capitol Hill buttresses the original constitutional division of government not only within Congress itself but also between Capitol Hill and the White House. The complex maze of individual power centers plus the strong personalities of many Congressional leaders fortify the constitutional scheme of checks and balances. Those who fear arbitrary power in the White House should be comforted by the fact that members of Congress have internal power incentives that dictate a position in opposition to the President. This may be a negative view but suspicion of government is in the mainstream of our political theory and practice.

Capitol Hill is the last bastion of free enterprise, of the political entrepreneur. While political scientists and historians have described at length the White House domination of public policy, Congress has always been an integral partner in policy development. Its legislative innovations are generally overlooked by outsiders who focus on the more easily understood and glamorous White House. The individualism and entrepreneurial nature of Capitol Hill have produced creative legislation to improve health and the environment, promote good labor relations, and to advance education.

Ironically, it may be that the very isolation of Capitol Hill increases its effectiveness. The growth of a professional and specialized staff provides legislative expertise. The multiple power centers of Capitol Hill guarantee that a broad consensus of members must exist before legislation is passed.

The private world of Congress is not at odds with democracy or the Constitution.

Appendix

Congressional Record—Daily Digest, February 6, 1978, pp. D99–D103

CONGRESSIONAL PROGRAM AHEAD

For February 7–11, 1978

(Committee meetings are open unless otherwise indicated)

Senate Chamber

On Tuesday, Senate will consider and conclude action on S.897, nuclear non-proliferation bill.

On Wednesday, Senate will begin consideration of the matter of the Panama Canal Treaties.

Senate Committees

Committee on Appropriations: February 7, Subcommittee on Labor-HEW, to resume hearings on proposed budget estimates for fiscal year 1979 for ACTION, 10:45 a.m., Room S-128, Capitol.

February 7–9, Subcommittee, to hold hearings on proposed budget estimates for fiscal year 1979 for public works projects, 2 p.m., Room S-126, Capitol.

February 8 and 9, Subcommittee, to hold hearings on proposed budget estimates for fiscal year 1979 for the Department of the Interior, and related activities, 10 a.m., Wednesday in 1114 and Thursday in 1318, both in Dirksen Office Building.

February 8 and 10, Subcommittee on Defense, closed, to resume hearings on proposed budget estimates for fiscal year 1979 for the defense establishment on Wednesday to hear an overview on defense programs, and on Friday to receive testimony on Air Force programs, 10 a.m., 1223 Dirksen Office Building.

Committee on Armed Services: February 7, to hold hearings on proposed authorizations for fiscal year 1979 for the Department of Defense, 10 a.m., 1114 Dirksen Office Building.

Committee on Banking, Housing, and Urban Affairs: February 7 and 8, to hold oversight hearings on the proposed budgets of the Federal Deposit Insurance Corporation, the Comptroller of the Currency, and the Federal Reserve System, 10 a.m., 5302 Dirksen Office Building.

Committee on the Budget: February 8 and 9, to resume hearings in preparation for reporting the first concurrent resolution on the fiscal year 1979 congressional budget, 10 a.m., 6202 Dirksen Office Building.

Committee on Commerce, Science, and Transportation: February 7, Subcommittee on Science, Technology, and Space, to hold hearings on the future of space science and space applications, 9:30 a.m., 235 Russell Office Building.

February 8, Subcommittee on Surface Transportation, to hold hearings on proposed authorizations for fiscal year 1979 for the U.S. Railway Association, 10 a.m., 235 Russell Office Building.

February 9, full committee, to hold hearings on the nominations of Edith B. Sloan and Susan B. King, both of the District of Columbia, each to be a Commissioner of the Consumer Product Safety Commission, 9 a.m., 235 Russell Office Building.

February 10, Subcommittee on Science, Technology, and Space, to hold oversight hearings on the implementation of the National Science and Technology Policy Act (P.L. 94-282), 9:30 a.m., 235 Russell Office Building.

February 9, full committee, business meeting, 11:30 a.m., 235 Russell Office Building.

Committee on Energy and Natural Resources: February 8 and 10, Subcommittee on Energy Production and Supply, to hold oversight hearings on the Federal coal leasing policy and its impact on western coal development, 10 a.m., 3110 Dirksen Office Building.

Committee on Environment and Public Works: February 7, to hold hearings on proposed authorizations for fiscal year 1979 for the Federal Highway Administration, and to receive testimony on the Administration's highway legislative proposals, 9:30 a.m., 4200 Dirksen Office Building.

February 8, full committee, to hold hearings on proposed authorizations for fiscal year 1979 for the Nuclear Regulatory Commission, 9:30 a.m., 4200 Dirksen Office Building.

February 8, Subcommittee on Transportation, to hold hearings on issues relating to the Federal highway program, including the level of Federal support, completion of the Interstate System, and the costs of maintenance of the Federal highway system, 9:30 a.m., 1318 Dirksen Office Building.

February 9, full committee, to hold hearings on proposed fiscal year 1979 authorizations for various Regional Commissions of the Public Works and Economic Development Act of 1965, and the Appalachian Regional Commission, 9:30 a.m., 4200 Dirksen Office Building.

Committee on Finance: February 7 and 9, Subcommittee on Public Assistance, to hold hearings on S. 2084, the proposed "Better Jobs and Income Act", Tuesday at 10 a.m., and 2:30 p.m., Thursday at 10 a.m., 2221 Dirksen Office Building.

February 8, Subcommittee on International Trade, to hold hearings on H.R. 5643, to implement the United Nations Convention on the means of prohibiting and preventing illicit import, export, and transfer of ownership of cultural property, 10 a.m., 2221 Dirksen Office Building.

Committee on Foreign Relations: February 7, to meet in closed session jointly with the Select Committee on Intelligence for a briefing on certain issues relative to the Panama Canal Treaty and Treaty Concerning the Permanent Neutrality and Operation of the Panama Canal (Exec. N, 95th Cong., 1st sess.), 10 a.m., Room S-116 Capitol.

February 9, Subcommittee on Arms Control, Oceans and International Environment, to hold hearings on S. Res. 49, expressing the sense of the Senate that the U.S. Government should seek the agreement of other governments to a proposed treaty requiring the preparation of an International Environment Impact Statement for any major project, action, or continuing activity which may be reasonably expected to have a significant adverse effect on the physical environment or environmental interests of another nation or a global commons area, 11 a.m., 4221 Dirksen Office Building.

February 10, Subcommittee on African Affairs, to hold closed hearings on foreign military activities in Africa, 10 a.m., Room S-116, Capitol.

Committee on Governmental Affairs: February 7, to continue hearings on S. 1785 and S. 2026, to require public disclosure of certain lobbying activities, 10 a.m., 3302 Dirksen Office Building.

February 7, Subcommittee on Federal Spending Practices and Open Government, to resume hearings on alleged irregularities in certain spending practices of the Small Business Administration, 10 a.m., 457 Russell Office Building.

February 9, Subcommittee on Civil Service and General Services, to mark up H.R. 3447, 3755, and S. 1559, bills relating to civil service survivor annuities; H.R. 6975, increasing the number of hearing examiner positions which may be established by the Civil Service Commission at the GS-16 level; and S. 1265 and S. 1267, bills relating to the maintenance and orderly disposition of public records, 9 a.m., Room S-210, Capitol.

February 9, full committee, to hold hearings on the handling of discrimination complaints in the Senate (pursuant to Rule 50 and Section 310 of S. Res. 110), 10 a.m., 3302 Dirksen Office Building.

Committee on Human Resources: February 7, to hold hearings on the following nominations: Robert C. Benedict, of Pennsylvania, to be Commissioner on Aging; Cecilia Denogean Esquer, of Arizona, Steven L. Engelberg, of Maryland, Hillary Diane Rodham, of Arkansas, Richard A. Trudell, of California, and Josephine Marie Worthy, of Massachusetts, all to be Members of the Board of the Legal Services Corporation; Robert B. Lagather, of Virginia, to be Assistant Secretary of Labor for Mine Safety and Health; William P. Adams, of Virginia, to be a Member of the Railroad Retirement Board; Harold Howe II, of New York, and Frederick H. Schultz, of Florida, each to be a Member of the National Council on Educational Research; and John W. Snyder, of the District of Columbia, to be a Member of the Board of Trustees of the Harry S Truman Scholarship Foundation, 9 a.m., 4232 Dirksen Office Building.

February 7, Subcommittee on Health and Scientific Research, to conduct hearings on S. 2410, amending certain sections of the Public Health Service Act relative to health planning and health resources development, 9:15 a.m., 4232 Dirksen Office Building.

February 7 and 8, Subcommittee on Aging, to resume oversight hearings on proposed extension of amendments to the Older Americans Act, Tuesday at 9:30 a.m., 6202 Dirksen Office Building, Wednesday at 9 a.m., 457 Russell Office Building.

February 8, Subcommittee on Child and Human Development, to hold hearings to review the current programs on child care and child development, and the need for additional legislation, 9:30 a.m., 4232 Dirksen Office Building.

February 8, Subcommittee on Health and Scientific Research, to hold hearings on the extension of NIH research authorities and community mental health centers, 9:30 a.m., Room S-207, Capitol.

February 8, Subcommittee on Education, Arts, and the Humanities, to hold hearings on S. 2473, to improve the basic educational opportunity grants program, 10:30 a.m., 318 Russell Office Building.

February 9, Subcommittee on Child and Human Development, to hold hearings on the reauthorization of the ACTION agency (Public Law 93-113), 7 a.m., 4232 Dirksen Office Building.

February 9, Subcommittee on Health and Scientific Research, to hold hearings on S. 2474, proposed extension, through 1983, of the Public Health Service Act, 9:15 a.m., 6226 Dirksen Office Building.

Committee on the Judiciary: February 7, business meeting, to consider the nomination of William H. Webster, of Missouri, to be Director of the Federal Bureau of Investigation, 10 a.m., to be followed by hearings on the nominations of Jack E. Tanner, to be U.S. district judge for the eastern and western districts of Washington, Robert F. Collins, to be U.S. district judge for the eastern district of Louisiana, A. David Mazzone, to be U.S. district judge for the district of Massachusetts, and Almeric L. Christian, to be a judge for the district court of the Virgin Islands, approximately 10:30 a.m., 2228 Dirksen Office Building.

February 8 and 9, Subcommittee on the Constitution, to hold hearings on S. 35, proposed Civil Rights Improvement Act, 9:30 a.m., 2228 Dirksen Office Building.

February 9, full committee, to hold hearings on the nomination of Paul A. Simmons, to be U.S. district judge for the western district of Pennsylvania, 10:30 a.m., 2228 Dirksen Office Building.

February 9, Subcommittee on Criminal Laws and Procedures, to resume hearings to examine the erosion of law enforcement intelligence gathering capabilities, 10:30 a.m., 457 Russell Office Building.

February 10, Subcommittee on Juvenile Delinquency, to hold oversight hearings on the Drug Enforcement Administration's efforts to control drug trafficking on U.S. borders with Mexico, 9:30 a.m., 2228 Dirksen Office Building.

Select Committee on Intelligence: February 7, to hold a closed business meeting, 2:30 p.m., Room S-407, Capitol.

February 7, full committee, closed session to receive a briefing on issues relative to the Panama Canal Treaty and Treaty Concerning the Permanent Neutrality and Operation of the Panama Canal (Exec. N, 95th Cong., 1st sess.). See Committee on Foreign Relations for schedule.

February 8, full committee, to hold hearings on S. 1566, to establish procedures for electronic surveillance in the area of foreign intelligence information, 10 a.m., 6226 Dirksen Office Building.

Select Committee on Small Business: February 7, to hold oversight hearings on the SBA procurement programs, 10 a.m., to be followed by hearings on S. 2259, the proposed Small Business Procurement Expansion and Simplification Act, 10:45 a.m., 1318 Dirksen Office Building.

February 8 and 10, full committee, to hold hearings to delineate the problems of attracting capital to small and medium-sized independent enterprises, 10 a.m., 424 Russell Office Building. . . .

House Committees

Select Committee on Aging: February 8, Subcommittee on Federal, State and Community Services, to hold hearing on life extension and tomorrow's elderly, 9:30 a.m., 2253 Rayburn Building.

Committee on Agriculture: February 7, 8, 9, to continue hearings on the general agricultural situation, 9:30 a.m. and 2 p.m., 1301 Longworth Building.

Committee on Appropriations: February 9, Subcommittee on Agriculture, Rural Development and Related Agencies, to hold hearing on Farm Credit Administration, 1 p.m., 2362 Rayburn Building.

February 7, 8, 9, Subcommittee on Labor-HEW, to hold hearing on Department of Labor on February 7, 10 a.m. and 2 p.m., 2358 Rayburn Building.

February 7, 8, 9, Subcommittee on Public Works, to hold hearings on North Central Division and Ohio River Division on February 7, 10 a.m., 2362 Rayburn Building.

February 7, Subcommittee on Transportation, to hold hearing on Interstate Commerce Commission, 10 a.m. and 2 p.m., 2358 Rayburn Building.

February 7, 8, 9, Subcommittee on Defense, to hold hearings on fiscal year 1979 Army and Defense posture statements, 10 a.m. and 2 p.m., executive on February 9, H-140 Capitol.

February 7, 8, 9, Subcommittee on HUD-Independent Agencies, to hold hearings on the Veterans Administration, 10 a.m. and 2 p.m., H-143 Capitol.

February 7, Subcommittee on Interior, to hold hearing on Bureau of Indian Affairs school construction, 10 a.m., B-308 Rayburn Building.

February 7, 8, 9, Subcommittee on Military Construction, to hold overview hearing on the Defense budget on February 7, 10 a.m., B-300 Rayburn Building.

February 7, 8, 9, Subcommittee on State, Justice, Commerce and the Judiciary, to hold hearing on Federal Communications Commission on February 7, 10 a.m., H-309 Capitol.

February 7, 8, 9, Subcommittee on Treasury, Postal Service and General Government, to hold hearing on National Council, Commission for Purchase from Blind and Other Severely Handicapped on February 7, 10 a.m., H-164 Capitol.

February 8, Subcommittee on Foreign Operations, to hold hearing on Export-Import Bank, 10 a.m., B-308 Rayburn Building.

Committee on Armed Services: February 7, 8, 9, executive, to continue hearings on military posture, 10 a.m. and 2 p.m., 2118 Rayburn Building.

Select Committee on Assassinations: February 7, Subcommittee on the Assassination of Dr. Martin Luther King, Jr., executive, to continue hearing, 10 a.m., B-352 Rayburn Building.

Committee on Banking, Finance and Urban Affairs: February 9, Subcommittee on International Trade, Investment and Monetary Policy, to hold hearing on trade with South Africa, 10 a.m., 2128 Rayburn Building.

Committee on the Budget: February 7, 8, 9, 10, to continue hearings on the first budget resolution for fiscal year 1979, 10 a.m., and 2 p.m., 210 Cannon Building.

Committee on the District of Columbia: February 7, to meet on committee business, 9 a.m., 1310 Longworth Building.

Committee on Education and Labor: February 7, Subcommittee on Employment Opportunities, to hold hearing and markup on H.R. 50, Full Employment and Balanced Growth Act, 9:30 a.m., 2175 Rayburn Building.

February 7, 8, 9, Subcommittee on Elementary, Secondary, and Vocational Education, together with Advisory Study Group on Indian Education, to hold hearings on H.R. 9810, Indian Basic Education Act, 1:30 p.m. on February 7, 2261 Rayburn Building.

February 7, Subcommittee on Labor Standards, to hold hearing on H.R. 6256, to amend the Fair Labor Standards Act, 11 a.m., 2261 Rayburn Building.

February 8, full committee, to mark up H.R. 314, to amend the Service Contract Act; H.J. Res. 649, calling for a White House Conference on the Arts; and White House Conference on the Humanities; and H.R. 10570, Environmental Education Act authorization, 10 a.m. 2175 Rayburn Building.

February 9, Subcommittee on Postsecondary Education, to hold hearing on Middle Income Student Assistance Act, 10 a.m., 2175 Rayburn Building.

Committee on Government Operations: February 7, Subcommittee on Legislation and National Security, to hold hearing on the Air Force and Navy audit agencies, 9:30 a.m., 2203 Rayburn Building.

February 7, 9, Subcommittee on Intergovernmental Relations and Human Resources, to hold hearings on the Federal role in dealing with urban decline; and H.R. 4406, Intergovernmental Coordination Act of 1977, 11 a.m., 2247 Rayburn Building.

February 8, full committee, to consider reports entitled "Dam Safety" and "Aircraft Noise and the Concorde", 10 a.m., 2154 Rayburn Building.

February 9, Subcommittee on Environment, Energy, and Natural Resources, to hold hearing on crime in Federal recreational areas, 10 a.m., 2203 Rayburn Building.

Committee on House Administration: February 7, 8, Subcommittee on Accounts, to consider committee funding resolutions, 10 a.m., H-328 Capitol.

February 9, full committee, to consider pending committee funding resolutions, 10 a.m., H-328 Capitol.

Select Committee on Intelligence: February 7, executive, to discuss committee business, 9 a.m., H-405 Capitol.

February 8, Subcommittee on Legislation, to continue hearings on foreign intelligence electronic surveillance, 9 a.m., H-405 Capitol.

February 10, Subcommittee on Program and Budget Authorization, executive, to continue hearings on intelligence and related activities budget for fiscal year 1979, 9 a.m., H-405 Capitol.

Committee on Interior and Insular Affairs: February 7, Subcommittee on Indian Affairs and Public Lands, to markup H.R. 1907, to designate certain lands as wilderness (Absaroka-Beartooth Wilderness) to be followed by hearings on private bills, 9:45 a.m., 2253 Rayburn Building.

February 7, Subcommittee on General Oversight and Alaska Lands, to continue markup of H.R. 39, Alaska National Interest Lands Conservation Act, 9:45 a.m., 1324 Longworth Building.

February 8, full committee, to consider H.R. 1609, to amend the Mineral Leasing Act of 1920 (Coal Slurry Pipeline Act), 9:45 a.m., 1324 Longworth Building.

February 9, Subcommittee on Indian Affairs and Public Lands, to hold hearing on S. 1214, to establish standards for the placement of Indian children in foster or adoptive homes, to prevent the breakup of Indian families, 9:45 a.m., 1324 Longworth Building.

February 9, Subcommittee on Energy and the Environment, to continue hearings on Nuclear Regulatory Commission authorization, 9 a.m., 2237 Rayburn Building.

Committee on International Relations: February 7, Subcommittees on International Organizations and on International Economic Policy and Trade, to markup H.R. 3350, Deep Seabed Hard Minerals Act, 2 p.m., 2200 Rayburn Building.

February 7, Subcommittee on International Operations, to continue hearings on Department of State authorization for fiscal year 1979, 9 a.m., 2200 Rayburn Building.

February 7, 8, Subcommittee on Africa, to hold hearings on economic assistance program for Africa, 2 p.m., 2255 Rayburn Building on February 7; 1310 Longworth Building on February 8.

February 8, full committee, to markup H.R. 3350, Deep Seabed Hard Minerals Act; and amendments to H.R. 9179, OPIC Amendments Act of 1977, 1:30 p.m., 2172 Rayburn Building.

February 8, Subcommittee on International Operations, to continue hearings on Department of State authorization for fiscal year 1979, 10 a.m., 2172 Rayburn Building.

February 8, Subcommittee on Europe and the Middle East, to hold hearing on fiscal year 1979 aid request for the Middle East, 2 p.m., 2200 Rayburn Building.

February 8, Subcommittee on International Development, to hold hearing on rethinking U.S. foreign policy toward the developing world—Nicaragua, 3:30 p.m., 2255 Rayburn Building.

February 9, Subcommittees on Africa, on International Organizations and on International Economic Policy and

Trade, to continue joint hearings on United States-Uganda relations 2 p.m., 2172 Rayburn Building.

Committee on Interstate and Foreign Commerce: February 7, Subcommittee on Health and the Environment, to markup H.R. 6706, Child Health Assessment Act, 10 a.m. and 2 p.m., 2322 Rayburn Building; 2218 Rayburn Building for 2 p.m. meeting.

February 7, 8, 9, Subcommittee on Energy and Power, to hold hearings on H.R. 9852, Comprehensive nuclear Regulatory Act, 9:30 a.m., 2123 Rayburn Building.

February 7, Subcommittee on Transportation and Commerce, to hold hearings on the transportation of coal and other bulk commodities by slurry pipeline; and H.R. 6248 and 6643, Coal Transportation Act of 1977, 10 a.m., 2218 Rayburn Building.

February 7, Subcommittee on Oversight and investigations, to meet on committee business, 2 p.m., 2322 Rayburn Building.

February 8, 9, Subcommittee on Health and the Environment, to hold oversight hearings on health effects of low-level ionizing radiation, 10 a.m., 2322 Rayburn Building.

February 9, Subcommittee on Consumer Protection and Finance, to markup the Fire Prevention Study Act of 1977, 10 a.m., 2218 Rayburn Building.

February 10, Subcommittee on Energy and Power, to hold hearing on The National Coal Policy Project, 10 a.m., 2322 Rayburn Building.

Committee on the Judiciary: February 7, full committee, to markup H.R. 9622, diversity of citizenship; and H.R. 9400, civil rights for institutionalized persons, 9:30 a.m., 2141 Rayburn Building.

February 8, Subcommittee on Immigration, Citizenship and International Law, to hold oversight hearings on the Immigration and Naturalization Service, 10 a.m. 2237 Rayburn Building on February 8; 9 a.m., 2226 Rayburn Building on February 9.

February 8, Subcommittee on Administrative Law and Governmental Relations, to continue markup of H.R. 664

and related bills, Contract Disputes Act, 10 a.m., B-352 Rayburn Building.

February 8, 9, Subcommittee on Courts, Civil Liberties and the Administration of Justice, 10 a.m. 2226 Rayburn Building on February 8; B-352 Rayburn on February 9.

February 8, 9, Subcommittee on Criminal Justice, to continue briefings on revision of the Criminal Code, 9 a.m., 2141 Rayburn Building.

February 9, Subcommittee on Civil and Constituional Rights, to hold hearings on H.R. 3504 and 7787, fair housing, 9:30 a.m., 2237 Rayburn Building.

Committee on Merchant Marine and Fisheries: February 7, 9, Subcommittee on Merchant Marine, to hold hearings on fiscal year 1979 authorization for certain maritime programs of the Department of Commerce, 10 a.m., 1334 Longworth Building.

February 8, full committee, to mark up H.R. 9508, rebating practices in U.S. foreign trade, 10 a.m., 1334 Longworth Building.

February 7, Subcommittee on Fisheries and Wildlife Conservation and the Environment, to extend funding authorization for Fishery Conservation and Management Act of 1976, 2 p.m., 2359 Rayburn Building.

February 7, Subcommittee on Fisheries and Wildlife Conservation and the Environment, to hold hearing on Marine Mammal authorization, 2 p.m., 2253 Rayburn Building.

February 9, Subcommittee on Oceanography, to hold hearing on Sea Grant authorization, 10 a.m., 2167 Rayburn Building.

Select Committee on Population: February 7, 8, 9, to hold overview hearings on world population, 9:30 a.m., 2212 Rayburn Building on February 7, 8; 2200 Rayburn on February 9.

Committee on Post Office and Civil Service: February 7, Subcommittee on Compensation and Employee Benefits, to continue oversight hearings on Federal Employees' Life Insurance, 9:30 a.m., 304 Cannon Building.

February 7, Subcommittee on Employee Ethics and Utilization, to continue

hearings on H.R. 10657, White House authorization, 10 a.m., 311 Cannon Building.

February 8, full committee, to consider H.R. 2722, collective bargaining representation for postal employees; and committee budget for 1978, 9:45 a.m., 311 Cannon Building.

February 9, Subcommittee on Employee Ethics and Utilization, to mark up H.R. 10657, White House authorization, 10 a.m., 304A Cannon Building.

Committee on Rules: February 7, to hold hearings on H.R. 5981, American Folklife Preservation Act authorization; and H.R. 3813, amending Redwood National Park Act, 10:30 a.m., H-313 Capitol.

February 8, full committee, to mark up subcommittee's report on broadcasting, 10:30 a.m., H-313 Capitol.

Committee on Science and Technology: February 7, 8, 9, Subcommittee on Advanced Energy Technologies and Energy Conservation R.D. & D., to continue hearing on DOE authorization, 8 a.m., 2318 Rayburn Building on February 7.

February 7, 8, 9, Subcommittee on Space Science and Applications, to continue hearings on NASA authoriztion, 10 a.m., 2318 Rayburn Building on February 7.

February 7, 8, 9, Subcommittee on Energy and Atmosphere, to hold hearings on EPA authorization, 2 p.m., 2318 Rayburn Building on February 7.

February 7, 8, 9, Subcommittee on Fossil and Nuclear Energy Research, Development and Demonstration, to continue hearings on DOE authorization, 10 a.m., 2325 Rayburn Building on February 7.

February 7, Subcommittee on Science, Research and Technology, to hold hearing on Federal Fire Prevention and Control authorization, 2 p.m., 2325 Rayburn Building.

February 7, 8, Subcommittee on Transportation, Aviation and Weather, to hold hearings on NASA authorization, 10 a.m., 340 Cannon Building on February 7; 2325 Rayburn on February 8.

February 8, Subcommittee on Science,

Research and Technology, to hold hearing on Office of Standard Reference Data of the National Bureau of Standards, 2 p.m., 2325 Rayburn Building.

Committee on Veterans' Affairs: February 7, 8, 9, Subcommittee on Compensation, Pension and Insurance, to hold hearings on pension reform, 8:30 a.m., 334 Cannon Building.

Committee on Ways and Means: February 7, to markup Airport and Airways Trust Fund, 1:30 p.m., 1100 Longworth Building.

February 7, 8, 9, Subcommittee on Welfare Reform, to continue markup of H.R. 9030, Jobs and Income Act, 10 a.m.

February 8, 9, full committee, to continue hearings on Highway Trust Fund, 9:30 a.m., 1100 Longworth Building.

Joint Committee Meetings

Joint Economic Committee: February 7–10, to resume hearings on the President's Economic Report, 10 a.m., Tuesday in 2154 Rayburn Office Building, Wednesday in 2337 Rayburn Office Building, Thursday in 5110 Dirksen Office Building, and Friday in 345 Cannon Office Building.

Conferees: February 7, on H.R. 3816, authorizing funds for fiscal years 1978 through 1981 for the Federal Trade Commission, 9 a.m., Room S-146, Capitol.

Notes and Sources

Much of this book is based upon personal interviews and the experiences of the authors on Capitol Hill. Footnotes are limited to published works and public documents.

Chapter 1: The Lure of Power

1. James Sterling Young, *The Washington Community, 1800–1828* (New York: Columbia University Press, 1966), pp. 71–72.
2. U.S., Senate, "Senate Committee System," *Hearings before the Temporary Select Committee to Study the Senate Committee System*, 94th Congress, 2nd sess. (1976), p. 22.
3. David Mayhew, *Congress: The Electoral Connection* (New Haven, Conn.: Yale University Press, 1974).
4. See Clem Miller, *Member of the House* (New York: Scribner's, 1962) for this collection of letters.
5. Richard Fenno, *Congressmen in Committees* (Boston: Little, Brown, 1973).
6. George E. Mowry, *The Era of Theodore Roosevelt and the Birth of Modern America, 1900–1912* (Indianapolis: Bobbs-Merrill, 1958), p. 118.
7. James E. Watson, *As I Knew Them* (Indianapolis: Bobbs-Merrill, 1936), p. 175.
8. "Tammany Hall Speech," July 4, 1910, *Clark Papers*, cited in Geoffry Morris, "Champ Clark and the Rules Revolution of 1910," *Capitol Studies*, vol. 2 (Winter 1974), p. 55.
9. Norman J. Ornstein, "Causes and Consequences of Congressional Change: Subcommittee Reforms in the House of Representatives, 1970–73," in Norman J. Ornstein, ed., *Congress in Change* (New York: Praeger, 1975), p. 89.
10. Norman J. Ornstein and David W. Rohde, "Seniority and Future Power in Congress," in Norman J. Ornstein, ed., *op. cit.*, p. 84.

11. Woodrow Wilson, *Congressional Government* (New York: Meridian Books, 1956). This work was first published in 1885.

Chapter 2: Power, Status, and the Legislative Process

1. Woodrow Wilson, *Congressional Government* (New York: Meridian Books, 1956), p. 193.
2. *Ibid.*, pp. 194–195.
3. See Richard F. Fenno, Jr., *Home Style* (Boston: Little, Brown, 1978).
4. *Ibid.*, p. 215.
5. Morris P. Fiorina, *Congress: Keystone of the Washington Establishment* (New Haven: Yale University Press, 1977).
6. The preceding and succeeding quotes from Rushford are in Gregory G. Rushford, "Why Senator Eagleton Fired Me," *Washington Monthly*, December 1977, p. 22.
7. The Eagleton quotes are in *ibid.*
8. Both Senator Eagleton and his legislative assistant contested Rushford's account of the events that led to his dismissal. The legislative assistant wrote, "Senator Eagleton is not a person who would forego an opportunity to correct an injustice in the hope of advancing himself within the Senate. Contrary to popular belief, the level of integrity in the Congress is quite high." Senator Eagleton responded: "Just as prisons are full of innocent men, I don't suppose there was ever an employee fired for good cause — to hear the employee tell it. . . . The fact is that I fired Mr. Rushford because he failed to perform the duties he was assigned and because he was unable to get along with fellow workers." Commenting upon the investigation, Eagleton stated, "Mr. Rushford produced nothing to justify his unshakable belief that somewhere there was bound to be corruption in the program." See the *Washington Monthly*, January 1978, p. 4.
9. *Congressional Record*, July 14, 1978, p. S10785.
10. *Ibid.*
11. *Congressional Record*, August 3, 1977, p. H8416.
12. *Congressional Record*, August 1, 1977, p. H8183.
13. *Ibid.*, p. H8185.
14. *Ibid.*, p. H8183. Emphasis supplied.
15. *Congressional Record*, August 2, 1977, p. H8283.
16. U.S., House, "Biomedical Research Ethics and the Protection of Human Research Subjects," *Hearings before the Subcommittee*

on *Public Health and the Environment*, 93rd Congress, 1st sess. (September 27, 28, 1973), p. 1.

17. *Ibid.*

18. *Ibid.*, p. 2.

19. U.S., House, "National Cancer Act Amendment—1974," *Hearings before the Subcommittee on Public Health and the Environment of the Committee on Interstate and Foreign Commerce*, 93rd Congress, 2nd sess. (February 5, 6, 1974).

20. For an earlier example of Roger's legislative style, see Eric Redman, *The Dance of Legislation* (New York: Simon and Schuster, 1973). Redman, an aide to Senator Warren Magnuson at the time, described the intricacies of the legislative maneuvers that surrounded passage of the National Health Service Corps from his vantage point in the Senate.

21. *Ibid.*, p. 89.

22. U.S., Senate, "Annual Expenditure Authorization Resolutions," *Hearings before the Committee on Rules and Administration*, Transcript of Proceedings, February 28, 1975 (Washington: Hoover Reporting Company, 1975), p. 4.

23. This and the preceding quotes may be found in *ibid.*, pp. 4, 6, 12.

24. This Cannon-Kennedy exchange is in *ibid.*, pp. 13–14.

25. *Ibid.*, pp. 18–19.

26. *Ibid.*

27. *Ibid.*, pp. 19–20.

28. *New York Times*, January 27, 1968, p. 28.

29. U.S., Senate, Committee on Rules and Administration, *op. cit.*, p. 23.

30. The Kennedy-Cannon exchange is in *ibid.*, pp. 23–24.

31. *Ibid.*, p. 28.

32. This and succeeding quotations from the floor debate over the airline deregulation bill are in the *Congressional Record*, April 19, 1978, p. S5849 ff.

Chapter 3: Committees, Power, and Status

1. A valuable history of the development of Congressional committees is Lauros G. McConachie, *Congressional Committees* (New York: Burt Franklin Reprints, 1973). This work was originally published in 1898.

2. Woodrow Wilson, *Congressional Government* (New York: Meridian Books, 1956), p. 82.

3. *Ibid.*, p. 87.

4. *Ibid.*, p. 62.

5. *Ibid.*

6. *Ibid.*

7. Bella Abzug, *Bella!* (New York: Saturday Review Press/Dutton, 1972), p. 15.

8. *Ibid.*

9. *Ibid.*

10. *Ibid.*, p. 36.

11. *Ibid.*, pp. 36–37.

12. *New York Times*, January 21, 1978, p. 21.

13. The Senate debate over the creation of the Intelligence Committee is in the *Congressional Record*, May 17, 18 and 19, 1976.

14. *Congressional Record*, May 19, 1976, p. S7557.

15. *Congressional Record*, May 18, 1976, p. S7408.

16. For further elaboration of the differences between the House and Senate Budget Committees see John W. Ellwood and James A. Thurber, "The New Congressional Budget Process: The Hows and Whys of House-Senate Differences," in Lawrence C. Dodd and Bruce I. Oppenheimer, eds., *Congress Reconsidered* (New York: Praeger, 1977), pp. 163–192.

17. *Congressional Record*, April 21, 1977, p. S6203.

18. *Ibid.*

19. *Ibid.*, pp S6204–6205. Emphasis supplied.

20. *Ibid.*, p. S6207.

21. *Ibid.*, pp. S6211–6213.

22. *National Journal*, November 26, 1977, p. 1851.

23. U.S., Senate, "Nomination of Harold Brown to Be Secretary of Defense," *Hearings before the Committee on Armed Services*, 95th Congress, 1st sess. (January 11, 1977).

24. U.S., Senate, "Consideration of Mr. Paul C. Warnke to Be Director of the U.S. Arms Control and Disarmament Agency and Ambassador," *Hearings before the Committee on Armed Services*, 95th Congress, 1st sess. (February 22, 23, 28, 1977).

25. *Ibid.*, p. 42.

26. *Ibid.*, p. 98.

27. *Congressional Record*, March 8, 1977, p. S3667.

28. *Congressional Quarterly Weekly Report*, May 29, 1976, p. 1334.

29. Marguerite Michaels, "The Biggest Bully on Capitol Hill," *New York*, March 8, 1976, p. 39.

Chapter 4: Staff: The Surrogates of Power

1. U.S., Senate, "Senate Committee System," *Hearings before the Temporary Select Committee to Study the Committee System, 94th Congress, 2nd sess.* (1976), p. 105.

2. *Ibid.*

3. Samuel Louis Walsh, "Senate Committees Personnel Practices," in *Committees and Senate Procedures* (Washington: U.S. Government Printing Office, 1977), p. 72.

4. *Washington Post*, February 16, 1975, p. A8.

5. *Washington Post*, February 20, 1975.

6. Senator Joseph Clark's famous attack upon the Senate establishment is in the *Congressional Record*, February 19, 20, 21, and 25, 1963.

7. The history of Congressional staff is discussed by Harrison W. Fox and Susan Webb Hammond in *Congressional Staffs* (New York: Free Press, 1977) and by Kenneth Kismehl in *Professional Staff of Congress* (West Lafayette, Ind.: Purdue University Press, 1977).

8. *Congressional Record*, March 3, 1893, p. 2478.

9. *Congressional Record*, June 9, 1975, p. S10136.

10. This and other quotes from the debate on S. Res. 60 are in the *Congressional Record*, June 9–12, 1975.

11. *Washington Post*, February 23, 1975.

12. *Congressional Record*, June 10, 1975, p. S10278.

13. This and subsequent quotes from the floor debate on S. Res. 60 are in the *Congressional Record*, June 9–12, 1975.

14. David H. Weaver, G. Cleveland Wilhoit, Sharon Dunwoody, and Paul Hagner, "Senatorial News Coverage: Agenda-Setting for Mass and Elite Media in the United States," in *Senate Communications with the Public* (Washington: U.S. Government Printing Office, 1977), p. 41–62.

15. David Price, *Who Makes the Laws? Creativity and Power in Senate Committees* (Cambridge, Mass.: Shenkman Publishing Co., 1976), p. 31. Price provides a detailed picture of the relationship between Magnuson and the Commerce Committee staff at this time.

16. *Ibid.*, p. 78.

17. U.S. Senate, "Legislative Branch Appropriations, "*Hearings before the Senate Appropriations Committee, Subcommittee on the Legislative Branch*, 94th Congress, 1st sess. (April 21, 1975).

18. *Washington Post*, October 31, 1977.

19. *Washington Post*, March 31, 1977, p. A10.
20. *Washington Post*, December 8, 1977, p. B7.
21. The quotes in this paragraph are in the *Washington Post*, February 5, 1976 (emphasis added).
22. New York Times, September 25, 1977, p. E4.
23. *Ibid.*
24. *Washington Post*, July 13, 1977.
25. *Washington Post*, April 20, 1978, p. B11.

Chapter 5: A Word about Perks

1. Quoted in Arthur Levine, "Down and Out on Capitol Hill," *Washington Monthly*, January 1975, p. 30.
2. The preceding quotes from Goldwater are taken from a Washington speech given on February 4, 1976, and reported in *U.S. News and World Report*, February 16, 1976, p. 22.
3. Quoted in Bernard Weinraub, "New Senators from House Enjoy Power, Miss Spirit," *New York Times*, March 8, 1977.
4. The quotes in this paragraph are in *ibid.*
5. This and the preceding quotes may be found in U.S., Senate, "Legislative Branch Appropriations Fiscal Year 1979," *Hearings before the Subcommittee on the Legislative Branch*, 95th Congress, 2nd sess. (1978), pp. 159–160.
6. U.S. Senate, "Annual Expenditure Authorization Resolutions," *Hearings before the Committee on Rules and Administration*, Transcript of Proceedings, February 28, 1975 (Washington: Hoover Reporting Company, 1975), p. 29. Following quotes are from this source.
7. U.S., Senate, "Committee Budget Resolutions," *Hearings before the Committee on Rules and Administration*, Transcript of Proceedings, May 18, 1977 (Washington; Hoover Reporting Company, 1977), p. 19. Subsequent quotes from these hearings are taken from this source.
8. Quoted in Eric Nathanson and Norman Ornstein, "The Space Race," *Washington Monthly*, January 1975, p. 36. This article is an excellent capsule description of the politicking that occurs in the House over office space.
9. *Ibid.*, p. 35.
10. *Ibid.*
11. This story is related in *ibid.*
12. *Congressional Record*, September 8, 1976, p. S15407.
13. The story of the Brooks Report and the reaction to it is in the *Washington Post*, January 11, 1977, p. A2.

14. The Schweiker statement is in the *Congressional Record*, August 4, 1978, p. S12574.

15. This and other quotes from the debate over the North Capitol building may be found in the *Congressional Record*, September 8, 1976, p. S15397 ff.

16. U.S., Senate, "Toward a More Modern Senate," *Final Report of the Commission on the Operation of the Senate*, 94th Congress, 2nd sess. (December 1976), p. 13.

17. U.S., Senate, "Legislative Branch Appropriations for Fiscal Year 1979," *Hearings before the Subcommittee on the Legislative Branch*, 95th Congress, 2nd sess. (Washington: U.S. Government Printing Office, 1978).

18. The first day of debate in the House on Senate Concurrent Resolution 98, which authorized the Magna Carta trip, is in the *Congressional Record*, March 9, 1976, p. H1715.

19. This and the preceding quotes in this paragraph may be found in the *Congressional Record*, March 17, 1976, pp. H2010-2024.

20. *Congressional Record*, April 5, 1976, p. S4957. The preceding quotes from the Senate debate are in *ibid.*, pp. S4956-4957.

Chapter 6: Power and Reform in Congress

1. Richard Bolling, *House Out of Order* (New York: Dutton, 1965); Richard Bolling, *Power in the House* (New York: Dutton, 1968).

2. For an excellent and thorough recounting of the story of the Bolling Committee, see Roger Davidson and Walter Oleszek, *Congress against Itself* (Bloomington and London: Indiana University Press, 1977).

3. U.S., House, "Committee Organization in the House," *Hearings before the Select Committee on Committees*, 93rd Congress, 1st sess. (1973), vol. 1 (Washington: U.S. Government Printing Office, 1973), p. 4.

4. Dulski's testimony is in *ibid.*, p. 131 ff.

5. *Ibid.*, p. 468.

6. Sullivan's testimony is in U.S., House, *op. cit.*, vol. 3, p. 86 ff.

7. Davidson and Oleszek, *op. cit.*, p. 159.

8. U.S., House, *op. cit.*, vol. 1, p. 25.

9. Davidson and Oleszek, *op. cit.*, p. 227.

10. *Congressional Record*, October 8, 1974, pp. 34468-34469.

11. *New York Times*, May 10, 1974, p. 45.

12. U.S., Senate, "Committee System Reorganization Amendment of 1977," *Hearings before the Committee on Rules and Administration*, 95th Congress, 1st sess. (1977), p. 3.

13. *Ibid.*, p. 546. Subsequent quotes from the hearings are taken from this source.

14. This and subsequent quotes from the debate over S. Res. 4 are taken from the *Congressional Record*, February 1–4, 1977.

15. U.S., Senate, Committee on Rules and Administration, "Open Markup Sessions on S. Res. 4," 95th Congress, 1st sess. (1977), p. 66.

16. *Ibid.*, p. 270.

Index